Writing out your life

University Centre at
Blackburn
College

Telephone: 01254 292165

Please return this book on or before the last date shown

| | |
| | |

Jo Stanley

Writing out your life

A guide to writing creative autobiography

Scarlet Press

Published by Scarlet Press
5 Montague Road, London E8 2HN

Copyright © Jo Stanley 1998

The author asserts her moral right to be identified as the author of this
work in accordance with the Copyright, Design and Patents Act 1988

British Library Cataloguing-in-Publication Data
A catalogue record for this book is available from
the British Library

ISBN 1 85727 073 8 pb

Designed and produced for Scarlet Press by
Chase Production Services, Chadlington, Oxford OX7 3LN
Typeset from disk by Stanford DTP Services, Northampton
Printed in the EC by J.W. Arrowsmith Ltd, Bristol

Contents

Dedication

To Vee and Val in Great Crosby. For their different valuings of the me beyond the stories, their different enablings, different distances, and their own different – but always ready – lifestories. For Jess and Joanne in Brighton, for the flames that they always, and so unexpectedly, pass on to me.
Thanks.

Preface

This preface is my story of how I came to write this book. It begins in summer 1995 at the Photographers' Gallery at a launch party for two books which photographer/educator Jo Spence had initiated and to which I had contributed.[1] I asked Avis Lewallen from Scarlet Press if Scarlet would be interested in publishing my manuscript on women working at sea. She said no, she didn't think they could sell enough copies, but asked if I was interested in writing a handbook on how to write your autobiography – for women.

Yes, I thought, I'm ready to write that. Yes, it's already tumbling out of me. Yes, as I read – anything – I re-write my version in my head, ready to say, 'These are some good ways to write autobiography.' I was pleased at being given the opportunity to offer some of the fruits of my own learning, my teaching and others' shared exploration of lifestory creation.

The ideas in this book have been gestating for 15 years; my apprenticeship as a writer of lifestories and understander of others' lifestories developed from my enjoyment of working in the early 1980s in a community publishing project, Centerprise, and its women writers' group led by Rebecca O'Rourke, as well as from my autobiographical writing through a divorce-triggered breakthrough.[2] I'd always thought I was a creative writer but I had concentrated on journalism. From 1982, however, I wrote fiction and autobiography and poems, daily and copiously – and soon left full-time news writing.

Through the late 1970s and the 1980s I was part of a London feminist way of life which led to many illuminations: going to consciousness-raising groups; reading Marion Milner (her books are listed in Appendix 2); attending creative journal workshops; talking and listening, finding out how much we are united by the struggle to understand how our lives have come to be as they are. I began writing a novel about my family and I started to draft my own autobiography – the first of many.

At the same time, the historian and the family-explorer in me went further. I was able to ask hundreds of women about their lifestories when creating community-based oral history projects such as the Wandsworth Women's Working Lives (with Bronwen Griffiths) and cooperating with others in editing their writings for *To Make Ends Meet*.[3]

I stepped through a crucial gate into an even more satisfying and sophisticated approach when in 1989 I gave a paper at Liz Stanley's Feminist Auto/Biography conference, met other practitioners and heard their ideas. This event was held at Manchester University and the venue was decorated with balloons. It felt like arriving home for a celebration of having come so far. This really began the process of putting together the deep, patchy, unwritten self-knowledge I had gained through psychoanalysis, with the knowledge gained from working alongside women who were seeking to represent their lives in fictional and non-fictional ways.

This process dovetailed with three years of regular self-exploratory/study meetings of the Educated Working-class Women's Group and with friendships with phototherapists Rosy Martin and Jo Spence, as well as with my training as a Pellin (Gestalt) counsellor. I began writing another autobiographical project looking at the psychic and social influences on the women in my Liverpool Irish family and gave it the working title 'The Family Autobiography'.

Since then, I've taped maybe a hundred or more people in community history projects at Battersea Old Town Hall and Hackney Hospital, made books and exhibitions with older women from Deptford and Islington, and helped to develop a lifehistory show with older women in Hackney. As a tutor, I've sat with many adult students as they struggled to get fiction and lifestories down on paper and introduced many to a career as information addicts through trips to archives such as the British Newspaper Library. As a trainer for Age Exchange, the reminiscence centre, I've listened to a multitude of wonderful and fragmented memories and learned from reminiscence experts such as Joanna Bornat and Peter Coleman.[4]

I re-write my autobiography obliquely all the time, through fiction and non-fiction about women who sail away; foresisters who chose mobility, sometimes as a way to deal with displacement and dislocation. At the same time, I state it more openly and academically for feminist journals and anthologies, getting feedback all along the way. I paint it with gluey fingers at the Mary Ward Adult Education Centre, go on about it in counselling at Willesden as Dorothy Badrick pummels lavender oil into me, and scribble it in my umpteenth diary in cafes and on trains whenever I'm stimulated. It's a very voiced history, mine, and it's absolutely part of other women's voiced lives.

The serious writing for this book began in 1995 when I was researching the lives of seafaring women in Newfoundland, Canada. Some of the examples I have used in this book come from the women I met while I was travelling. Although not writers and not interested in writing autobiographies as such, they were women who were interested in their lifestories and those of other women. One of the encouraging things about writing this book was discovering how much women everywhere want to know each other's histories. They hunger not for the glamorous stories (although these can be usefully inspiring) but the ordinary tales, the victories, the romances and, above all, the stories about how other women manage in similar circumstances.

On a personal level I gained too – on buses, in boarding houses and at conferences – talking to other women about my personal agony following a triple disaster that had just happened to me. The questions that I asked were: Am I mad to feel so bad? Why is it so hard? Can it be borne? *How* can it be borne? The women I met in passing told me stories of similar situations. Parallels, parables and examples seem to help more than direct advice ever does. One of the best justifications for telling lifestories is that they are so helpful to other people, for living. Autobiographies are not just 'good reading' or someone being 'self-indulgent' but crucial sources of wisdom in our changing, difficult times.

Throughout the winter and spring of 1995–6 the book kept renewing itself, sending out new shoots, in unexpected directions. Teaching the course in lifehistory helped – as I knew it would. As did those heavyweight hardbacks borrowed from Senate House library – Philip Lejeune, Alessandro Portelli, Bella Brodzki, Luisa Passerini and so on – and favourite autobiographies read again to discuss with my students: Colette's *Break of Day*, Carolyn Steedman's *Landscape for a Good Woman*, Doris Lessing's preface to her *Golden Notebook*. The people who helped me on the first, most intensive part of this book's creation were old friends who were writers, lifehistory workers, feminist historians, teachers, therapees and therapists, artists, workers with older people, and art therapists.

Ready to write up a new chapter in winter 1996, I'd open up the file and there would be eight pages of notes scribbled on trains; I'd forgotten I'd got so far. And then, when I was researching Hollywood stars' autobiographies for another project, I saw their reasons for writing: in particular, the actress's desire to show herself as herself, and not her screen persona. It was at this stage that I started to create some of the examples given here, composites of several women's stories. Not all the women in this book are real individuals, but they are all based on real women.

In June 1996, I began talking to an editor interested in commissioning me to write my autobiography. I started to feel that many of the suggestions I had so far made in this book were eyewash; that I, too, like many people I'd challenged on this, was faced with a desire to take years of reflection and to tell only small parts of the truth. Above all, I felt that I was lying in my autobiographical drafts: that I wanted to give the publisher fascinating stories that reflected well on me – not frankness. I realised that the way I wanted to write – levelling with a trusted friend, speaking from what I see as my core – was at odds with the performance anxiety that made me want only to have acceptable things printed.

At the same time, I was moving perhaps 80 box-files of my history around in my flat. I looked inside some – for example, four boxes on Grenada and three diaries of trips to that island alone. Suddenly I saw that I couldn't stand to have a deadline, that an autobiography must be written in its own time; certainly, mine must be. 'Can't you just knock it out, a pro like you?' my friend asked. No, I can't. Not my lifestory – it requires a different sort of reflection and a different relationship with data. Anyway that project was shelved when the publisher's editor changed her mind.

Throughout the summer of 1996 this handbook went on, changing from being a slim guide into something very rich and satisfyingly fat with examples. I came to see it as a generous and deeply exploratory book, especially as seemingly no one else had written a handbook using the ideas of the latest feminist critiques of autobiography as a means to explore ways of doing it yourself. In this summer re-writing I was influenced by much academic work on autobiography, women's psychology and philosophy, as well as re-readings of some favourite autobiographies. The most accessible and seminal ones are listed in Appendix 2. I hope that their legacies will help you as they help me. Good luck with your autobiographical journeyings.

Jo Stanley, Gauxholme

Acknowledgements

Many women helped directly in this book. Not all of them wanted to be identified. To them and the hundreds and probably thousands of women who have been in this lifehistory-exploring world and contributed to it, a thank you for the climate that you richly created. Your lives and ideas for thinking about them have taught me a lot.

Some of the greatest help came from the students, past students and staff on the unique Certificate in Life History Work at the University of Sussex – a course on which I feel deeply proud of lecturing. The people who did the exercises, commented and suggested include Chris Abuk, Joanne Gulbkenian, Margaretta Jolly, Jess Richards and the course's creators Dorothy Sheridan and Al Thomson. This was further helped by the women I met on the weekend autobiography workshops I have taught at the City Lit and for Spread the Word, especially therapist Wendy Monticelli.

In the final stages, my companions in Todmorden – Margaret Andersen, Kathy Wandering Star, Tiger Lily, Henry and Linus – gave the most conducive company, and Bob Fellowes loaned me the monitor that enabled the final editing. Dominic Sweetman helped in many practical ways and Sylvia Fiorelli flat-sat reliably. Carol Burns, who has taught lifestory writing at the City Lit for 24 years, read several draft chapters and encouraged me to go on. Margaretta Jolly and Dorothy Sheridan did the final read-through with astonishing alacrity as well as enthusiasm, despite their own commitments. Audrey Jankovitch supported me through a terrible grief that threatened the editing process.

Other people were important in creating a particular climate for me. They include Dorothy Badrick, Astra Blaug, Stephanie Buick, Anna Davin, Edgar Ernstbrunner, Helen Lucey, Rosy Martin, Shirley Read,

XIV/WRITING OUT YOUR LIFE

Jane Roberts, Liz Stanley, Myna Trustram and Val Walsh. My family were always rooting for me.

I'm especially grateful to Ann Devlin-Fischer for her early encouragement – and to Skip Fischer whose generosity provided the means to do so much in Newfoundland where the book first began to leave my head and become notes on paper. Finally I acknowledge the help of the women at Scarlet Press for their respect, efficiency and incisiveness. Thank you all.

Introduction

If you have picked up this book then you are probably quite a long way along the road of thinking about writing your autobiography. You may well be wanting company in this process, or some ideas about how you might go about it. That is what this book is for. *Writing Out Your Life* will help you with some ideas about ways to write autobiography (I will be using the word interchangeably with lifestory); it offers you stories about how other women have done it; and it asks lots of questions, leaving you your own space in which to think about your responses. Let the process be as joyful as possible; that will help you to work all the better. I've written it in what I hope is a straightforward manner.

HOW TO USE THIS BOOK

The first section of the book deals with thinking about what you want and what the overall process means. The second section offers direct suggestions about how to tackle various elements of your book; for example key people and significant times. Section III suggests ways to perfect it once you have written the first draft. Section IV is about the stage when you show it to others for feedback and then perhaps to publishers and readers.

You may want to read this book and write as you go along, making notes. Or you could try a fast-track method and read it quickly all the way through once. Then, as step two, re-read more slowly the bits that you found interesting or difficult. Do some of the exercises. Next, as step three, make notes about the bits you think you need to read again in order to help you to write in the way that works best for you. That is, use the book to help you design your own journey. For step four, read those parts carefully (or ditch them if they turn out not to be right, after all).

After that, you should have some idea of your own way forward. Towards the end of writing the first draft of your lifestory, you will probably need to pick up this book again to re-read the chapters on structure and polishing. Later, it will help when you are thinking about publishing and what to do next. I recommend that you read selectively, or even randomly if that is the most creative course for you. Make notes as you go along, so that you remember all the good ideas you had as you read.

Inevitably, writing a lifestory entails self-exploration. It is your right and responsibility to do so only to the extent that feels OK for you. In other words, please take good care of yourself. If in any of the exercises you feel you are going in more deeply than you can handle, then stop. Use friends and professionals and relaxation to help you with your feelings. This book is offered generously as a way to make your thought processes clearer and more interesting, not to involve you in traumatic revelation. It is to help you to get the most out of the process of telling your lifestory – enjoyably. It's about freedom rather than oppression, and about self-determination rather than being determined by others as we speak out. If you find yourself thinking, 'Oh, no, do I have to do all this looking and uncovering?', the answer is: No, no, no. Just take the suggestions that work for you and ignore the rest. These are just a range of optional ideas, not The Right Way. There is no such thing.

STYLES OF WRITING

Some autobiographies are written in a straightforward linear way. They start with family roots and then go on, year by year, to the present. Examples of this popular genre include Helen Forester's *Twopence to Cross the Mersey*, some of the contributions in *Truth, Dare or Promise: Girls Growing up in the Fifties* (edited by Liz Heron), or the autobiographies of contemporary women politicians such as Helen Suzman and Margaret Thatcher. Such writers don't discuss their difficulties in formulating the story and in finding a voice in which to tell it, nor do they challenge the dominant form of lifestory-telling.[1]

Others use *complex* methods to tell the story in an unstraightforward, bitty, multi-vocal way, and explore the process of telling as well as *what* they are saying. Examples listed in Appendix 2 include Carolyn Steedman's *Landscape for a Good Woman*, Ronald Fraser's *In Search of a Past* and Louise Erdrich's *The Blue Jay's Dance*.

I want to suggest ways to write about the full depth and breadth of women's experience, to allow complexity in if you want. While some women may prefer to avoid unnecessary palaver, others may welcome the freedom 'to problematise' as a good and necessary activity, not a bad one. To 'just do it', by contrast, is to reduce our ability to speak wisely about the profound challenges of gendered life as it is – rather than life as it is in daydreams, newspapers and the many accounts that take a traditional 'Great White Male' version as the norm.

WHY/HOW ARE WOMEN'S AUTOBIOGRAPHIES DIFFERENT FROM MEN'S?

Why is this book especially for women? As western women, many of us have been trained to undervalue ourselves. We feel that we're not worth writing about. And our lives have been scripted in advance by men. There are certain stereotypes that we are supposed to conform to (wonderful mother, braver than any man, so charmingly feminine) and there are stereotyped ways in which we are expected to present our stories. These can inhibit us from writing wholeheartedly about life as we experience it.

But now, today, as a woman writing your lifestory, you can enjoy describing precisely how it felt for you, what had significance for you, how different (or similar) you were to these standard models of 'woman'. You can experiment and have fun. If you want to experiment in a sophisticated way, Chapters 1, 2 and 3 discuss ways to do so, as do the academic books about autobiography in Appendix 2; or you could leap straight into Chapter 4 and get on with it immediately.

What is different about us, as women, is that we have had different experiences to men (such as childbirth, sexual objectification, domestic work). Therefore the topics we write about will be different, differently weighted and differently expressed. We usually have different viewpoints and different values. For example, women tend to be more affiliative and go for group experiences more than men. So a woman's autobiography might include far more about friendships and about the agency of others in her life than a man's traditional account of a process he has undergone in a more solitary way. Motherhood – our own and those of the women around us – is a key feature in the lives of many of us. The monthly evidence of the womb's activity and western society's particular placing of women's bodies both ensure that we are in touch with our physical selves, which can mean we may tell a more embodied story than do men. Women throughout history have written their lifestories in much more fragmented, disjointed and interesting ways than traditional male accounts.[2] This is despite living in a society where men dictate many of the norms because they have the power, including publishing power. Today we have a very rich heritage. And the great bonus of writing in the late twentieth century is that we can write without the same reference to inhibiting norms, even though publication can still be a restrictive process.

Section I

Thinking it out

What is it anyway?

This chapter deals with the main questions people ask when thinking about writing autobiographies. These include: 'Can I do it?', 'What does autobiography mean anyway?', 'Why do people do it and why do I want to? (Am I mad or justified in wanting to?)' People usually think about the connection between themselves and the published autobiographies they see in shops and libraries. 'Will publication be possible?' And the biggest question of all is: 'How can I write my lifestory well?'

CAN I DO IT?

This question can mean both: 'Am I *capable* of it?' and 'Am I *permitted* to do it?' Implicit in this also is: 'Can this me-who-I-don't-think-very-much-of do something so grand?'

If you can speak, if you can write, then, yes, you are capable of creating your lifestory. In fact, you already do it, daily. Many of your conversations, diaries, letters, shopping lists are autobiography: making your self manifest. You hear autobiographies every day if you listen to *Desert Island Discs* and *In the Psychiatrist's Chair*. You see them on *Video Diaries* and in miniature on the Ricki Lake and Oprah Winfrey shows, in every TV documentary or news item where someone is explaining something about her life, be it a plane crash or a mugging, a lottery win or a miraculous reunion with a long-lost sister.

Every day you produce an autobiography of one sort or another. Telling the doctor about your sickness and its connection to your history is a kind of lifestory. Filling in an application for a credit card is another lifestory. Telling someone at the bus stop about the procession you have just seen go past is an autobiography. How you account for yourself if you are picked up by the police is an autobiography. Giving a social worker an account of why you are a fit person to adopt a child is an autobiography. Writing a curriculum vitae for a job is most certainly an autobiography. And of course there are many versions, tailored to fit different needs and situations.

However, 'writing an autobiography' sounds like a grandiose enterprise entailing a major investment of time, effort and self-belief. Some people think: 'Do I have to have done a lot of important things before I'm considered worth writing about?' It seems like something extraordinarily arrogant; a project that has already been defined by people who, you are supposed to think, 'know better' than you.

So you may want to know what you yourself mean by autobiography, what you *think* it involves and what it may actually involve. Many thousands of women have found it *can* be done and have loved the fulfilment of doing it. There are high pleasures and delights, and some unexpected costs too. Chapter 2 talks about some of the gains, pains and beneficial side-effects.

As for the second meaning of the question 'Can I do it?' – 'Am I *permitted* to write an autobiography?' – the glib answer is a shrug: Who is to stop you? Who's got the right to prevent anyone writing their story? Should anyone be allowed to stop someone doing something they want to do, if it will cause no harm and may even be fun?

The ideas of enjoyment, danger and speakable knowledge are crucial. Women in this society are taught to keep a lot secret and are often the family's repository for all those cats that mustn't be let out of the bag. People – or our idea of them – *can* stop some would-be writers. So one of the issues tackled in this book is how to deal with censorship and self-censorship. How do you write despite objections, how can you get rid of the gags that you or others tie round your own mouth (often for the best of reasons)? How do you write loud and proud, respectful of others yet happy in your own voice?

Exercise: Dealing with constraints on writing

Only do this exercise if you're not feeling OK about writing your lifestory. It is entirely optional.
- Write down who says you can't write your lifestory.

- Write down who says you can.
- Give each person a value (a mark out of ten) for how much weight should be given to their views. (You may want to give two marks, one reflecting the person's former/imagined power, one reflecting their here-and-now rights to determine your actions.)
- Have an imaginary dialogue on paper with those 'people'.
- Then have a real dialogue with them, if possible.
- Talk afterwards to someone you trust, so that you can get a distanced view of the opposition's agenda and how you can handle it.

The point of this exercise is to help you identify what you are up against so that you can tackle it, including understanding that sometimes when you say others are stopping you, really it is yourself. If you can see where the obstruction lies you will be more able to tackle it. See Chapter 3 for self-censorship and more ideas on dealing with inhibitions.

This exercise might be a useful one to keep in the back of your lifestory ring-binder when you make one, or in a separate place for your notes on process, in case you are faced with feelings of constraint later.

Sharon wanted to write about her family's Irish roots for part of her autobiography, because it was important to her sense of no longer quite belonging to her Donegal past:

Within a few months of starting to talk about the lifestory project I started thinking my dad would say – somehow – that I couldn't. And I realised with that exercise on assigning value that I'd give ten out of ten for the weight of his past power over me, but only three out of ten for his present power over me.

It turned out that my dad was so ashamed of our early poverty and so upset at the thought of anyone knowing about it that he came near to wanting to tear up all my work. He hated the whistle being blown on him. Luckily all the writing was on disk and he didn't know how to erase documents. But it meant I had to choose to write despite not having his go-ahead. I don't want to upset him or betray him. But I don't share his standards over pride. I know that poverty is caused by societies and not by personal failure. So it isn't a shame issue for me as it is for him. And I absolutely needed to go ahead and write what I needed to write. So I *could* do my autobiography, my way. But there was a price. And the bonus was discovering that he had only got a three out of ten score for his real power over me now.

The respectful and complex answer to the question 'Can I [am I permitted to] write my autobiography?' is: 'Yes. Yes. Yes again.' Such a sense of receiving permission, even freedom, can take quite a lot of learning and re-learning. It isn't a sense that, once discovered, is then possessed for ever. For some women, a sense of having to be cautious is real. So, yes, you are permitted to write it. And, yes, this book is full of ideas intended to help you act on that knowledge.

WHAT IS AUTOBIOGRAPHY?

What is a lifestory, or an autobiography? It is the story of someone's experiences as told by her for others. It is an attempt at making an overview, creating some sense and coherence out of lived experience. The roots of the word 'autobiography' are *bios* meaning life, course or way of thinking; *autos* meaning self, and *graphos* meaning to write.[1] An 'autobiography' has come to mean a published, book-sized account that at least 2,000 other people will want to buy. But it will be much more helpful in thinking about writing your lifestory if you temporarily divorce this polished and exceptional commodity 'autobiography' from the organic process of exploring yourself. A lifestory does not have to end in a book.

Is there an alternative word, such as 'lifewriting' or 'lifestorying' or 'lifestory-telling', that you want to use? You may want to play with the idea that you can label this thing in whatever way turns out to be appropriate or feels comfortable.

Autobiography can be:

- an assertive act: 'I matter. I deserve time spent on me'
- a deeply creative and exploratory act with volatile, unstable and rewarding ingredients

- a recuperative act: you seize elements of your neglected selves and give them the status and dignity they have always needed; esteem returns, you re-member yourself, reassemble lost parts
- a versatile act: you might dress in many costumes in which to act your various parts
- a fundamental recording act: 'Yes, I *do* exist.' You bear witness to yourself, in a world that exists independently of you
- an illusion-chasing act if you are trying to capture the essential you. It's better to relax and do whatever you can with all that you come up with
- a tightrope-walking act: you can maximise and minimise the constraints on you, playing with all the stories and fictions you use about yourself, balancing how much truth you use – including literal truth and emotional truth
- a constructing and determining act: you are building a contextualised self, a thing you call 'I', as you write: 'This is how I was, this is how/what I became'
- an opportunity-grabbing act: 'Here's a chance to speak – fully. I'll take it – fully. I'll voice complaints, state observations,[2] rant, explore, collapse correctly and publicly if appropriate, be self-conscious, be critic-and-composer all in one go'
- a readerly act: you enjoy reading about 'you' (these versions of you) as they appear from your pen
- a critical act, not only because your lifestory may contain criticisms of yourself, others and your society but also because, implicitly, it states that you are critical of others' accounts of you and that you want to write (and right) your own account
- sometimes a generous act – a gift to others (but it doesn't have to be – you can keep it just to/for yourself alone)

Cathy, a former aid worker in South Africa now writing her story, said:

I didn't know in advance what kind of act I was doing at any one time. And that didn't matter. It took quite enough energy just doing whatever deep thing it occurred to me to do at any point. Knowing that it could be – was – so many kinds of act helped because I just relaxed and let myself be diverse.

Does writing an autobiography differ from other lifestorying?

Is an autobiography better than letters or diaries or gossip? No, but it is different because it is usually bigger and more public. You are attempting to give others the whole story, or at least to cover a wide range of areas of your life.

Writing a lifestory is like preparing a banquet for many people, whereas gossiping and writing letters are private snacks, sometimes meals. A lifestory can't be whipped up from packets or microwaved and served up in minutes. There's the fancy tablecloth to be found, the candelabra, the flowers for the table, let alone the food to be prepared and the right guests to be invited. Again, writing a lifestory is more like building a whole fleet of customised cars than just sorting out the battery in your familiar old jalopy. However, diaries, letters and gossip – processed – can become an important part of your final lifestory.

WHAT IS THE CONNECTION WITH PUBLISHED AUTOBIOGRAPHY?

Some people absolutely pine for publication and don't want to get started unless it's guaranteed, but such guarantees are rare. Almost all the autobiographies you see are published books, so it's hard to believe any other sort counts – or even exists. Sometimes people say, 'I just want to get it down, I don't care if no one sees it,' but actually they do care and feel too conflicted about the desire to admit it. It can be painful to want something that seems so presumptuous. Maybe some people genuinely don't care about being read, but so far I have not met any of them. Most of us desire, above all, recognition – even mass acclaim – for our stories. This is especially true when writing a lifestory entails revealing a terrible injury to our sense of ourself which has so far been hidden.

It can be infuriating when someone says kindly: 'Why not just enjoy the process of writing?' For many people, the private process is not enough. There is, however, a middle ground between doing it for the sake of the process (and remaining unread) and doing it for a mass market. Options for self-publishing are discussed in Chapter 20. If you are wondering whether there is any point in writing if no one else is ever going to read it, then turn to that chapter now. It may help you decide on your final product and also encourage you on your way in the next few hours.

What do you hope to achieve?

It may help you to deal with the worry about 'Will it become a proper book?' if you recognise your deeper intention. Do you *need* it to be a published book, or just some pages of self-explanation? Is it a way of self-healing and therapy? Do you want it to be a significant contribution to women's body of knowledge, or a sort of ode to your formerly hidden self? It may be any of these things and more.

Marlene Kadar, who has written extensively about autobiography, proposes that the highest goal of this new genre, women's lifewriting, is self-knowing, which is linked to the notion of self-care. Knowledge is power. Knowing about yourself in this enduring and fundamental way can enhance your self-esteem as well as increase your effectiveness in the world.[3] Chapter 2 talks about why women write, and should help you to explore the connection between your work and other published works. What matters to you?

What will be good enough for you?

Because of all the inhibiting notions about what a 'proper' autobiography should be, it's worth reflecting on what would be good enough for you and you alone if these notions didn't exist. Do you want to do what you think you are capable of, or something more than that? What will satisfy you as an autobiography?

Cathy thought:

I wanted to summarise the whole problem of aid distribution by way of my African lifestory: a 250-page illustrated book that MPs would respect. In fact, I found that this was far too big a project, not least because of all the background research I needed to do ... I re-appraised my intentions. It took me eleven months to let myself off the hook. Finally I wrote 16 pages of poems, illustrated them, and read some of them aloud at charity readings. That turned out to be good enough. That was what I could do. And I did it well.

Other women may find that there is much more that they *can* do, but first they have to jettison the low expectations they have of themselves.

Jean said:

I had learned to type in school, been a typist. But it's one thing to type up other people's one-page letters. It's another to think about a book of 300 pages – about me. But then my mum died, I didn't have her to look after any more and I thought, what the hell, if this is what I want to do with my spare time I can. So I wrote my lifestory as I chose – by hand. 500 pages. It was much less effort by hand than by machine.

HOW CAN I DO IT?

This section deals with some basic concerns about how to proceed with autobiography. *How* precisely can it be done? I'll deal with the practical problems first as these sometimes mask deeper fears. Then I'll go on to the intellectual and emotional problems.

Occasionally, people are daunted by the idea that they won't be able to write well enough once they get started. It's normal to feel a bit wary. This is a big enterprise. Common fears that arise are:

- It sounds so far-fetched that people will not believe it's real!
- My English is rotten, embarrassing.
- Nothing I did is that interesting.
- Have I got enough to write about?
- I've got too much to say – and no time to say it.
- I lose my point – I can't tell any story dramatically.
- I can't type.
- I haven't got a typewriter/word processor.
- I can't get down on paper what I say aloud – people are interested till I start writing, then I get dead dull.
- A publisher would not be interested as I'm not a professional!
- No one will understand it. They'll make judgements about my choices/decisions. They'll misinterpret me.

Sometimes these are real obstacles. Sometimes they are just blinds because you fear to start on such a big self-centred project – especially if you have dependants. Some writing tutors argue that you need to learn how to be creatively selfish, how to use metaphorical earplugs to block out the demands that conflict with your creative needs.

Practical problems

But I've never written anything more than a shopping list
Most people have written more – and better – than they think they have. And this book is here to help you. Chapters 15 and 16 on structuring and Chapter 17 on polishing offer some good ideas. Books on creative writing can help you with some of the technical problems. Creative writing classes can help you to make things sound as interesting as they really are. Reading and learning from others' autobiographical techniques can help. Try the books in Appendix 2. If one particular book works for you, read it twice and consciously adopt some of its devices. Try Vivian Gornick, Carolyn Steedman or Jane Lazarre, for example. Experiment with styles – humorous, descriptive, critical and so on – and see which ones work best for you.

But my English is rotten
Even well-known writers have their problems with writing 'correctly'. Louella O. Parsons, Hollywood's first gossip columnist who could make or break movie stars with her revelations about their private lives, wrote on the first page of her autobiography, *The Gay Illiterate*:

> I have been described – perhaps too accurately for comfort – as a gay illiterate. There have been articles written about how I split infinitives with rare abandon and treat history with gay disregard for dates and places. Some of these boners I admit to. Others are typographical errors. That's my story and I am going to stick to it. The story has always been the most important thing for me – and to Shakespeare! Let the King's English get in the way of the news, and the participles can dangle where they may – in the ruins along with the spilt infinitives.[4]

You yourself know that the content of any story is far more important than the correct use of commas. In the same way, the body you have for life matters more than the clothes you can take or leave. The point *is* the body, the story. Clothes (the grammar) can come later.

Respect your desire and ability to speak out. You yourself would probably urge someone else to let the story out in whatever way she could and ignore the trimmings. The next chapter talks about how imagining an audience can help in areas like this.

However, the story and its appearance do have a strong relationship with each other. Realistically, if your lifestory is eventually written in what others recognise as 'good English' it will be accepted by them with less unease than something idiosyncratic – as Gertrude Stein found when she first sought publication. Try looking at her *Everyone's Autobiography* to see how unusual uses of English can work (see Appendix 2). Classes on adult literacy can improve your grammar, as can diligent and aware reading of others' writing. *The Complete Plain Words* by Ernest Gowers is the standard handbook for looking up rules on splitting infinitives or hyphenation, etc. Also, you may hire a professional editor to work on your final draft if you really want to end up with a story that is impeccable in a standard way. But don't let these worries inhibit you. The trimmings are very much stage two.

But I can't type at all/very well/fast enough ...

It doesn't have to be typed, of course. But if you are aiming for publication, or just for a neat appearance, then it must be typed.

Local authority adult education classes teach the use of typewriters and computers. Try doing a class in such skills and then staying late to use the equipment. You may want to handwrite your autobiography at home and then type it up at the class if you can. Alternatively, there are people who will type for you. Usually, it is an enormous boost. You can see the finished work clearly and decide where it needs to be revised. You can even admire it!

But how can I find the time?

Writing your lifestory requires a big commitment in time – perhaps several years if you plan to write the full story. If you write only a page a day (350 words), five days a week, then the first draft of a book-length manuscript (a standard 80,000 words) could be done in less than a year – even allowing for a month's holiday. I'm not suggesting you do it this quickly or regularly, but clearly it doesn't have to take for ever. It might help you to write down how many hours per week you think someone (not you) should be allowed to spend on their autobiography and then apply that to you.

Stress experts believe at least 25 per cent of our time needs to be spent doing just what we like, if we are to survive healthily. So, if writing an autobiography is a way of doing what you like, it could be seen as a helpful contribution to your greater well-being. And it may help others around you too.

I would also recommend that you use a kitchen timer as you write. This has two advantages. If you set it for an hour then you will find that you work very hard and put an immense amount into what can seem like 'too little time'. Second, breaking the job down into manageable chunks – 'I'll do an hour tonight and 30 minutes in the morning' – encourages you to feel the whole project is 'do-able'.

Intellectual/emotional problems

But will I be able to remember?

Usually, once people start writing they find they remember much more than they expect to. The older you are, the more clearly you will remember your past, because long-term memory usually improves as short-term memory declines.

Some of the things that can help you remember well and vividly are:

- Questioning: of your self and any significant other people; this will help you to amplify and clarify key elements.
- Not feeling you have to over-simplify and explain exactly how and why it all happened so long ago. Let some things remain fuzzy or unexplained. If you over-simplify you risk being reductive and even patronising to your readers and to yourself. You need the space to be complicated when necessary.
- Reflecting: this can help you see recurring themes and underlying patterns which may then release related memories.
- Always jotting down the fleeting memories, however briefly. Get the notebook habit.
- Using objects to stimulate your memory, including smells. Of all the senses, smell is the one that triggers memories most directly, be it cloves or cauliflower, marigolds or melting tar.

The resources chapter (Chapter 14) suggests many ways in which you can supplement your memory lapses – and most autobiographers expect to do such research. No one can remember everything.

But can I remember properly?
This is a pernicious question. No, you can't. There is no 'proper' memory. It's a fallacy to believe that there is a factual past that can be recaptured, one that really was true and that everyone agreed with. Sidonie Smith, who has written extensively about autobiography, believes that in writing as women there are four fictions involved. The first of these is the fiction that any memory is. (The other three are the 'I', the imagined reader and the story.)[5]

Helen M. Buss, who has looked at many archives of women's autobiography, says:

> Memories are as much acts of imagination as they are acts of recall; they are 'a play of seeking, choosing, discarding words and stories that approximate but never recapture the past'. Women autobiographers, seeking a less unitary 'I' than the male autobiographers of the past, have often played a different game with the 'remembering' process, one that acknowledges the tentative and conditioned nature of memory.[6]

As a woman, you may enjoy sorting out how differently you remember if you feel free to judge yourself generously.

If you want to work with memories in an open and fluid way it will help to be very relaxed instead of conforming to a pre-set agenda. Let your intuition challenge you all the time. The better developed your powers of discernment, the more precise (though not necessarily 'true') the memory. Stereotyped and obsessive ruminations should be discarded. Note them as signposts if necessary, but put them aside. This is a time to remember boldly and freely.

But there is no one 'me'
Movie stars' autobiographies – for example Katharine Hepburn's – frequently make the point that the authors want to reveal themselves as they actually are and explode the myths surrounding their public persona. Indeed, part of what is called the Autobiographical Pact is that readers expect to find the writer revealing frankly the authentic under-story, the 'whole truth'.[7]

In writing your lifestory you may be trying to create an account of your progress towards selfhood and to tell it in a way that feels authentic. This is a key debate at present. Postmodern philosophers such as Michel Foucault and Roland Barthes argue that we are multiple selves – none of them 'false', none of them 'true'. The counter-argument is that we have multiple aspects that make up a recognisable and authentic self.

If you really are concerned that you are not telling the truth about something, relax and accept that this is clearly a difficult area for you. You can only be as honest as you can be at any time. Respect all your various views of yourself and write all of them down. Don't charge head-on at the issue that is distressing you. Go to one side of it, with descriptions of the surrounding circumstances, or describe others in a similar situation.

For example, Helen, an agricultural student working on her history as family member, found she could not bear not knowing precisely what she thought of her sister's wedding:

> So I described the dress, the ceremony, the reception, what I thought others were feeling watching this bizarre couple. First I realised how bitter I was, and that my disapproval was masking my jealousy. And then I realised how sad and confused I was, that someone so close to me should act like not-me. I felt very very bereft. And then I felt joy that she was going off out of my life, to Cyprus, and I could have some parental attention at last. But describing her stupid frock and the fatty roast duck and all that was a way to find how to say all the things I needed about that event.

Another way to tackle the splits between your different aspects as you write is to explore them and to encourage them to relate to each other, using Gestalt. Gestalt (German for whole) is a type of psychotherapy founded by Fritz Perls; it involves recognising different aspects of the self and letting them dialogue in order to find a synthesis or reconciliation. Throughout this book I'll be suggesting you make use of Gestalt techniques. For example, Helen tried it in writing about her sister's wedding:

> I got the roast duck to talk to my dad's suit – I wrote it out like a play. And through that I found my anger with wasted money (the duck) and my sense of loss – because my dad's expensive hired suit 'spoke' of his grief at letting Stephanie go. It was the last thing he could do for her – look good. Make that tribute. And I got Stephanie's blue garter to 'speak' to Photis's knees and I found a tenderness and fear of each other that then reminded me that I too had those

feelings. Gestalting things really works when you want to know about all your feelings. Because they know about each other in depth they can then live respectfully together. It's fearing the unknown other that causes the tension.

But I don't know how to sum it up

Humanistic philosophy saw lifewriting as the harmonious unfolding of a human being. You sat down and gently prised open all the folds of the life you'd already lived, smoothed them out and made them into a book. I find this idea seductive, disarmingly suspiciously seductive. Oh, if only writing my lifestory really could be like gently unrolling a pack of cottonwool pleats and turning it into something soft, continuous, nice, flat, accessible, contained! How satisfying that would be. That model suggests that lifewriting is like playing back a tape, time-travelling, or whooshing the wet paintbrush over a magic colouring book and finding all those past elements still there, ready and waiting.

To some extent it is like that, but it is also like a wrestling match – and so it should be. To write as 'passive victim' of the story isn't quite enough for most questing autobiographers today. They – and maybe you – prefer to question and disrupt this story that is easy to tell because it has been so often told. It's a basic misconception to expect to find yourself coming out all of a piece. You are unlikely to be able to narrate a coherent story of you-who-lived, a tale without discrepancies or inexplicable glitches and absences.

Writing a lifestory also determines what's still to come. In philosophical terms, the act of writing produces meaning. As you write about this past you, you are creating that thing you will henceforth call 'me'. You lay down tracks for the peculiar wagon that is your future life to roll along.

So don't expect to be able to sum up your life easily. Discussing, attempting and failing to do this as you tell the story are enriching aspects of the whole process.

But I feel so separate from the me who did those things

Some people expect to feel at one with the self who lived the life that is being described. It's enjoyable, and hard, to achieve that feeling. And it's necessarily an illusion. Like the self you see in the mirror, it is not quite you.

This is what all autobiographers have to live with it. It's inescapable and the more you can comment in your writing on the gaps between these 'selves', the more interesting your autobiography will be.

Feel the fear and do it anyway

It's a good idea to respect your fears about writing autobiography but do not allow them to stop you. Fears and objections are very deep-rooted. You may like to try some techniques to circumvent those anxieties that aren't amenable to other approaches. Try any of the following:

- meditation
- writing them down
- hypnotherapy
- listing the good and bad feelings brought about by writing

Feel your reluctance and understand its causes. Make a friend of it rather than fighting it. It may have useful things to tell you.

HOW ON EARTH DO I START?

It's worth thinking deeply about what you want from the whole process. Any task is better handled when it's broken down into smaller parts, ideally with rewards after each stage achieved. I suggest that at this point you start making a list of what you need, practically and emotionally, to support you.

Cathy's list went like this:

Emotional/practical things I need:

A clear regular space and place each week of five hours for writing (Sunday mornings?).

Food that lights the lamp at the base of my spine (Virginia Woolf's words for what writers need).

One friend to say she loves every syllable.

One friend to criticise my grammar.

A fairy godmother to pay for some inputting.

One weekend course at the City Lit in ending and beginning pieces of writing.

Someone knowledgeable to help me do my first day's research at the Public Record Office (possibly Janet F?).

Mum's cooperation over my access to the family Bible and albums.

Courage. (If not, try whisky and friendship from someone doing their autobiography.)

A deadline of two years' time. If I don't like it I don't have to finish it. Or I can extend the deadline.

A statement: 'I like and esteem myself enough to let myself be confident in my writing.'

Material needs:

Unlined notebooks with Liberty covers for rough thoughts (and the self-given permission to rip them out later when I need to file them in the main autobiography).

Two reams of paper.

3b pencils and enough putty rubbers.

A laptop computer with a decently lit screen.

A new disk called 'autobiography', and a backup disk and an extra disk called 'odd bits/junk/extras'.

Half a dozen box-files for storage (new ones to encourage me, not secondhand as usual).

The knowledge that 'I'll let myself buy enough ring-binders for each chapter.'

You will certainly need a ring-binder (99p from Smiths) and several reams of paper (about £4 each), a hole-punch, several pads of 'Post-it' notes and some means to divide the writing into sections or chapters: coloured sheets of paper are cheap. The prices throughout this book refer to no-frills 1998 prices.

Different people have different needs: for example, privacy, time, company. It can make the experience much happier if you identify your needs in advance and sort out any obstacles. It pays to not be overly optimistic and think: 'Oh, I can get by with just this scrap of paper, just using this corner of the bedroom.' This is the start of a slippery slope of not providing a worker with her necessary tools. Take what you need. Buy whatever you can afford. Allow yourself all you can in the way of treats, equipment, reassurance and knowledge.

Respect that worker. She's going to do something important to her. So she deserves all the support going. She's you – starting something delightful and challenging. She's you – probably finding she has all sorts of unexpected resources to help her along. She's you. Good luck.

What is it for? Who is it for?

One of the things that will help is to know genuinely who you are writing this autobiography for, and why. You may know it only on an unconscious level, but some bit of you will honestly comprehend your intentions and you can gain from becoming fully aware of that knowledge. Understanding your motivation will affect the freedom and the carefulness with which you write.

WHAT ARE YOU WRITING IT FOR?

You may have many reasons for writing this autobiography. US women's rights leader Elizabeth Cady Stanton, for example, had a two-fold goal as she wrote her lifestory in the 1890s: 'to gain personal and professional acceptance as both an ordinary *and* an exceptional woman, and to propagandise for the cause of women's suffrage'.[1]

Exercise: Understanding what you are writing for

- Make a list of what you want to write your lifestory for.
- Leave it for a time, say two days or until you are in a totally different frame of mind.
- Come back and write in your second thoughts.
- Tear each item off and then arrange them on the floor in a different order.
- See what happens to your understanding when you rearrange the ideas and put the first last. Play with the thoughts.

The aim of this exercise is to help free you up to understand your precise intentions and needs so that you can make the autobiography work for you. Try pinning up the summary near your workspace or putting the outcome of the exercise in the space where you keep your notes on your working process – say in the back of your ring-binder.

Reasons why women write autobiography

- to understand themselves better – to find the deep strands
- to sum up, to write a clear account
- to show their descendants what it was like to be them, in their time – and where they came from
- to confess[2]
- as revenge (as writer Tillie Olsen said, writing is the best revenge)
- to be witnessed in all their depth
- to earn money
- to become famous
- to educate and inspire others who are like them and misunderstood
- to tell people who they are
- to put the past to rest – to review their lives and put right what can still be corrected
- because it's safer than therapy – no one need hear them
- to be able to take control of their lives as they live them
- to see if they can do it – as an adventure and experiment
- because it's absolutely time they spoke out

Exercise: Understanding how other autobiographies may be affecting the way you write yours

- List the ten autobiographies that have had most impact on you.
- Rank them in order of importance and write the titles down one side of a piece of paper.
- Note by the side of each why you think the writer wrote it. (Go back to the original and see what she said about this – weigh up the truth of this, if you like.)

- After a few days go back to the list and reflect on which of those reasons are also your reasons for writing. Where is that OK and not OK?
- Now make a list of why *you* want to write. How do you feel about the discrepancy between your reasons and those of your model autobiographers?

You can use this exercise as a way to ditch any old, unhelpful reasons about why you should write. Keep it where you keep notes on your working process for this lifestory.

Beneficial side-effects

You may set out with one or two reasons for writing your lifestory and end up discovering you were writing it for entirely different reasons. The things that happen along the way may well turn out to be good reasons for writing it, although you hadn't thought of them in advance.

'Nothing is more difficult than writing an autobiography', said Russian revolutionary leader Alexandra Kollontai at the start of her *Autobiography of a Sexually Emancipated Woman*.[3] Whether or not you agree, there will be times when the process is hard and so you may like to know about some of the beneficial side-effects.

- You can discover whole new subject areas you want to learn about.
- You can gain a greater sense of meaning and coherence about your life.
- You can remind yourself of your triumphs over adversity.
- You can enjoy the pleasure of sharing after being private for a long time.[4]
- You can take pleasure in creating something.
- You can relive all of your happy, funny and interesting times.

Julia, working on the lifestory of several women, including herself, whose family connections were with former Yugoslavia, found the payoffs included browsing the library shelves when stuck, and becoming interested in Virginia Woolf's life and then that of her husband Leonard Woolf:

Most of all I enjoyed the sheer sense of indulgence which came from closeting myself away with my memories. Close after that followed the sense of achievement from putting the past into context and finding natural connections between hitherto unrelated events. My relationship with my three friends assumed a new dimension.

Negative side-effects

Most women I've talked to have found the negative side-effects of writing lifestories to be far less significant than the benefits.

Negative side-effects include difficulties with handling your memories, becoming sad and angry at mistakes, at changed lives and losses, and at your current state. These feelings can best be tackled by accepting that certain events did happen, but you did all the good you could. Getting some support when experiencing these feelings can also be useful, and knowing when to duck them because they are too hard is invaluable. Remember, *you are under no obligation to write about everything*. An autobiography is a place where you have supreme control and you can confront or skim over whatever you choose.

You may regret that the amount of work involved takes time away from other things. This can be tempered by accepting its necessity for now. You could also continue to do the things that give you pleasure, but perhaps for shorter periods of time and less often than you would prefer.

WHO IS IT FOR?

The best person to write for is you. You are the point. It's your story. You don't need to use possible future audiences to justify it. Someone might say: 'I'm only writing it for my grandchildren, really. I'm not that vain.' But it's not vanity to write your lifestory; that's a meaningless word, bandied about by people who are not true friends. They may be feeling jealousy, inferiority or even terror that someone close to them is speaking out.

What, actually, could be more just and important than each human being summing up aspects of her life in the way she wants? After all, you only have one life – and it belongs to you. Marlene Kadar asked the rhetorical question: 'Whose life is it anyway?' Well, then: Whose life is your life?

Writing it because it matters – to you

Some people write lifestories because they feel they *should*; someone may have told them to. That's not necessarily a good basis to work from. It's much better to write it free from any sense of obligation, if you can. Try the exercise that people sometimes use in therapy.

Exercise: Sorting out what matters deeply to you

- Take three sheets of paper.
- On the first piece write all the things you would do if you were told you had only six weeks to live.
- On the second piece write all the things you would do if you were told you had only a year to live.
- On the third piece write all the things you would do if you were told you had only three years to live.

If you don't write 'Writing my lifestory' on any of these sheets then it sounds like you'd be happier doing other activities instead.

Who do other women write for?

The act of writing autobiography usually includes the desire to be witnessed and understood. So although the main point in writing it may be to do something for yourself, the very fact that you are no longer keeping the story inside you suggests that you also want to be seen/heard in some way. Some of the people women write for (or think they are writing for) include:

- themselves
- grandchildren
- friends
- 'people out there' who read published autobiographies
- 'women of my type' (such as other lesbians, other black women)

- people who are so totally different that the writer wants to teach them something
- unknown audiences who might applaud them

Novelist Storm Jameson dedicated her autobiography thus: 'Written for my judges – the forgotten men and women who made me.'

Exercise: Finding who you are writing for

- Try making a list of the people you are writing for. Write their names on the right-hand side of a piece of paper.
- On the left, write down – in any order – reasons you are writing it for them.
- Use a highlighting pen to indicate who matters most – and least.
- Reflect. Is this good enough for you or do you want some other people to write for? If so, what/who would they be? What qualities do you require?

The point of this exercise is to help you feel clear about your target audience – and who you don't need to bother with. I suggest you store it in the place where you keep notes on your process. You may decide to have a photo or symbol of that person by the space where you are working.

Why do you need to know who you are writing for?

This knowledge will drastically shape how you write it, including, for example:

- the sense of duty or freedom with which you write
- the language level – if you are writing simply for grandchildren you may have to reduce the complexity of the things you want to say
- the things you omit – if you are writing a didactic autobiography, to teach people, then you may well exclude any shameful bits
- the sense of 'self' that you can filter it with; how you *show* what you feel about yourself
- moral/ethical decisions
- the commitment you give to it, in terms of both time and focus

WHO ARE YOU WRITING IT TO?

The people you are writing the final product *for* are not necessarily the people you will be writing *to*, as you go along. For example, you may be thinking that it will be about some aspect of your life, such as surviving domestic abuse, that you want the world to know about. But while you are writing this for the world, you may want to have one single addressee in mind, a person who'll respond well as you write. In Denise's case:

> I wanted to write my story about my life in the West Indies for my great-grandchildren here, but I kept writing it with my teacher in Georgetown in mind. The children are too young to write to yet – a lot of them aren't even born. So I had to 'tell' somebody else – and I told Miss Williams, because she always encouraged my English.

Finding your good listener

Think of someone – s/he could be imaginary or real – you want to address. S/he should be someone who understands you almost as well as you do yourself, but perhaps more generously. S/he may have some insights you haven't got because s/he has lived a somewhat different life and sees you from the outside, objectively. You'll need to know this person and feel s/he is listening to you as you speak/write. Write her/his name somewhere where you'll notice it, such as over the computer.

How it helps to write 'to someone else'

If you write to someone else it can work for you in the following ways:

- By providing you with a companion in what can be a lonelier slog than any other form of writing (because it is so much for and about you and is so much about the hunger to be understood). Keep her in mind as you work. If you flag, you can address her: 'Jenny, I'm getting bored with this bit. What would you like to hear instead?' See her as friend, companion, equal in the process.

- By writing to/for someone (preferably real) whom you nominate as your business manager. Agree targets and deadlines with her. For example, Jean told a woman in her creative writing group: 'I'll do the chapter on my hysterectomy by October 15, and it'll be 4,000 words long.' Use the business manager as your super-ego, to discipline you – charmingly – if you go off track.
- If you are writing 'to' someone, as in a letter, you are on your best behaviour – in a good sense. You describe things vividly and wittily. You make sure that the reader will know what you are talking about. You don't witter on and go off the point because you don't want to bore her.
- By writing to something symbolic, a spiritual guide, or even a particular animal, you might provide your deepest self with someone it is useful to be in touch with. A native American might write to her foremother using a telling name such as Laughing Water.
- Similarly, you could try writing to the child or wise crone in yourself. That is, select a positive aspect of yourself at a stage in your past or future, and write to her. This is one way of not only levelling with your deepest self but also having a long-range perspective.
- By writing to/for someone who does not know or see the 'real' you, for whatever reason, you will introduce greater clarity into your writing.

Exercise: Thinking about the right companion/recipient

Thinking about the above options, make a list of the right companion/audience figure for you. Take on the one that you fancy. Employ her, marry her, lie under her mantle. Have a one-page dialogue with her. Ask her any of the following: What can you give me? What do you need? How do I know I can trust you? What sort of things might you tell me? What can I do to get the most value out of you? How will you surprise me? What can I give you?

You don't need to write to/for any of these figures, certainly not all. But you do need company in doing long tasks, especially ones in which you can get lost because you are so involved. Identify the kind of companion – imaginary or real – who is best for you, the very best that you deserve (no half-measures). Then use her. If she's real, make sure you agree this frankly. Maybe offer her something in return so that it is a real contract.

See Chapter 18 on using using real people for company in writing and for feedback. But do use others. Psychologists are just now discovering how very important it is to be coaxed as we learn to do new tasks.[5] You particularly benefit from support and encouragement when writing lifestories because they can be so fundamentally concerned with anxieties about how others see us.

HELPING YOURSELF

This chapter has aired some of what I see as the key issues about what you write for and who you write for and to. It's particularly important to have an encouraging and permissive listener to bear in mind as you write. You need to know your lifestory will be received in the right way, if you are going to write something so important to you. Just as you don't yell your lifestory in the midst of a blizzard to a gang of distracted, angry coyotes who speak only Coyotese, so you need to utter your lifestory in the right setting. Find the right conditions for reception even if it is only an imagined reception. So this chapter has also tried to assist you in finding the right companion or target to address your labours to.

Do let some of the ideas filter into your unconscious. You are starting a difficult job. Some analysis of your own reasons for writing may help you to enjoy the challenges that lie ahead.

Speaking out

For many women, especially those writing an in-depth autobiography rather than a social history of themselves, the first thing they need to know is whether they can say what they want, whether they can speak out. So I'll say to you what I often find hard to believe about my own lifestory: *writing your autobiography is an OK activity*. And you can write it as and how you like. It's your right. The decision about *showing* it to others and publishing it is the second stage and does require negotiation and taking other people's rights and feelings into account. But stage one is for you.

CONCERNS ABOUT SPEAKING OUT

Repercussions are real. Fears are real. Women, especially doubly marginalised women such as lesbians, black women and women with disabilities, have been silenced because others' responses to speaking out can be so threatening. Some people may be harmed by your speaking out (and damage you in return). Some things may have to remain unspoken. A long and nasty court action was brought by actress Brigitte Bardot's husband and son who attempted to excise one-third of her published autobiography; they didn't like what she wrote about them. Insisting (as I sometimes do) on the right to say anything at all is simply not adult, not if you need to operate in the world with others who also have needs (to be safe, for example). You may feel fine about speaking out, but if you are worried then see if the following exercise helps.

Exercise: Assessing the scale and validity of your fears

Write a list of any fears you have about writing your lifestory. Then look at that list on several different occasions, perhaps with different friends. Try writing the actual odds on the feared result happening. Respect the fear. Try a dialogue with it. Get to know the fear, and decide, firmly, that you – not it – are going to be in charge.

The point of this exercise is to help you assess fears realistically so that you can deal in an adult fashion with the risks involved. You may want to extract a useful message from your exercise and put it near your workspace. It's useful to remember that what is worrying to speak about one day often seems harmless when looked at several weeks later. We can get things out of proportion.

HOW WE CENSOR OURSELVES

There are many ways we censor ourselves and many reasons why we do it. You are not alone. You will have internalised various 'shaping stories' (the OK way that things can be told) and ideas of what cannot properly be said. You have numerous barely noticed inner voices that instruct you to do things. Such voices use a million different tones, from peremptory to persuasive. And they are believable. Their repeated statement is: 'You can't say that.' Getting to the stage of reading this book may already be a major breakthrough, because you realise that you *can* express your lifestory.

'You can't say that' might mean one of two things: either that you yourself cannot/should not speak because the effect will be unbearable and have terrible consequences for you; or it refers to the wounds you may inflict on others by speaking out. This second meaning is a complicated one often linked to the first.

Sometimes we are more worried about losing the love or friendship of those people than actually caring about their well-being. 'Protecting' them can really be about safeguarding ourself. Also we can over-estimate how much protection they need, in a mix-up over what we are reluctant to say. 'They wouldn't like it' can actually be a cover story for 'I don't want to say it.' It saves taking personal responsibility for wanting to withhold things. Feeling we have to say it all, absolutely all, can be a disempowered and disempowering position. Choosing precisely how much and how little we want to say – and saying it – can be very liberating.

Ways we silence ourselves accidentally

There are many ways that, as women, we inadvertently cheat ourselves of what we want to say. They include the following.

1. Inventing a whole narrow narrative format – either unconsciously or consciously – that tells a story which reduces the complexity of what actually happened. This is usually done unconsciously in self-defence.

It's a good idea to identify what your message is, if you have one. You may not be aware of yours so try asking yourself: 'If I knew this person [me] what might I suspect her message of being?' Once you know what your message is, you'll know if you actually want to convey it or leave it out. That is, you need to know your organising story – if there is one – whether you want to guard against it, utilise it, expose it honestly to your readers at the start, or even change it during the writing process.

2. Excluding facets of yourself you imagine others can't take. For example, as Estelle C. Jelinek points out in her study of women's autobiography, nineteenth-century suffragists:

> were confident and relentless fighters, [but] on the whole their autobiographies manifest varying degrees of insecurity about their acceptance, especially as women. Suffragists, it seems, more than any other female reformers, were under the often unspoken but nevertheless present charge of proving their 'femininity'. In order to counteract the public's image of them as 'mavericks' or as 'unladylike' they devote more of their autobiographies to their early teens than their later careers. Some spend a disproportionate amount of time on their lifestudies demonstrating what a normal, happy, religious upbringing they had. As adults, they depict themselves as people with whom other white, middle-class, conservative and religious women can identify without feeling threatened.[1]

Exercise: Not omitting aspects of you

This is one way to deal with the tendency to skew lifestories in this particularly reductive fashion, which might very well be unconscious.

• Identify what you fear people might disapprove of in you.
• Make a list.
• Make a second list of how you would like them to think of you.
• Discuss with an honest friend the extent you want to accede to others' standards and ways you can help yourself be brave enough to speak it as it feels.

Use this exercise for quite a deep level of knowing what you need to guard against. You may like to use it as a checklist later during the process of revising your book.

WAYS TO BEAT THE SELF-CENSOR

These are some ways to help yourself feel free enough to write auto-biographically. You may think of more. Different ones will work better for you at different times, just as in life deliberately chosen bravery is more useful on some days than a friend's comforting support.

Know that there are two parts to this autobiographical process
One part is what you say privately, what you need to say. The other part is letting others see it. Do it just for you, first. You don't have to do the second part if you don't want to. Let the private just-for-me part of the process last for ever if you want. If this autobiographical process is for you, then you have the right to withhold it from all other eyes, or from certain eyes, or even your own eyes, for whatever length of time feels right for you. It can be therapeutic, and that's more than good enough. Letting others see it may well turn out to be only a secondary goal. You may feel that the expression is the point and that you are concerned with the process rather than the product.

Let yourself be as in/visible as you need
Invent a pseudonym for yourself and write as that person. It could be a sensible name or one that indicates your attitude: Dagger Teeth, Flowery Poser, Truth Teller or The Judge. Feel free to lock doors, use

code, even write in semi-darkness under a table. Hide out if you need to. Let your story be 'invisible'. Let yourself be secretive, oblique, incomprehensible, for stage one. Paint abstract statements rather than a clear narrative. Scribble drafts in writing that no one else can read. Buy lockable books and keep them in a double-padlocked safe deposit box in a lockable/secret cupboard or at a friend's house, if necessary, or at the bank. Leave instructions that your writing should be destroyed unopened when you die or left for 50 years or whatever you like.

This can be particularly useful if you want to express fully your hatred for someone else. It may be that you need to write a hating, unfair, ranting version of your story before you can write a balanced one. It can be enormously liberating to permit yourself a short period in which you write an irresponsible 'minority report', against the grain of everyone's expectations of you as a fair human being, especially if you rant wholeheartedly and in a safe enough place. Write the filthiest, most over-t!-top things you can possibly say. But then go on to the next stage.

Do it at the right speed for you
Some of you will need to write your lifestories slowly, so that you can evaluate the wisdom of saying what you want to say and work out good ways to say it. Alternatively, try writing it fast so that your anxieties are temporarily outstripped. Virginia Woolf recommended writing so fast that the critical devil sitting on your shoulder couldn't keep up. This advice for fiction writers may work for you too: to hell with all the typographical errors or the bad handwriting – just slam it out and on to paper.

Don't try to be 'in the right'
'Right and true/wrong and incorrect'. For any writer, it is difficult to feel they have permission to write. How to get that freedom is a particularly important question for autobiographical writing because you are not only reporting on yourself but also others. Each aspect of yourself has a version, as do all the different aspects of other people involved. It's a contest – and there will be winners and losers. Just as you don't have to position yourself as a right enough person to produce an autobiography, so you also don't have to get all the contents right. You don't have to sum everything up correctly and accurately. Your job is just to write. Try enjoying being in the wrong, imperfect, during

this precious period of exploration. Forget that right/true and wrong/inaccurate even exist. I believe there is no wrong to be in anyway, there are just other people's anxieties.

Position yourself as a woman

In recent years, a number of feminist academics thinking about the craft of writing autobiography have discussed the position we write from as women. Not the physical position of 'Here I am hunched over the keyboard with my neck at a funny angle' but from what place, in the sense of your 'idea of yourself in the world'. One US writer on women's autobiography, Sidonie Smith, for example, believes that nineteenth-century women who wrote autobiographies assumed that they were addressing privileged and powerful male readers who had the right to set the tone.[2]

You may well like to write just as it comes out or you may like to consider if you are positioning yourself in some way. That is, are you writing from the perspective of being in a particular role, rather than as multi-dimensional, non-superficial you? Are you, perhaps, writing as a daughter, as Mary Wollstonecraft did in her autobiography-cum-travelogue, *Letters Written during a Short Residence in Sweden, Norway and Denmark* (1796)?[3] If so, what does that mean in your head? Are you writing/thinking as a challenging daughter, an appeasing daughter, a boasting daughter, a defensive daughter, or a lost daughter who now says: 'You were right, Mum'?

Perhaps you are writing as a metaphorical mother, trying to encourage the little ones to follow your example, trying to show them why you've had to become so ruthless, trying to marshal the world into coherence. You might be writing as a sophisticated, experienced guide to extraordinary lifestyles and want to ensure your readers feel confident to follow you, or that they'll admire you or be shocked by you. Or you may write as critic, showing what you and others did wrong in your life or indicating that you trod an exemplary path.

There are many positions to write from as woman – including a sense of yourself as more like a father, son, boss, cross-dresser, outsider from another planet, mad visitor. You may not know what position you are writing from until you start writing. And it may change many times in different moods. But if you know the psychic place in which you are composing and telling this story, it will help you to go further and write from other positions as well, or help you to shake free of positions that are bad for you. Do feel free to allow ambivalence. It can be deeply enabling to say you have mixed feelings or feel differently about different things at different times. (It can also be disabling if you allow yourself to flounder, to dodge difficulties.) In the process of writing you may well learn when ambivalence is disabling and when it is enabling.

Identify and befriend the internal critic

All writers need to befriend their internal critics. Make use of your critic's positive critical abilities and stop it from becoming a nagging drone. You're going to have a long relationship so you need to be on the same team.

Speak from whatever distance is necessary

Part of the decision about how you position yourself is to figure out the distance you need. It recognises the importance of knowing you are far enough from your subject or audience when you need to be. Take the space you need – just as you select on a train how near or far you sit in relation to others. I'm not talking about a cool, objective, scholarly distance that might be deemed academically correct, but about the need to be metaphorically at a distance from society and its expectations.[4] In situations where caution is necessary, you may need occasionally to say 'she', lie, write fiction or in some way disown yourself for the time being. One of the great bonuses of a word processor is that you can tell it to change all the 'I' s to 'she's (and back again, as often as you like) so that you can experiment with how much you want to own and how much distance you want to create.

Use a therapist for support

Aspects of yourself may be too painful to confront. In writing you could encounter the most formidable of walls, the most plausible of rationalisations in yourself. Be ready for floods of recognition when a barrier comes down or a dam breaks. Therapists can help.

Know what you want to withhold but save it

It can help to give yourself permission to note any section of your writing you feel anxious about and then highlight it in some way and put it safely aside. If you're using a word processor you might like to set it in italics, put it in footnotes, or create a special section called 'bin' that is not really for rubbish, just for things you need to discard for now. If you're handwriting or typing, try using a highlighting pen. Photocopy the offending bit and put it somewhere safe, tearing up the original. You might then – knowing your power to destroy information – decide which bits of it you do actually want to keep. You might want to have a special coloured pen to use when you are in libel lawyer mode, marking out the dodgy bits for yourself. The principle is to keep the information safe in some way while also acknowledging fully to yourself that it is dangerous and that you may eventually choose not to use it.

Challenge truisms

If you find yourself writing truisms or clichés, stop (or at least underline them and go back later to look at them). Truisms, platitudes, familiar statements that sound stale may well be cover-ups. You may be saying what you are supposed to say rather than what you want to say. Try inserting negatives, even where you don't believe them to be true, as a way to explore whether the opposite of what you are saying could actually be the case. For example, Jean says:

> I mistrusted the feel of it when I wrote 'Mother and I always did get on well.' I inserted two words so that the new sentence then read 'Mother and I did not ever get on well.' Having experimentally uttered that dreadful calumny meant I then felt free to tell the curate's egg truth: that sometimes we did get on but not nearly as often as she liked to think we did.

Write several versions

It may help to know that you don't have to speak out from the start. You can write more frankly in a later draft, once you've practised and tested what it's like to speak out. For example, Lucy Brewer (aka Louise Barker) wrote two lifestories of her experiences of rape, brothels and adventures. The second, *The Female Mariner* (1816), was 'far more vivid and concrete in its details and more angry about the indignities she had suffered' than her first attempt, *The Adventures of Lucy Brewer*.[5] You can have more than one go at this. A really helpful book which encourages you to approach yourself from many different angles is Stephanie Dowrick's *The Intimacy and Solitude Self-Therapy Book*,[6] and another is Deena Metzger's *Writing for Your Life: A Guide and Companion to Your Inner Worlds*, especially the exercises.[7]

WHY YOU SHOULD SPEAK OUT

The whole point of writing a lifestory for some women is to have the freedom to speak out at last. It's a chance to bellow truths that demolish, to state feelings that have festered. It can be very healing. US feminist Kate Millet, in her autobiography, *Flying*, wrote about how embarrassed and vulnerable she felt in writing frankly. She talked to novelist Doris Lessing about this and reported that Lessing said:

> The most curious thing is that the very passages that once caused me the most anxiety, the moments when I thought, no, I cannot put this on paper – are now the passages I'm proud of. That comforts me ... Because through letters and readers I discovered these were the moments when I spoke for other people. So paradoxical because at the time they seemed so hopelessly private.[8]

WHY YOU SHOULD SOMETIMES NOT SPEAK OUT

Sometimes there are good reasons for silence. You may simply not know what to say yet and to attempt to force it would be a way of injuring yourself. You may believe in judicious speaking or reticence rather than full confession. Sometimes breaking silence can injure you and/or other people and worsen situations.

Only you can judge how much you should protect yourself and others and how much you can reveal. You are the expert (though you can also benefit from advice) on how much you really need to be safe.

Deciding your policy on this may take some time and experimentation. It may be that you reverse your decisions along the way. Chris said:

> I have thought a lot about how much to disclose about my early life ... Gradually I have got used to the idea that it is possible – and good – to disclose a lot. But there are still some things that serve no purpose to be said. I am not of the blood and guts school – my aim is to be socially constructive. Sometimes it is better, as far as I am concerned, to write obliquely. Verbal disclosure – or letters of disclosure – have been a window on my life and thoughts. And, with a few exceptions, people to whom I have addressed them have

responded with tremendous support. That is one of the main encouragements I have to write my own story and to value its importance to other people.

What I haven't written about includes much that is hurtful or possibly controversial. As a head of a family, a member of a community or several communities, I have decided that it is necessary to be careful in what I say or I might hurt my family or be ostracised. I am working on rethinking and renegotiating these boundaries all the time ... there is a lot I could write about my marriage – but I think fiction is going to be the most constructive form in which to tell much of it. These are difficult decisions and they are often what stops me writing.

There are several ways of being silent in positive ways.

1. Direct omission. If you are going to omit, you may like to own up to it by saying 'I am omitting something here', adding a short explanation if you wish. Such an acknowledged omission might excite curiosity but at least it is a more respectful way to behave towards your audience.

2. Changing names and details so that problematic people (including you) can't be recognised. If you do this a little, but still want to call the final thing 'an autobiography', you can own up to the alterations. The preface or an appendix might be a good place to do so. A difficulty is that people's reactions can't be predicted. Some readers may be so fearful that they will identify themselves anyway, through all the layers of disguise. In other cases, people can be so unaware of how they come across to others that they might not recognise themselves however blunt you are. If you are changing the details so much that the book is more of a fiction, you may want to consider what to call it – 'fiction/autobiography' or 'fictionalised lifestory', for example.

3. Restricting the circulation of the whole autobiography. It's your right to decide that no one can see your story, or to put an embargo on its release. If you decide early on in the process that you will prohibit free circulation of the finished item, it can free you up during the process of writing.

For some women the questions of how and when to speak out and how to do so judiciously are tricky ones. We are silenced and some of us may, appropriately, want to refuse that silencing. Many decisions about self-censoring are cultural. What is intolerable 'blurting out' for one woman might be just moderate self-disclosure for another. In thinking about speaking out we are thinking about the very core of women's condition – and our potential free future.

Getting down to it

4

Ingredients

This chapter is about exploring what kinds of ingredients you might like to use in your lifestory. If making your lifestory is akin to making a cake, then you will need to consider what kind of cake it will be – apart from wonderful. Which bits will count as fruit? What will be the flour and the milk? This can be the oddest cake in the world, as well as the most enjoyable. Or if lifestorying is like creating a map, which are the continents and which the tiny islands? How many seas and rivers, brooks and lakes are in this story? How much of the ground is high and which are the densely populated territories? How do they all relate to each other? And with what symbolic materials are you making this map – fine pen or plasticine, plastic flags or a mélange of anything that will do?

What should an autobiography include? This autobiography is primarily for your pleasure, so you may want to ask yourself: 'What do my favourite autobiographies include?' Notice what you enjoy reading about and which bits you'd hate to have been missed out. Cast your thinking wide. Think not just about published work, but other people's stories that have been related to you.

Jane, a public relations consultant from Bath, wrote down that her favourite lifestories included the following:

- deep truths, things that people don't usually tell you
- some ideas I haven't thought of – so bits of philosophy are fine
- funny bits, that you might feel a bit ashamed to write about
- really frank and interesting stuff about the kinds of people I don't usually meet (like gamblers), the kind of places I don't

usually go (like jazz clubs and religious retreats), the kinds of things I don't usually do (like skiing in Scotland)

WHAT ARE YOUR KEY ELEMENTS?

In the cake analogy this would be where you decide on what fruit and flavourings you'll be putting in the cake. In a map, this would be where you decide on how many and how large the continents, how secluded and numerous the islands, where the streams flow and where the mountains become barriers. The continents may well be key relationships, key occupations or activities, key dwellings in other places. The little islands might be important but fleeting experiences, such as a brief encounter with a mentor or stranger. Rivers might well be the on-going feelings and ideas that flow through all your life, linking the most outlandish places. Oceans can be huge periods when nothing apparently significant happens and yet the tides pull on. Lakes can be times of calm vision or easy experiences such as an enriching, unproblematic friendship. Mountains can be situations of enormous difficulty and isolation. Later chapters suggest more ways to write about these in full. This section paves the way.

MAIN THEMES

Some of the main themes in women's autobiographies, the rivers flowing through every part of the story, include the following:

- love – not only romances but family love, passion for places, the struggle to love despite obstacles, love of self, love of actions, love of creativity, or even (as the Russian novelist Dostoevsky said, 'Hell is the condition of those who cannot love') not loving
- creation – which can include creating a home, children, building up a business, making yourself into what you want to be, writing, painting, photography and so on
- coping with difficulties and crises – this can include beating addiction, learning how to survive socially, handling tricky relationships, surviving illness
- hopes – their fulfilment and their disappointment

- changes – their unexpectedness/expectedness, their demands, what you learn from them, what they leave in their wake (for example the loss of a parent), emigration, completing a project, moving, new/old relationships
- beliefs – what spiritual notions and what ideas you use to guide you, how these work and how they have been adapted in the light of events in your life
- knowledge and awakenings – what you know, how you learned it, how you applied it, what others taught you, how you came to make fresh realisations
- adapting to new times/people/living styles/environments – and refusal or inability to adapt
- observation of others – changing, growing up in relation to you
- tensions between key forces or viewpoints – for example, the ordinary domestic you versus you as the exotic eccentric; you as pragmatic compromiser versus you as lone heroine

Exercise: Themes like rivers

Sit down quietly when you have an hour in which to be calm. What are the rivers? What aspects of the way you think and feel have meandered (or sometimes flooded) through your life? Do this in list form, leaving plenty of space for later thoughts. There will probably be many later additions, as this is a profound exercise. Feel free to draw these rivers in relation to the high ground (they are *connected*, they can't be drawn in isolation).

Keep the lists or drawings in a safe and prominent place. They will be crucial for your unconscious planning of how you tell the story and you will probably want to alter them extensively as you write more and more, particularly as you write about the high ground. You may enjoy the idea that writing can be a way of stepping into the same river twice: the water in it has long gone but the route, volume and nature of it remain the same.

Physical relics

You may want to look at the physical relics of your history at this point, the things in your attic or stuffed in old suitcases: dolls, letters, clothes, guitar, earrings, your baby's first bootees, your sister's old records. If you have kept them, it is usually because they remind you of something important, which you will want to consider for the book. It is your evidence. These objects can be the prompt for your memory. Objects can also include gravestone epitaphs, photos, even people and places if you are looking at them as material objects for evidence of your past.

These physical remains can also be counter-information that reminds you of the significant contrasts between what you think happened (the story you have subsequently created) and the events that happened at the time. The discrepancy between the two – your memory versus the relic's evidence – can be useful. Don't think you need to write 'the truth' as it was. Present the two versions side by side if you like.

Exercise: Using objects

- Take, or think of, an object from your past; for example, a comfort blanket, a plastic nursery rhyme mug, school badge, your child's birth certificate. Put it in front of you, in a quiet place. Reflect on it for three minutes, using a timer. If your attention wanders just note that it has and pull yourself gently back (be gentle; beating yourself up will take too much time, you can use the energy for better things).
- List all the things the object meant to you then, so far as you can remember.
- Then think of a time when this object was your companion in something profound, and write down what the object said, thought, felt. That is, treat this as a Gestalt exercise; the object may 'know' things that you do not consciously 'know'.
- As a postscript, describe the object briefly, for someone with no vision. This may bring you to a whole other train of thought. Go along with it if you like or just makes notes for another time.

Keep the outcome of this exercise – which you may want to do with several objects on different occasions. These stories around objects may be one of the basic building blocks of your autobiography. They may also change your whole unconscious thinking about how you tell the story, so do keep them and let them work their own quiet alchemy while you get on with the next thing.

If you are someone who likes to plan very early on, then try the next exercise using objects. (If you want to be free of any structure for your autobiography, then fine, leave this exercise out entirely.)

Exercise: Preliminary chapter planning

- Using the idea of significant objects from above, select 18 objects that matter to you. Try to make them objects that represent very different experiences or times in your life. (If they are not physically available to you, then draw them, however badly, or write their name and characteristics on a sheet of paper.)
- Arrange on the floor 18 pieces of paper numbered chapter 1, chapter 2, chapter 3, etc., up to chapter 18.
- Place on each piece of paper one object or several objects (or sketches of/notes about the objects) in any order that feels right for you.
- Now stand back and reflect. Are these possible chapters for your book? Think of 'chapter' as another word for 'grouping', if the word feels inhibiting. If they are suitable foci for a chapter, then note, draw or photograph (Polaroids are great) this arrangement before you clear it away, because it will be useful throughout your writing process – and quite easy to forget.

What may well happen is that you will discover other things you want to include. Fine. Make notes on these and keep them somewhere safe. You may want to do this exercise several times during the months of writing your lifestory. Different objects will become significant as you go along. I think this is an exercise that can never be done too often because it helps you ground the book in a very material way. If your aim is not to be fanciful, then this will help you achieve that aim.

Moments of being

There are moments in your life when you suddenly become hyper-aware of yourself. Virginia Woolf famously called these 'moments of being'. For example, I had such a moment visiting my parents at home one day when I was in my mid-thirties. It was just after my first marriage had ended. I saw myself in the wardrobe mirror of my old bedroom. I was wearing my nana's old dressing gown, and I moved by mum's painting table (she was using the room as a studio) towards my London bag containing (someone's second-hand) ballet shoes which I'd brought to practise being my dancing self in and my (Oxfam shop) tambourine which I'd brought to show myself I wanted to be a wild percussionist and not a neat Swan Lake grey sexless cygnet. By my side was the junkshop typewriter. It was a moment of startling clarity. I recognised: 'Ah, this is what made me. This is all that I am composed of' and felt great relief and joy at the continuity, at witnessing this proof of the rich elements that had constructed my identity as artist-writer-traveller-human.

You too might like to think of any moments when you suddenly saw yourself and life with a very heightened sense. That moment when you suddenly feel: 'That's it. That's what I've been searching for without knowing it all this time. That crystallises something that's been brewing for years!'

There will be many other things you want to include as key ingredients in your story: turning points and stepping stones, influences and cultural affects, coincidences and hiccups. Many more ideas are suggested in the later chapters about meaningful places and people, ideas and events, and in the chapter about your body. This section has attempted to break the mould of standard lifestory-telling: your story does not have to include births, jobs, marriages, deaths and house removals in any standard way – unless you want it to. You can create a much more spiritual, exploratory and informal landscape, if you so choose.

THE BACKGROUND CONTEXT

In the cake analogy, this is the flour and the fat and the liquid for mixing. These are the bog-standard, taken-for-granted ingredients without which you cannot usually make a cake. It pays to have your curriculum vitae, if you have one, by you in doing this lifestory. Remember that this section is at least as much about all the things you haven't included in the CV – the background and 'barely-worth-mentioning' context – as it is about these documented and impressive things that you can tell others about: the GCSEs and jobs and certificates.

Confession albums

To help you recognise the 'barely-worth-mentioning' ingredients, you might like to think about confession albums, which were a favourite Victorian party game. Hosts asked visitors to fill them in and then later enjoyed looking at all the different confessions their various house guests had made. The questions might appeal to you now in this lifestorying as a way of reminding yourself to tell readers things that you might otherwise think are self-evident.

The usual questions were as follows – the responses are by Agatha Christie:

My ideal virtue: courage.
My idea of beauty in nature: a bank of primroses in Spring.
My idea of beauty in art: Bruegel's tower paintings.
My favourite study: archaeology and fresh aspects of history.
My favourite flower: Lily of the Valley.
My favourite qualities in men: integrity and good manners.
My favourite qualities in women: loving and merry.
My greatest happiness: listening to music.
My greatest misery: noise and long vehicles, crowds.
My favourite amusement: a good play.
My favourite residence: my own home.
My favourite authors: Elizabeth Bowen, Graham Greene.
My favourite poets: T.S. Eliot, Yeats, Tennyson.
My favourite musical composer and instrument: Elgar, Sibelius, Wagner.
My favourite heroes in real life: none. I am not a hero-worshipper.
My favourite heroines in real life: Little Sisters of the Poor.
My favourite actors and plays: Alec Guinness; *Murder in the Cathedral*.
My favourite animal: dogs.
My favourite names: Isabella, Charles, Rodney.
My favourite quotation: 'Life is pure flame and we live by an invisible sun within us' (Sir Thomas Browne).
My present state of mind: peaceful.
My motto: 'The business of life is to go forwards' (Dr Johnson).
My signature: Agatha Christie Mallowan.[1]

Feel free to play with these questions, delete, add and alter at will. When I did this exercise with some students, most of them were irritated by the superficiality of the Victorian questions and invented new ones instead. Try confessing 'The person I hate most; The part of my body I most like; The thing I'd never confess to a living soul; The crime I'd most like to commit; The thing I'd like Jim to fix; My most secret of secret pleasures.'

You could also use the confession album as a way to sum up yourself at different stages in your life. Fill it in *as if* you were 29 or twelve or five or whatever age you want to explore. Try altering your handwriting to fit the you-then. Maybe even decorate the page by dropping jam sandwiches on to it or making doodles of daisies as you might have done at that age.

Bridges

In the transition between different events and stages in your life there will have been metaphorical bridges: pathways that enable you to cross with relative safety from an old place to a new site (and to travel back to the old, at times, if need be). If you are someone who has literally journeyed a lot or is living in a country not of your birth, you may have undergone some sort of rite of passage. On ships crossing the equator first-timers take part in the Neptune ceremony, a traditional group celebration of an initiation into a new group: people who have crossed the line. This is a kind of statement of there being two territories (north and south) and the ceremony is a kind of bridge.

Such bridges, whether or not they are recognised by rites, are the mixture of factors (including prior experience) that help you change and separate from the old you and the old lifestyle. They can be imagined and fantasised about before they happen (and re-written after they happen). You may have mentally travelled to the 'new country' first. You may feel you made your transition without a bridge. Try thinking what bridge you might have liked. Or you may have had a bridge but denied it. Bridges can be overlooked when you tell your lifestory, because the point is usually to describe the arrival at a destination and not the journey. Exploring your bridges may be one way of exploring overlooked aspects of your character and journeys through life.

Exercise: Your bridges and their building

Take a piece of paper and reflect on one bridge in your life. You may even like to draw a bridge to remind yourself of what they look like – little old humpbacked stone bridges across slow streams or wildly swinging rope bridges over dangerous ravines.

You may like to write it all metaphorically, as an adventure in which 'she' and not 'you' featured. What was the nature of your bridge: what was it made of? How long was it? Had you glimpsed it in the distance before you reached it and did it look different then? When you looked back after crossing it, did it look different again?

What do you think you needed to traverse your bridge well? Metaphorically, where did you buy all the provisions that you carried over in your secure waterproof pack? What did you take with you and did you have a bearer, a luggage trolley, a packhorse? Were you a bag lady or a free spirit? Did you explore the bridge, dropping something over it to see how fast the water was flowing? Was the bridge safely above the torrent? Who else was on it?

At the far side, look back. Did you leave anything on the bridge? What did you leave behind? What initially greeted you on the new land: what was the metaphorical equivalent of champagne or custard pies? How were you different for having crossed it? Who made that bridge? What other bridges have there been in your life?

The point of this exercise is that it is a way to think about transitions and stages. So it could be a form you use to structure your lifestory. Every chapter could begin or end with or focus on a new bridge. Or it could be a way to reflect more generally on the twists and turns of your life and the things that assisted you on your way.

Work

Many lifestories, for example those submitted for the National Life Story Awards at the National Sound Archive[2], miss out the thing that takes up at least eight hours of most days, most days of the week, most of the active years of your life: work, whether paid or unpaid, in the house or outside. In lived life, work is the thing that defines your identity – in others' eyes. It can obsess you when you haven't got a job or when it it isn't right, and even when it is. It is crucial to your material well-being, enabling you to support at least some of your chosen lifestyle, but few lifestories give it such weight.

Usually, occupations and daily labour feature in the lifestories of people who are famous for their work, such as film-makers and novelists. Their produce is publicly displayed (however privately achieved) and gives hundreds of thousands of people pleasure. Readers want to know the private person behind the public figure. If you are not famous, then the main reason for you to write about work is to describe what meanings it had for you and how it structured/structures your life.

For example, for some people work means satisfaction, for others frustration. You can view it as a waste of good living time, or a way to contribute something to the world. For women, it has particular meanings: it may not be what you wanted to do but what you ended up doing for lack of opportunity or to fit around bringing up children. It may have been a place of conflict, pain or humiliation that had to be endured because the wage was so crucial at that time. Your job may be one proudly achieved later in life, after many delayed starts. If you don't want to write about work then feel free not to do so. Only write about it if it illustrates something about your identity that you want to explore in this lifestory: for example, your abilities, diversity, success, ambitions, split loyalties and so on.

You might want to start thinking about your achievements (such as the number of millions of plates washed!). List your main jobs. Now tear that piece of paper so that each job is on a separate slip and arrange them in order of importance. Jean decided on categories: 'jobs that paid me the best, jobs I liked doing, jobs that taught me something important about myself'.

Look at your CV and try to find patterns in it, such as being drawn to a particular kind of work, or employer or workplace. Think about how work affected the way others saw you or you saw yourself at any one time.

One of the challenges of writing about work is to represent both its daily nature and its qualities. When people talk about their past jobs they mention the high points, telling anecdotes about adventures or achievements, but seldom convey the 95 per cent of ordinary daily slog. You may want to find a way to do this, especially if a lot of your time has been spent in this unremarkable way.

It's important in writing autobiographically to understand how much you act on your work. It's not just something you are a victim of but something in which you are active, not only by making a product and contributing it to the world, but by the way your very presence subtly changes the workplace and work practices. It's different because of you, you specifically, being there. How?

Exercise: Understanding how work affected you

Ask yourself: if I was standing outside me drawing or photographing or writing about this woman worker, what would I say and see?

If I was an anthropologist or sociologist, what insights would I have about this woman's relationship with her work? How does it relate to her life at home? How is/was that work different to the way she first saw it?

Use this exercise to fill in as much detail about this element of your life as is appropriate. Its aim is to find new perspectives on what it meant to you.

Conversely, you may want to look at the role of play in your life. What effect have fun, relaxation, being silly and not working had on your progress?

THE METHOD

Chapter 13 describes how to explore some of the structuring ideas with which you, the cook, will put these ingredients together. This section discusses the task of mixing the ingredients, the stage of adding enough water, milk, eggs, seasonings, and then baking. Or how the wise surveyor will appraise the task of judiciously laying out this map.

Using detail

It's a good idea to be aware from the start *how* you want to write the lifestory. Using the cake analogy, this is about deciding whether the cake is to be thick with fruit, covered with marzipan and iced, or if it is to be plainer. Is the fruit to be chopped coarsely or finely? Your lifestory will be enriched by specificity and illustration, so do include as much precise detail as you can. One of the basic rules of writing is 'show, don't tell'. Conjure pictures for your readers (including your future self).

Using dialogue

Appropriate snatches of dialogue are useful because they reveal the characters of the people who are speaking as well as their situations. For example, in *My Own Story*, suffragette Emmeline Pankhurst writes about what happened when she was freed from Holloway gaol. The governor asked if she had any complaints to make. ' "Not of you," I replied, "nor of any of the wardresses. Only of this prison and of all men's prisons. We shall raze them to the ground." ' [3] This illustration of how she speaks illuminates her personality far more immediately than any indirect description of the conversation.

Using pictures

Do use illustration, whether actual photographs and drawings or just illustrative writing. Make it a rich book. If you've publication in mind, then the number of photographs is usually between six and 20. But at this stage, feel free to use as many as will assist you in your creative process.

WHAT NOT TO INCLUDE

One answer to the question 'What shall I include?' is probably 'Everything that occurs to you, to start with.' You should do this in note and sketch form initially as otherwise you'll make the project unwieldy. But then feel free to put aside those areas that don't seem important. Usually these are bits I think I 'should' write – but don't actually want to. In that case, I put notes on them in a file called 'Maybe' and put it on a high shelf to show myself I don't need to bother with them, unless I actively want to.

Do take care that you don't amass so much material that you feel daunted. Chapter 5, How do I start?, has good suggestions about organising the project so that you can move freely throughout this fascinating process.

The minute you feel bogged down, stop. It's not good for your flexibility and creativity. Get off your chair. Exercise for a few seconds. Then set your timer for five minutes. Just note down headings for what you might include. Then put it away for another time in a file called something like 'Material to be considered later' or 'Bogs to be negotiated when I've got the energy and a pair of thigh boots'.

Not everything, not everything in order

Don't expect to be able to include all of your life and every story. You do *not* have to. Some people imagine that a lifestory should be a blow-by-blow account in chronological order. This is not so. You are free to include and omit whatever you like.

Leave out anything that does not seem directly relevant to the meaning you are trying to convey.

Don't be side-tracked

It's very easy to be side-tracked when writing your autobiography. You must decide when it is a fruitful path that should be followed to its destination and when it is a diversion from your main road. If it is a diversion, make notes on it but put it aside. Mark your main writing with an asterisk or reference number so that you can easily re-make the connection with the diversion material if you want to at any later time. If you're in doubt about the relevance of it, ask yourself: 'If I had only one more hour left in which to write my autobiography, would I include this?'

No 'shoulds'

Don't, for a minute, include anything you feel you should include, in the sense that someone else might say it *should* be there. It's your book and it should be your place of joy and exploration. (Later, if you have an editor, you might have to consider what others think you should include.) For now, feel free to play highhandedly with the material *you* choose. You are a free woman of the city of yourself. Enjoy the exploration. Come back from your foraging trips with many useful things you want to incorporate in this story of you.

How do I start?

How do you start? In whatever way feels right for you. Some people write whatever they feel like, then organise it later. Others prefer advance planning. Already you probably have a hunch about how to kick off. Feel free to begin in the way you want. If you'd like a suggestion, try the six-stage action plan on pages 65–8.

HOW TO TACKLE IT

Letting it happen organically

I prefer to do months or even years of dreaming, thinking and writing odd pages of notes. Then I draft chapter topics that seem to have emerged from that process, drawing them together. I like doing it bittily because it gives me more room to develop as oddly as I like. I do mean develop and I do mean odd. I love the discoveries that happen because I *haven't* planned. I subscribe to the view that a little bit of chaos is necessary to artistic creativity. However much you plan, it will alter anyway because you will be changing as you write. Such a big task can't help but be ramshackle and uneven at times.

Pre-planning

In contrast to this organic, from-the-bottom-up model, Julia found, in doing her academic lifestory work about women and former Yugoslavia, that a top-down approach worked well for her:

I would advise other women writing life history ... to invest in the planning stage, particularly deciding the main outcomes and themes. Having these to focus on acts as a natural stimulus to memory and helps in the process of sifting through information. Even where there is no expert tutorial support available it should be possible to discuss ideas with friends and to take note of their constructive feedback.

You probably know it already

You may already have developed many ideas by reading this far; they will be in your unconscious, waiting. Most people find that they and the lifestory project have many fleeting encounters and several false starts to their relationship. Listen to your own ideas first before responding to my suggestions. You will know best. If no ideas for starting occur to you, here are a few ways of tapping into your own creativity.

Exercise: Listing possible approaches

Try heading a piece of paper 'Ways I could start'. Then write a list for yourself of your good ideas about tackling this project. If that doesn't work, try heading it 'Ways she could start' and be your own instructor. Cathy's list included:

- start writing about the three most important things I want people to know about me – then see what happens
- write the ten most self-evident things about me
- try getting a set of ring-binders and making chapter headings – and see where that gets me and what I already know I want to say
- go on holiday with three years' diaries and write up what's important from them, rather than just conjuring memories out of the air

Exercise: Doing it as dialogue between you and the lifestory project

See the project as a thing you are going to speak to and collaborate with. It has its own wisdom so you can discuss anything intelligently with it. You could use a few stage directions too if that would help. Are you and your lifestory project going to smile at each other from across a huge or tiny room at your first encounter? What – metaphorically – are you both wearing? For example, working overalls, playsuits? Are you bare-skinned but facing a lifestory project that is power-dressed? What metaphorical landscape are you going to do this in? By the side of a quiet sunny lake? In a dark, private, lockable place? Write the script of this encounter.

Exercise: Planning it like a business project

The methods used for planning business projects may appeal to you if you like to prepare. Type out a form leaving gaps that you can fill in. The headings could be as follows:

- project title
- two-sentence description of project
- goal
- projected date of completion
- number of hours per week to be spent on it
- obstacles to achieving goal
- resources needed/available for achieving goal
- personal strengths which will be brought to project
- target completion date for stage one, stage two, stage three and so on
- comments

Getting your goals clear

Understand your own intention, frankly. It pays to be as up-front with yourself as you can at this stage. For example, how much time do you want to spend on it, what kind of story is it going to be (familyish, full of fantasy, non-chronological), how do you feel about eventual publication? Are you going to enjoy this or will it be a slog? Put up notices for yourself about anything you need to be reminded of.

Listing

Make lists of what you are going to cover: lots and lots of lists and lots of sub-lists, each on a separate piece of paper. Keep them brief. This is your brainstorming time and these will be valuable parts of the skeleton of your structure. The lists may well reflect the headings in this book, such as what I want to write about, places I want to mention, things my body showed me.

At some point you might also create another list of *how* you want to write; for example, bravely, beautifully, quirkily, with the freedom to be dishonest.

Reflecting

Reflect on these lists. Attach an extra sheet to any that especially appeal to you, noting where you might go to next with them. Keep it very brief at this stage. Reflect on your old diaries. Reflect on your family album. Reflect on the stored stuff in your literal or metaphorical attic. Reflect, reflect, reflect – and write down or paint the outcomes of this reflection. Catch the thoughts; don't let them slip away.

Collating

Take a ring-binder and some sheets of coloured paper to use as temporary dividers (those ready-made card dividers may feel intrusively dictatorial at this stage, neatening up and professionalising your thoughts before you are ready to be so proper).

Then see if any of the lists you've made can be fitted into any kind of order. For example, if one of your 'what' lists included 'childhood games I played that taught me how to be in later life', you would put that near the start of your ring-binder if you think the lifestory is going to be chronological.

You might want to create chapter headings at this point. Again, do them on separate sheets of coloured paper and let yourself know you can change them. If you want, write 'Introduction' on one sheet and 'Conclusion' or 'The end' on another. It's one way of making the process seem do-able, not infinite.

Researching

You may want to summarise how much and what kinds of research you will do. Perhaps someone may do it for you. Now might be the time to get an overview on how much you intend to supplement your memory and how.

Preparing to put it together later

If you like to pre-plan, try reading Chapters 15 and 16 on putting it all together. Just skim through them. Any ideas you have from this may well help you to avoid going down some wrong paths now and can save you both work and time. Jot down casually at this stage what sort of structure you think it might have.

Fix the time allowed

Make a deal with yourself about the time and length of this whole lifestory-creating process. Some of us like to work fast, some slow. You'll know best if you dread having something hanging over you. Julia, writing about her and her friends' experiences of former Yugoslavia, found 'meeting deadlines was not always easy but it did ensure the adrenalin *kept flowing* and provided a firm structure within which to complete the work'.

Some writers make a deal with the family about the amount of hours they will be available for the next few months – and stick to it.

Fix a provisional date, say a day and date in three years' time, when you'd like to have the whole thing finished, or even a first draft. Agree with yourself how many drafts you'd ideally like to do. And make a contract with yourself to allow a certain number of hours per week.

It is OK to write it all fast: speed does not automatically mean your story will be superficial. Vancouver holds an annual festival for writing a novel in three days and I've been greatly helped by a handbook called

How to Write a Movie in 21 Days.[1] One of the key things it recommends is numbering 300 sheets of paper, marking some as the start of new acts and scenes. You can do this with your lifestory if you like. Seeing the pile of numbered sheets, with chapter headings every 15 pages, is an enormous help because it proves the project isn't impossible. These decisions can be revised and revised again but knowing the physical ground you have to cover usually helps tremendously.

GOLDEN RULES FOR GETTING STARTED

Rules work because they allow you space to think and re-think without causing you the trouble of doing any rearranging. They give you room to explore. Try them and then add your own.

• *Leave plenty of blank space*
Expect that almost every page will be half empty. Leave blank spaces – especially at the bottom – for afterthoughts, notes to yourself and later summaries about what you think you had *intended* to say on that page. Write on one side of the paper only. Leave the back of every sheet blank so that you can cut out bits and stick them somewhere else if you want.

Always leave a lot of space between lines. Write on every other line if you are handwriting, set the typewriter or word processor for double-spacing if you are typing.

Leave wide margins (say 3 cm) on both sides, in which to make additions. I know all this makes the process more expensive and it uses up more trees but, believe me, you'll be using up that paper one way or another. The margins won't stay blank for long so the paper won't be wasted.

• *Feel free to be messy*
Don't feel you have to write in a linear way, word after word, line after line, event after chronological event, page after page. Do use the brainstorming idea of blob charts. In a blob chart you put a key word in the middle of the paper and then scribble in any other key words you associate with it; drawings and scraps of poems too. The point of doing this is that it frees up your creativity. It may look messy but it will help you get to exciting points far faster than the usual methods. (See books on creativity such as those on using the right-hand hemisphere of your brain.)[2]

• *Always write more*

Write too much. Continue even after you think you've said enough. You'll be surprised at what you uncover. Say the obvious in case it isn't obvious to others.

• *Do use asides, but on the side*

I've found that many lifestory writers feel appalled at how many asides they want to make; that is, the number of diversions and comments and explanations and supplementary points. Asides are good in a way. Their insistence on existing shows how fully you are thinking about your lifestory. They're normal, especially when you are doing a lot of remembering. Life can't be summed up along one clear pathway. As women we usually have the ability to think widely and associatively; that gift should be celebrated and made room for. The usefulness of asides is that they allow you to note what may or may not prove to be irrelevant later. It may be important information that you just don't know how to situate at this stage.

Asides can also become unwieldy, intrusive and diverting. So try writing your asides in brackets, footnotes or italics or in the margin (some people use the right-hand margin for asides, and leave the left-hand margin for intellectual afterthoughts and editorial comments). The idea is to make these asides visibly different from what you are calling 'the main points', to give yourself clarity.

• *You can start more than once*

You may well have several false starts. Keep each version. They will all be helpful in the end, however disheartening they seem to you at the time.

• *Do it often*

Write several chunks a week of two or three pages. Frequency really helps. Re-read them a day or two later. If you leave it longer than this you'll probably have moved on too far to amend it in the same frame of mind. I prefer to make the first amendments within two days (and then later in a few months', or even a few years' time). Make notes on what you might like to add or summarise what you really intended to say and didn't quite get around to saying. If you are scared of the process, set the timer for ten minutes and say to yourself you'll write just for that time. This can be a way of going onwards.

• *Feel free*

Feel free to paint, or to write 'she' not 'I', or to go off into fiction or poetry
if at any time it feels appropriate to do so. (Keep a few journal notes
on that process if you do it; it can help a lot for your later understanding
of what you are trying to say.)

• *Any time is a good time*

Don't discard odd chunks of time as not long enough to be worth
using. Even in five minutes you can write a good list (say from one of
the exercises) which you can then think about on the bus or while doing
some physical tasks. Take up the writerly habit of carrying a notebook.
Only the most rare human being remembers that thing that is so
vivid that it can't possibly be forgotten. It can be – and usually is.

THE SIX-STAGE ACTION PLAN

Extract the bits of this plan that will help you and discard anything
that inhibits you. Design your own action plan using any elements
of this as a basis. You may want to attach time limits to each stage.

Stage one: Starting the writing

Flip through this book. If you haven't already done so, do the exercise
that most appeals to you (or even the one that you most hate the thought
of doing). Do it freely, not with sweaty diligence.

Then congratulate yourself. Making the first mark really is the final
stage of the starting-up process and the first stage of actually doing
the lifestory project. For those of you who dread it, you've got over the
worst bit. For those of you feeling positive about the process of writing,
this may well be one of the most exciting moments. If you like making
records, this is a moment to write about in your diary of autobiographical process.

From this point on, you should be well away with only the occasional
hiccup. Do any exercise you fancy next. Do the exercises that most
attract you and consider whether it would be worth trying the ones
you dislike – they may be offering you an important clue. And do any
writing that continues on from these exercises, including writing that
goes off at a tangent if you think this is appropriate.

Stage two: Starting to create order

Start putting these fragments together in your ring-binder. At this stage, and possibly only temporarily, chronological order may be a help. This is because it's one easy way to categorise the writings and find them again. If I file bits of writing under themes or topics I later find that I have forgotten what group I put them in. The category they seemed to belong to at the time of filing has since changed. So chronological order is a more memory-proof way of organising the data. The *date* when events happened is relatively non-controversial.

One way to proceed is by having a cardboard divider within your ring-binder for every five years of your life. It's up to you whether you refer to personal time or the world's time; that is, whether you sum up the periods as 'age 0–5', or '1955–60'.

This is advice about *storage* only. Your completed book does not have to be structured chronologically (Chapters 15–17 will discuss this). If a structure is already emerging for your lifestory, then let it come. Arrange the ring-binder in a way that will allow this – and allow change too.

Some people find such an approach is not relaxed enough for this necessarily ad hoc and fluid stage. You may want to use a box or a ring-binder without dividers. If you do the latter, keep a list of contents at the front of your folder so you can maintain an overview of what is accumulating. It's easy to forget. If you are very thorough you could photocopy your notes and arrange one set in chronological order and a second set in theme order.

Stage three: Seeing how you are shaping up

After a month or two, start to write or type some of the fragments in some kind of connected way. Chapter 15 offers ideas on ways to pull it all together. Ideally use a word processor so that you can revise and revise again. Glance at the ideas about structure and polishing in later chapters.

As whatever you write at this point is your *first* draft, it will necessarily be imperfect. Don't worry about perfection now. The main function of whatever you produce at this stage is to be a signpost to show you how you are coming along and what you need to do next. It should give you clarity.

You may find it advisable to not show what you have written to anyone else at this vulnerable stage. Any kind of influence at this point can become a setback. I prefer this stage to be private, relying only on my judgement and values. Other people's come later.

Stage four: Moving away from focusing on you and looking out into the world

This is the stage when you think about what else you want to include. Begin researching background information (see Chapter 14) whenever you like. Do remember your agreement with yourself on how much research you are going to do, so that you don't overload your lifestory with others' data instead of your own meaningful stories.

Begin interviewing people. (See Chapter 14.) Your schedule for this may have to be a compromise between interviewing those people who can give you information about an area of your life that is fascinating you at this very moment and interviewing those who are close to death and should be interviewed at once. One way to handle this conflict is to do the interview but put the tape aside until you are ready to listen to it. Of course, by doing so you may lose the chance to ask those supplementary questions that usually crop up after hearing the tape and that you would normally deal with in follow-up interviews. For most people the interviewing schedule is usually a tricky compromise that is never quite ideal.

Stage five: Structuring and polishing

At some point, you will want to start shaping and structuring your work. Read the later chapters for help on this and act on the suggestions that work for you. This is when chapters and sequences and re-thinking and totalling up come together. At this stage some people become a bit obsessive. You can't leave it alone because this is a whole way of thinking about your life, not just constructing something on paper. It's a philosophical and psychological task as much as a technical wrestling with putting data in the correct order.

Stage six: Revising

Minor revisions will probably be going on all the time. As you re-read you'll be crossing out sentences and re-phrasing certain points and re-wording as you go along – almost unconsciously.

Within a year of stage five (your shaping process) being roughly finished you may want to do a major revision. Read Chapter 17 on polishing and fine-tuning. If you want to leave your lifestory as it is, fine. Such decisions will be affected by your vision of the finished work and whether you are seeking publication. While you may not want to revise, a publisher will certainly need to have some things altered, tightened up, expanded, explained or even deleted. Some people fear this process initially, then enjoy it. For me it is usually exhilarating. I feel not only that I have been thoroughly understood but that someone is prepared to help me achieve a task I cannot complete alone. The joy of attention and assistance outweighs irritation at what the editors want to cut. I learn about the art of writing too.

But you may be writing your lifestory for yourself, as a personal exploration rather than for publication. In that case, and if you don't want to revise but just to put the lifestory to rest, then this whole process can be reward enough. Fine. Forget about any corrections that others might want or any ideas of 'proper' autobiography.

For now, get started. If you get stuck, Appendix 1 offers some good suggestions on how to start up again.

Writing about your body

One of the best places to start writing about yourself is to begin with your body. It's the undeniable companion which has been with you all these years: witnessing you, evidencing you, expressing the feelings or thoughts that lie deep in you, facing life's hardships with you. The last ten years have seen such a growth in women writing about the meanings of the body that there are plenty of texts to choose from if you want to look at a few of these ideas first.[1]

Some of the earliest women's autobiographies deal with the body too. Agrippina famously describes the breech birth of her son (who became the Emperor Nero). Medieval visionary Julian of Norwich spent much time describing the feeling that she was about to die before her visions came; her mother was so convinced Julian had expired that she even walked towards her to close her eyes. Today one of my gains from reading movie stars' autobiographies is in seeing how they have experienced illness, because that proof of their physical vulnerability is somehow endearing. Women artists such as photographer Jo Spence have made visual autobiographies (self-portraits) using their bodies as a way to show their resistance to victimisation.[2] Jo claimed back her power by taking pictures of the doctors and her body to show how she was treated and how she looked after herself when she had breast cancer.

For almost all women, identity is deeply tied in with the body, as autobiography after autobiography shows. 'It is not so much that the body is used instrumentally – as a means to some end outside the body. Rather to be in a certain bodily condition is to be oneself', say Mary and Kenneth Gergen, who studied the use of the body in many popular lifestories.[3] Bodies are the undeniable proof that you are who you are. They are also the aspect of yourself most visible to others' surveillance and control. And they are the most obvious way in which women differ from men. We have a whole extra system: the reproductive system. In writing about your body you are writing about yourself as a member of specific gender.

Feminist autobiographical theorists have observed that men omit the body's importance much more frequently than women. Not all do: South African President Nelson Mandela described his tribal circumcision, for example. But often men write only about the self that their head creates, rather than writing about themselves as fully embodied human beings with hungers and sensual pleasures, instincts and physical abilities. The mind–body spilt in western society means that people tend to think and speak about themselves in terms of what they think and say, as if they were walking brains rather than whole bodies.

Try starting with the following exercise as a way to think about the self you are going to be writing about, and writing with, for the next few months or years.

Exercise: Bits of your body

List the favourite bits of your body. In brackets briefly write the reason why. Write down the kind of bouquet or gift you might give it to thank it for being there and giving you pleasure in your life. If it's appropriate, go on to think about what parts have been most difficult for you. Give them a bouquet too, rather than blaming them. You may want to say how you are willing to relate to them in the future.

WHAT BODIES DO

These are some of the things that bodies do: leap, walk, make love, sing, cry, feed, bleed, succour, give birth, twine themselves round, cuddle, fart, excrete, grow, weaken, fail, strengthen, arch, play, swoop, swim, inhale, exhale, carry on enduringly, carry, get broken.

Explore those functions of your body that are meaningful to you. For example, you might be aware of how your body grew in height, evidenced by the way you grew out of clothes, and the way others handled it. On our birthdays my dad got my sisters and I to stand with our backs to the living-room door while he (who was so particular about keeping paintwork nice) marked our height on it with a pencil and we all compared this new mark to the previous marks. I liked the attention to my development but now I wonder whether I wouldn't have preferred my changes to be handled in a different way. What were my internal perceptions of my growth and its meanings? What less perceptible or ignored developments went unmarked: breasts, ability to speak to adults, courage, spiritual longing?

Body power

When did you discover just how much your body knew and could do? Perhaps you used it as an instrument of achievement. Perhaps you pushed it beyond your normal strength and walked on hot coals, bungee-jumped, survived intense cold by meditating yourself into being hot. Perhaps you dressed it up so it carried you through a social situation that required far more aplomb than you felt inside. Lavish some affection on this thing you are regarding and which will be so useful in writing a holistic story of you.

Exercise: Thinking about body power

List the times when your body assisted you to do something momentous, for example have a baby, win a race. Make notes about date, place, etc. Then focus on one particular time that you felt you had really learned about who you were and your capacity. Expand this into a short piece of writing. Include your reactions, such as shock, and what the experience then led on to you being able to do.

For example, Jean found: 'I was 55 when I first started going rambling in a group. I'd thought I was past it. Discovering that I was fit enough to climb a hill I never thought I could make was an important stage in realising I did not have to be confined by old age ... I used it as the opening for the second half of my lifestory.'

The point of this exercise is to get a view of your life from an oblique perspective. It will be part of the background knowledge you are accumulating – a kind of colouring in of the picture of you.

Writing about periods

Many women have written extensively about menstruation, a monthly event which frequently reminds us of our womanhood. You may like to write about periods too, if they have a significance for you.

> ## Exercise: Menstruating
>
> - When did your periods start and what did they mean to you (for example, shock, delight, horror, relief at your normality)?
> - What information had you had beforehand and did your actual experience tally with it or belie it?
> - What events made you see periods differently over time? (For example, once they started becoming painful with endometriosis? Or once you learned that it is not something to be ashamed of and that the onset of menstruation is actually celebrated in other cultures? Or once you began to notice how companies marketed tampons?)
> - Think about how this reflects other elements of your life: does the monthly pain actually determine how active you are? Does the joy you feel at the arrival of a period indicate how much you gamble with the possibility of pregnancy?
>
> The point of this exercise is to understand the significance of these monthly rhythms throughout your life. You may not want to include much of it in your lifestory but it could be useful background in thinking of yourself as an embodied female. If you want to go further, a stimulating book on menstruation is *The Wise Wound: The Myths, Realities and Meanings of Menstruation* by Peter Redgrove and Penelope Shuttleworth.[4]

When your body fails you

Has any part of your body been broken? In a society that values perfect bodies and regards health and ability as the norm, you may like to record the meanings for you – then and now – of the process of losing power or perfection in one area of your body and then recovering it. Illness, disability and injury, especially for people who have taken their bodies for granted, can bring wisdom but also emotional pain and difficulties, especially over others' responses. For example, for children in hospital for the first time the trauma can be increased by the family's absence.

What about you? Perhaps your body's failure taught you pride in your healing ability? Perhaps it was a non-event. Perhaps it gave you an abiding interest in TV hospital dramas such as *Casualty*, or even affected a later career choice.

Exercise: Exploring what happens when your body fails you

Think of a time, maybe the first time, when you discovered your body wouldn't always do whatever you asked of it. Write about the event as you *then*, in the present tense. For example, 'I am six years old. I am in this place full of people I don't know. I hurt. I am on my own ...' Write the details of the time, place, your response, the response of people who loved you, professionals' roles, the aftermath.

Alice, a medal-winning long-distance runner working on her career story, did the above exercise.

> For about three years after this car smash I felt my body had 'failed' me. I hated it. It had broken the deal. This perfected glorious body could no longer do all the things I'd worked to make it be able to do. I wanted to kill it. Doing this exercise I realised that I needed to do a lot of work on my relationship with my body, and with all my ideas of imperfection. It also gave me a frame with which to write my whole life story: that it was this sort of mad hill climb from babyhood to be this athlete my parents wanted. And then, like in the nursery rhyme, Jill had fallen down the hill. And the vinegar and brown paper and being in bed mending myself period was a time to leave room for what the next volume might say. But this volume was called 'The Uphill Struggle'. I know it isn't a new idea for a lifestory title but it was the image I wanted to enable me to write all that had happened so far. That was my shaping idea.

The aim of the exercise is to help you avoid presenting a false picture of yourself as a perfect performer and instead to reveal the normal, fallible, embodied being.

HOW BODIES LOOK

Exploring how your body looks and how this has affected your life entails looking at both how you think your body looks and how others think your body looks (and the overlap).

Describing your appearance

Whether or not your lifestory will be published and include photographs of you, you may want to describe how *you think* you look. (This of course will not be the same as what your readers think, having seen your photos.)

> ### Exercise: Distinguishing features
>
> Initially, write down the physical features that would appear on an official summary. Don't be judgemental and say 'weight – 2 stone too heavy', just state your weight. Then go on to add whatever else you like. I include the following:
>
> - height (later you can talk about it relative to others)
> - weight (later you can talk about its fluctuations and their meaning to you)
> - hair colour (later add texture, lengths and different styles)
> - eyes (later add the colour of your eyelashes, the thickness of your eyebrows, the common expressions in your eyes)
> - complexion (you may later want to refer to any cosmetics that change this)
> - any distinguishing features (later add the things that are not visible to a casual glance but which you think distinguish you; for example a false breast, having hidden scars)
> - remarks

Changes over time

In looking at popular autobiography and the body, Mary and Kenneth Gergen found that at puberty it is 'as if the body, which seemed a reasonably stable and controllable aspect of the girlhood self, begins to undo one's identity in adolescence. Simultaneously it can make one hideous and desirable, both of which are problematic shifts of identity.'[5] Folk singer Joan Baez in her autobiography, for example, said that on entering high school 'on the one hand I thought I was pretty hot stuff, but on the other I was still pretty self-conscious about my extremely flat chest and dark skin.'[6] Identification with your body is different in youth, in middle years and in old age. Changes of culture can also mean you drastically re-think your embodied identity. For example, visiting China can make you height conscious.

Getting older can mean that you become more and more interested in your body as health becomes increasingly precious. Looking back over many years, you may see cycles of neglect and indulgence, health and illness.

Exercise: Showing the changes

You may want to make a chart as below. Put the various features down the left and then ages or dates at the top. Mark any changes that have happened over the years.

AGE	0	5	10	15	20	30	40	50
height								
weight								
hair								
eyes								
complexion								
distinguishing features								
anything else								

The point of doing these exercises is to appraise yourself in an objective way, for the purposes of both deciding what information you want to give to readers and of understanding what's important to you about your appearance and its changes. Just use the above chart for reference and exploration rather than including it in an autobiography.

When others look at our bodies

It may be that when people look or looked at your body they had ideas about you that were incorrect as far as you were concerned. If beauty is in the eye of the beholder, then how much are other physical qualities also in the eye of the beholder? In other words, what did they project on to you because of how you looked?

You may want to write about events in your history that were affected by others' appraisal and misappraisal of you; people beheld you in a particular way, they mistook you or recognised you. Sometimes beholders will have been wrong but sometimes they will have been right – without your realising it. Appearances can be revealing as much as they can be deceptive.

With whose eyes do we look at our bodies?

As women we are encouraged to gaze at our bodies evaluatingly – are our legs long enough, breasts big enough, mouth smiling or pouting enough? But whose is the evaluating eye? Who constructs those standards by which we judge?

Exercise: Thinking about the evaluating eye

Take a time in your history when you were most anxious about your appearance. Write down the date. Draw a picture of you then or describe in words how you looked. Include clothes.

Now, what did you then, and do you now, think the people judging you *wanted* women to look like? What values did you have then? What options did you have for evolving your own system of values and applying it to yourself? How did this affect what you did?

Use this exercise especially to think about times of collision and unease. These can be key moments in a woman's struggle to deal with her identity. It can be a way of knowing the discrepancy between your self-evaluation and your views on appearance by contrast to others' views. You might like to repeat this exercise for several different times in your life, such as in your teens, after having a baby, after an operation, after the menopause.

WAYS BODIES ARE TREATED

In western society, women's bodies are more looked at, commented upon, exposed, handled, treated, mistreated and looked at than men's. The less privileged we are, the less respectfully our bodies are handled. I am thinking about how we treat our *own* bodies (which is coloured by how others teach us to treat our bodies) and how *others* treat our bodies – be they lovers or doctors, photographers or beauticians, plastic surgeons or hairdressers.

Bodily treatments

Alteration/reconstruction: operations, cosmetics, Alexander technique correction, osteopathy, healing, cosmetic surgery, implants, surgical removal (for example, of beauty spots, warts), sex change, enhancements such as ear/body piercing, tattooing.

Mutilation: by ourselves, for example nail-biting, scab-picking; and by others, torture, abuse, in group experiences such as war, and by accident.

Appreciation: stroking, loving, massage, good exercise, healthy food.

The way others treat you

The way you treat your body has connections to the way others treat you or have treated you. This behaviour can be useful evidence about you in an autobiography.

Exercise: Being physically treated by assistants/ professionals

List all the people who help you or have helped you with your body (for example, beautician, swimming instructor, orthodontist, dressmaker).

Then list any of the sensations you felt when they handled you (such as a sense of delightful abandonment to their expertise, wariness, worries about the money it will cost you, fear of news about the effects of aging they discover).

What does this mean? What does it tell you about your attitude to life?

Lally said:

> When I split up with my lover I got a ring put in my clitoris. When previous relationships ended I got another hole made in my ear for earrings or got a hair cut. I finally realised that it's my way of celebrating my new relationship with myself alone – undetermined by others. I think in my lifestory I might group every chapter round the new piercing I had done – because it marks a new beginning ... My body is subject to my wishes – even though my lovers may not be.

The point of this exercise is to understand what new meanings you give to your body as you change or help it.

Medical history

You may want to include your medical history – noting what happened and who treated you for it. What did you think of that treatment's appropriateness? Was there an underlying malaise that the illness was only a symptom of and if so was the treatment of use?

Exercise: Your medical history

Try either writing down the things you consulted the doctor for, or writing down the various periods in your life and then noting visits to the doctor at those times. You may discern some patterns. Write about a pattern or a symptom that seems to stand out. What does it tell you about the way you handle life?

The point of this exercise is that it can be a fast and deep way to understand what has been distressing you in life and how your needs have been attended to. It can be the most illuminating body exercise of all. Be careful not to grill yourself about 'Was it psychosomatic or real?' It's better to accept that body and mind work as one and that many useful messages are conveyed to us – fast – by our wise bodies.

Wrong use of your body by others

The next exercise refers to the reality of what happens to many women's bodies and minds in this society. The exercise may not be appropriate for you. Feel free to skip it entirely. If you think you have been sexually abused, then rather than writing about it for the first time here, write with the support of a workbook such as *The Courage to Heal*.[7] If you have worked through the abuse already, either on your own or with a therapist, then you may decide to use any notes or drawings you have already made as a way to reach the right stage for writing it in a lifestory. Some women, of course, have written whole lifestories solely about abuse, for example Elly Danica's *Don't: A Woman's Word* and Sylvia Fraser's *My Father's House: A Memoir of Incest and Healing*.[8]

Any invasion or abuse of the body can feel like a negation of your identity. For some people this might a painful subject, for others a necessary one. If you want to tackle the idea of physical abuse that has happened to you or significant women you know, try the following exercise. It might help to set aside a small amount of time for it and arrange a treat for afterwards. For example, ask your very reliable friend to pick you up and take you swimming in an hour. Explorations of such loss can sometimes bog writers down.

Exercise: Abuse

Write about a woman (imaginary) who has just one thing in common with you (anything, it could be the colour of her hair). Then make a list of ways in which her body might have been abused.

Now write about how she handled that. I'd recommend not thinking about how she suffered but rather how she dealt with that experience at the time and how she survived; stay detached rather than letting yourself be submerged in the feelings. You could explore how she constructed that experience afterwards; that is, the stories she told about it, and how the stories matched (or not) the idea of the event she had at the time.

You might want to think about the events surrounding such a time. If it's appropriate, write the view of the person who did the abuse. What did they think of what they were doing and what were they like before and afterwards?

Try asking yourself the question at one remove, as Caroline did after she experienced a violent physical attack:

What did the mirror see?
What does her mother see?
What do men see?
What do women see?
What does she see?
What do I see?
What don't I see?

The point of writing in the third person – as 'she' not 'I' – is to be freer to write difficult material without too much distress and without telling your standard account of the events. It can provide a fresh way of seeing.

This is not to suggest that other people only treat our bodies badly. You may also want to write about a lover's caresses, a mother's strokes, children's snuggling, kind handling by strangers after you've had a road accident, the pleasure of dancing or playing in a huge circle. You may also want to think about how you have treated others' bodies over the years and what this says about your development.

HOW BODIES FEEL TO US FROM THE INSIDE

It can be hard to know how your body feels from the inside. I don't mean a lover's or a surgeon's knowledge; I mean how you feel when you are peaceful and at one with your body, happy inside your own skin. This is usually at times of great calm and reflection.

There are other times when you do know your body from the inside – or aspects of it – because of some extreme way in which it is being tested, such as very violent exercise, torture or a difficult labour.

Exercise: Stillnesses

Don't write this but meditate on it. Lie down for ten peaceful minutes in a quiet room and think about these questions:

- When have you stood or lain still and just experienced your body getting on with it?
- What sounds do you hear from it: blood singing in your ears, your breath's particular cadences?
- Do you have a smell in repose that differs from the active you?
- What is this body when it is being rather than doing?
- When in your life have you had your best moments with it – calm and confident and absolutely at one with yourself?

Now get up quietly and write down anything that comes into your head, but only five words to a line. That is, show yourself by using this poetic form that you are not forcing yourself to write a linear narrative. These are just fragments for you to incorporate later.

Sensations

You may want to describe bodily sensations you've experienced: falling, being held, floating, glowing, drowning, flying, bursting, trembling, feeling reborn, expanding, shrinking, freefalling, leaping. All these can help the lifestory. Include your profoundest feelings; body metaphors are vivid metaphors. What were your earliest bodily sensations? Being bathed? Sucking? What are the ones that stand out for you since? What are the ones you'd like to die feeling? This could be a way to complete a lifestory if it has a chronological structure: you could try talking about final moments in contrast to your first moments.

WHAT THE BODY SPEAKS OF

Sometimes your body speaks when you can't or won't. It tells you about something that is going on. The English language is full of sayings that can be illustrative – or annoyingly restricting – in understanding what one bit of your body is telling you (for example 'My heart leapt when she said that'). You may well have had the experience that your body has acted without you at times – especially in shock. One woman I know recorded that when she left her violent husband her feet just took her out of the door, away from his threatening knife, running down the street and round the corner to her friend's house.

Exercise: Thinking about when your body has spoken or acted for you

First of all, make a list of ten or 15 occurrences connected with your body that were absolutely beyond your conscious control. Leave plenty of space. Now think about something your body did that surprised you because it expressed what you could not say in any other way. Maybe you became ill in order to avoid an exam, or you blushed when you least expected it.

Take one of these moments and explore it more deeply. What did it say? How did it say it? What would have enabled you to have said the same thing aloud in normal speech? How does this tie in with any patterns in your life that you want to consider?

The point of the exercise is to help you find out how much in tune your body and mind are, and to see how this has operated throughout your history. If it works for you, the information could even be used for chapter themes.

YOUR BODY AND SOMEONE ELSE'S

Sometimes the most profound knowledge you can have – of life, yourself and others – comes from knowledge your body picks up from another person's body. You learn from strangers' bodies, lovers' bodies, your mother's body. You gain information from what your eyes see of them, what your lips touch on them, what your senses pick up from their bodily reactions. For example, how has a lover's physical differences left you thinking about yourself by contrast? Interested in the unexpected commonalities of bones and muscles? When pregnant were you proud or raging at how your child's body drew on your physical strength, connecting you to other unequal power situations in your life?

What about the people who seem almost like extensions of your body: children, lovers, siblings, parents? What happens to you when something happens to their bodies, be it a war wound or an admiring stroke, self-mutilation or pregnancy, illness or facelift?

Exercise: The impact of others' bodies

On one side of the page make a list of the parts of your body. Then down the other side of the page note which other person's body impacted on that bit of your body. Then expand one of these items. What effect did it have? How did you see it then and now? What was the intention? What were you ready for?

Other women

How has your body affected the lives of other women you know and thereby influenced what you subsequently did? For example, did the early onset of your menopause unexpectedly lead to other women feeling so alarmed that you decided not to talk about it? How about a woman you shared a home with? Did you both start menstruating in synch, share clothes and start sounding alike on the phone?

Cycles

Fiona saw her life as a cycle of fatness and thinness:

When I was fat, women loved me and took comfort from me – like from a mother. So there have been times when I have been beneficent and times when I've been lithe and kind of untrusted by them. They think I'm too sleek to be relied upon, you know. And I drafted my lifestory with alternate chapters: the eight stone me and the ten stone me.

You may like to draw a picture of your whole life in terms of cycles, in order to get an overview.

OUT-OF-BODY EXPERIENCES

Finally, you might also like to add any out-of-body or paranormal physical experiences you may have had. For example, during a dangerous labour some women have experienced being up above the room looking down on themselves. In my dreams, I frequently fly; not fancy mile-high stuff but about 6 or 8 feet above the ground, just for speed and to overtake slower people. I glide into it like running or strolling: no fancy lift-off and landing procedures. What do such extraordinary bodily experiences say about your ordinary physical life? How can you use this in recounting your lifestory?

The world outside

Many of the things that shape our lives occur as a result of what is going on in the world around us. English writer Storm Jameson's two-volume autobiography, *Journey from the North*, for example, is valuable not least because her life spanned a long time (1891 Whitby to 1965 London) and very different periods: from the Boer War to the space race.[1]

Your lifestory may be shorter but as someone living through the 1980s and 1990s you will have seen many drastic changes, not least the information revolution, growing fascism, the ending of apartheid in South Africa. If one big experience affects a period, people tend to think of themselves in terms of that experience. For example, people born just after the Second World War are part of the 'baby boom' generation. Women who were teenagers in the 1960s, like the four women in Carol Dix's account, *Say I'm Sorry to Mother*, know they are linked by growing up in the era of the Vietnam War protests, the introduction of the contraceptive pill, the civil rights movement, the Beatles and LSD.[2] Different events have different impacts depending on the lifestage we have reached at the time.

Any autobiographical piece is more exciting to readers if it is time-specific. And it's more satisfying to you as a writer if you show how much of what happened was the product of a very particular time in your life and in social history. The collective autobiography *Once a Feminist: Stories of a Generation* is loved by many women I know because the stories speak about *that* time in *their* own history.[3]

Your lifestory will be rich because of the relationship between the external events you mention and your personal experiences: public time and personal time. The two go hand in hand and you should show where they overlap. Public timescales and personal timescales affect each other. For example, at the time of the Queen's coronation in 1952 I was a provincial, television-less three-year-old. I gathered from the wireless and the grown-ups that an event I should be excited about was happening, but that was all I could make of it at that time.

This chapter is about public time: the date-specific social events that everyone experiences at the same time. Chapter 8 is about personal time and Chapter 9, the last of these three chapters on 'when?', is about the overlap of these times: the stage you are at, personally, when a major public event happens.

WOMEN'S TIME

There is no universal time. Any experience is affected by you being the particular woman you are, living in the particular class and culture that you do. (A rich white English woman visiting South Africa in the 1980s, for example, might describe the anti-apartheid struggle differently from a black pensioner living in Soweto or a young black woman who cleans her hotel room.) Your unique experience will reflect that you are a woman living at a time when women have been differently treated by the dominant group and who has gained, lost and learned by being part of a particular culture at a particular time in that culture's history.

Exercise: Seeing what made your experience specific

Try briefly listing the factors that make your experience of time specific to you (gender, age, class and so on). Later, you will need to bear these in mind as you write and revise your lifestory, so that you can convey your unique experience of those times to people who don't have those factors in common with you.

The point of this exercise is to help you avoid making assumptions or thinking that your experience is typical and ordinary. No one has experienced the same unique cross-section of events as you. The background awareness of the specific you experiencing these events will help you tell it all the more richly.

How much information about public time should you use?

In speaking and writing, the innovative autobiographer Carolyn Steedman found that her readers didn't want history but she wanted to 'tell a story within a historical framework'.[4] And she did so. So you may want to bear in mind questions such as: 'How much do I want to put external events in history in this autobiography? Is it primarily for me or for others?' You may want to decide on the strategy of historicising it for yourself, during the process of writing it. Then afterwards you could cut out some of the more overt historical references if you feel it's too much like a history lecture. (It usually isn't.) It works less well in reverse because it can lead you to write an ahistorical account – seeing yourself as someone not affected by the outside world. That isn't on; we are products of our history.

You may not need to make such a decision in the abstract. Write what feels right and then note where some historical information might make your meaning stronger. Read other people's autobiographies with an eye for how they handle public history, then see if you would want to refer more or less or differently to historical events in your lifestory.

Some of your key aids will be:

- your memory (and it will be useful to think how it can falsify and rearrange actual events)
- information about events in the world in which you operated at various times – which you can get through chronologies and back issues of newspapers (see Chapter 14)
- family memories, including snaps
- books on history
- personal memorabilia and records – diaries, notes, poems, doodles
- maps and places – look up all the places you have lived in or visited
- old books of yours – even bookmarks (or bus tickets, pressed flowers) can hold information to stimulate more memories; as can old records, old clothes and so on

Your history/their history

Expect to find non-matching ideas about public and private time-specific events. Anticipate that events in the outside world will sometimes seem to have almost no relevance to your life. In a creative writing class I once taught, we used the *Penguin Chronology of World Events* to look up the students' favourite years. Most were shocked, angry or disappointed to find that this version of a year in no way reflected their experience of it. International political agreements signed, Nobel Prizes won, new exhibitions opened, new symphonies played, new inventions; all these things felt irrelevant by the side of 'That was the year I started school,' 'That was the year we built the new cowshed,' 'That was the year I realised all birds had different songs.'

In response to the inadequacy of public chronologies the students invented their own. They bought big notebooks, headed each page with a year, and wrote in the external and personal events they thought important – sometimes after much research and once as poetry! The official chronologies did come in useful after all. For example, knowing the date that Prime Minister Harold Wilson made his 'white heat of technology' speech helped Jean to identify that that was the year she decided she wanted to do science at university: 'His vision of our country's future affected my personal sense of mission (I didn't do it, though).'

EXTERNAL/PUBLIC TIME-SPECIFIC INCIDENTS

Some of the things that happened in the world that you may want to mention will include one-off events, such as Prime Minister Thatcher's doorstep tears as she announced her resignation. I found that such one-off incidents were less important in writing my lifestory than movements. By movements I mean particular cultures or periods – be it the brief flourishing of glamrock with silver-platformed Gary Glitter in the early 1970s; or the days and weeks of a protest, such as that against the Falklands War; or the months of pleasure and hope such as those immediately following Mandela becoming president of South Africa.

Bear in mind that there is time lived and time thought. Go down the following list and see whether you want to include any of the following.

1. Wars. These affect your daily material existence (e.g. the domination of the daily news bulletins, rationing, bomb-dodging, fear of call-up, habituation to danger and death), as well as how you think about the future (with pragmatism, hope, disbelief and so on).

When did it happen? Which people you knew were affected by it? What did it mean to you? (Dread? Endless family discussions about what government policies should be? Doing without food or certain people?) What did it mean for you to be/not be relocated as a refugee or evacuee?

2. Changes in laws and policies. They reflect a climate of ideas that subtly shaped your life as well as permitting or inhibiting you and others to do certain things. The 1944 Education Act enabled many English working-class girls to get a better education than ever before. Equal opportunities and anti-discrimination legislation have made some changes in thinking about women's status and even some material changes such as slightly higher pay. Many feminists wrote usefully about this in autobiographical essays in *Once a Feminist*.

3. Cultural changes – in literature, music, cinema, TV, the visual arts, fashion and food. Such changes enable you to think differently about yourself and often to act differently.

Exercise: Thinking about some of your key social/historical events

Stage one
- Write a list of key social/historical events that stand out in your life.
- Write by the side the age you were when they happened.
- Pick one that is of most interest to you.
- Note the one you care least about.
- Leave that list somewhere safe. You will use it – many times. If you have a file or folder of notes for your autobiography, put it there.

Stage two
- Now look again at the one that is of most interest to you.
- Why did it matter to you then?
- Try asking it – the event itself – why it mattered to you so much then.
- Describe the event in list form. Who was involved? What was the outcome? How did you know about it? (Through television news or newspapers or someone telling you about it?)
- What might it have meant if you had been five years older or younger at the time?

- How did it affect those around you who were different and similar to you, and how did their responses affect you?
- Try writing a letter as if from you then, conveying to someone in a different period what it was like.

The point of this exercise is to explore thoroughly any events that had significance for you. There may be a number of these you will use in a whole autobiography.

WHAT IT FELT LIKE: EXPLORING PUBLIC TIME

Your job in writing lifestory is to show the impact of the time on you. If you are expecting to have an audience you will need to demonstrate what it was like to people who were not there at the time. How can you show them, not just tell them, how it was?

You can evoke the period in many ways. Start off by feeding yourself clues. There's a good way to do it. Consult history books, especially picture books, to remind you. Try your library or video shop for the videos of individual years, which are usually made up of old cinema newsreel clips. There are also many compilations on record and CD – such as greatest hits of the '80s, classic wartime songs – which will help you remember the flavour of the period.

In writing about any time, ask yourself the questions which follow, but don't drown your story in historical detail. It is not your job to teach history. Only write about what matters to you. This is a personal story, and social and economic history are the background not the foreground. Your role is to select what mattered to you, and to show your feelings and experiences.

The following groups of questions are memory-nudgers. Don't let them overwhelm you. Exploit them confidently – and as much or as little as you want. Referring to your senses (hearing, seeing, smelling, tasting, touching) while writing about external history is the most direct way of remembering and successfully conveying memories.

Tasting the world then

What food did people (and you) in your area eat in your younger days? Remember the tastes of a time on your tongue, against your lips, curling up your nose, remaining with you after you swallowed. You may have been brought up in a northern working-class home in the 1950s and found later that 'southern' food, such as avocados and nectarines, came as a revelation.

Until 1953 there was still rationing of chocolate. In the 1960s diets became less traditionally British: yoghurt entered the new supermarkets. In the 1970s we became more conscious of cholesterol; cuisine minceur and nouvelle cuisine emerged. In the 1980s many people starting noticing E-numbers; it became chic to ask for diet cokes, not regular; cartons of fruit juice became normal fridge furniture; Marks and Spencer became the fashionable place to go for ready-made gourmet treats. In the 1990s people went off beef because of BSE fears; they avoided artificial sweeteners; and in London Thai restaurants seemed to be displacing Indian restaurants.

- What did you eat? How much was this also influenced by class, location, family, poverty, fads, marketing?
- What did you avoid eating, or spend a long time getting round to trying?
- How did you eat? For example, did you start eating on your lap, with a fork in your right hand? Why?
- How/why did your tastes in food or diet change?
- Proust, in *Remembrance of Things Past*, famously made eating madeleines dipped in tea into a major sensual experience. What is/was your equivalent of Proust's madeleines?
- How did you 'economise' in what you ate? How did you treat yourself?
- In what ways did your eating change when you became responsible for others, such as children?

Hearing the world then

You will probably want to focus on music not speech – because of its sensual impact. There's nothing like a song to bring back the memories.

- What was the impact of the music of different times on you?
- How did you learn this taste, and how did it change?
- What else went with this music? (For example, going on demos singing it; putting up pop posters; screaming at concerts; belonging

to fan clubs; dressing like the musicians; joining appreciation societies; learning to play yourself; carrying a walkman around.)
- How did the music reflect what else was going on in society at that time? (For example, the wartime need for cheer; growing commercialisation; protest movements.)
- What other noises did you hear then? (The odd horse on cobbles; 'received pronunciation' accents on the BBC Home Service; the very first chimes of an ice-cream van; silence.) What specific sounds conjure up a particular time or place for you?

Touching the world then

What was the feel of those times? How did clothes feel against your skin? Bodies must have felt the same, because human skin doesn't change, but because soap was more crudely scented when I was a child (Lifebuoy, not Bodyshop Dewberry), I experience my skin as different. For me, born in 1949, the main thing I remember is the change from natural fabrics to synthetic fabrics and then back again: crimplene instead of the scratchy wool of home-made jumpers. Fewer chairs now are covered in plush that prickles your bare thighs or moquette that sticks to them. We washed up with soft knitted dishcloths which felt so much more enjoyable than scouring pads. In the 1970s I still bashed hard on the keys of a manual typewriter but as technology changed my touch on the keys has become lighter and lighter, first with an electric typewriter, then with a computer. The TV is switched on by just the faint pressure of a finger on a frail button, not by a heavy switch that required a whole wrist movement. What do you remember touching that you no longer touch?

The look of the world then

The look of things will be something you describe again and again in lifestory. Think of the look of streets (narrower, dirtier?) and homes (try going to the Design Museum in London or looking in junk shops and old interior design magazines); the look of schools and workplaces (more compartmentalised, less user-friendly?); what people wore and how they did their hair (more formal, more uniform?); the look of towns and countryside (less crowded, a greater difference between the two?); the look of vehicles and equipment (extraordinarily cumbersome by today's eyes, lacking in beauty?).

If you are ever stuck as to how to start writing when you don't want to write about feelings and thoughts, or if you feel you aren't conveying the time context adequately, then try making a then–now list for a particular time. You might set it out like this:

	Then (state year)	Now
houses		
streets		
people's hair		
equipment		
vehicles		
schools		
towns		
country		

Naming names

You'll delight your readers if you can name some of the old names. One of the odd pleasures of reading even the most simply written autobiography is recognising trade names (for example, Cash's woven name tapes, the Betterware man, the Spirella lady, Jeyes disinfectant, Butterkist popcorn ... see!). And it's not a legal problem – unless you libel them. At the same time it can be easy to get caught up in the romance of remembering and listing every name you can recall. Don't. While remembering is a feat that you may feel rightly triumphant about, these things may not mean much to others. So only include the details (the clop of horses' hoofs) and brand names that have meaning to you. Show *why* they have meaning. For example, stiff Izal toilet paper was once supposed to be a sign of prestige in my world. It always puzzled me, though, because it was no more friendly to my skin than the other rolls of hard toilet paper, it was less comfy than newspaper and the leaves weren't quite the right size so you had to use twice as much. But the coming of soft, coloured Andrex was far more revolutionary – that really made a difference.

Clothes

One of the most direct ways of remembering and conveying the look of the time is by recalling your hairstyles, clothes and makeup. What clothes did you/others wear then? Remember to describe how they felt as well as how they looked.

In the war, British women made underwear out of parachute silk and cut down old coats for new skirts. In 1949 the end of clothes rationing brought the New Look. In the 1960s Biba and flower power created whole new ways for women to look; there were mini and maxi skirts. In the 1970s I started going unisex and wore jeans and knuckleduster rings. In the 1980s women fighting on men's terrain discovered shoulder pads. In the 1990s women are wearing flares, mini/long skirts and platform-soled shoes again. You may be from a culture where certain clothes were appropriate for certain ages. You may have chosen to discard a traditional veil, to wear a sari or to wear the uniform of a sect or group you belonged to.

- What did you wear and what did you not wear that others did?
- Why?
- How did you afford it?
- What did you make?
- How did you feel in what you wore?
- What do you think others thought of you in what you wore?

The smell of the world then

Your sense of smell is the most important sense of all; it has the most immediate access to the parts of the brain that remember. That's why reminiscence groups use it. Passing round the cloves and camphor is a rapid route past the memory haze. Think of the different smells that were in your world in the past:

- at the meal table
- at school
- at home
- in other people's houses
- at work
- out in the wider world

Evoking a smell for your readers can be an impressively productive way to trigger hours of memories of a period. So sniff wherever you go, and try and recall smells too. I find it's a good exercise to do while waiting at bus stops. I work at remembering a smell of a time I'm preparing to write about, then when I sit down on the bus I list the things associated with that smell.

Pulling it all together

To pull all these strands together, try the following exercise.

Exercise: Illustrating the time in question

Try remembering the smells and sounds that epitomised different periods for you.

- Write a list, down the left-hand side of the page, of dates for each half-decade of your life, such as 1960, 1965, 1970, 1975 and so on.
- Next to these dates, write down the smells and sounds new to you at that time.
- Now expand on those for one specific date.
- Make notes on what impact they had on you, these olfactory and aural evidences of external change. How did they change you? What did you lose/gain/learn/newly understand/look forward to trying (for example, foreign travel)?
- How did the people around you respond?

Use this exercise at any time as a way to place anything you are writing about in its particular period.

SIGNIFICANT OTHERS' CHRONOLOGIES

To some extent, events in the lives of the people around you are public events, in the sense that such things are not personal to you. They are things that happen out there in the world, to people who are not you. In order to help you write a full autobiography, you may choose to make some chronological charts so that you can review the ages and experiences of your significant people at particular points in time – both in *your* life and in public, historical time.

Exercise: Writing about another's life and its effect on you

Take a wide sheet of paper. Down the left-hand side write every year of your life, but begin ten years before you were born. So if you were born in 1968 begin at 1958.

Along the top write down six significant people in your life, including yourself.

Go down the years, writing in their ages and anything significant that happened to them. For example along the 1967 line Carol wrote:

Jane	Anna	Geoff	Mum	Me	Nan	Petronella
infant school	mature student	stroke	new job	junior school	widowed	emigrated to Tasmania

Or you might prefer to select odd key years for you and then insert others' details.

The usefulness of this exercise is that it gives you a perspective on the world you entered. Also it shows you what interests you about other people and what issues you are particularly concerned with, such as health, sex, class, art, clothes, locations, finances, hopes and dreams, landscapes.

If your autobiography is to be rich, it will refer to the historical context and the circumstances that produced you. It is important to be selective and write about what matters to you, not the whole history of your family. Be subjective – write your opinions on political/social/family changes. Say and evoke how you felt and how you feel now about these events and changes in your world. Remember the feelings and the thoughts you had at the time in response to these events. You are very much the product of the outside world, and what you have made of it illustrates much about your character.

Times in your life

This is the second chapter exploring the significance of *when* something happened in your life. It discusses some of the events that happen in people's lives that have very little, if anything, to do with what is going on in the outside world at the same time.

PERSONAL EVENTS

Some of the key time-specific personal events in your life may include the following:

- being conceived and any pre-birth experiences
- being born
- early sexual play
- birth of siblings
- starting school
- transferring to secondary school
- beginning periods
- first relationships
- leaving school
- casual/short-term relationships
- first jobs, further education or dole
- leaving home for the first time
- serious live-in relationships
- pursuing a career
- children – including other people's
- transition as children leave home

- increasing wisdom
- aging
- grandchildren
- menopause
- post-menopause
- facing death

There will also be many other personal experiences, including abortions, operations, creativity, moments of epiphany, major successes, discoveries, travels, broken friendships, moving house, joining of organisations and groups, relationships with animals, formal education, new skills achieved. The time in your life, as well as in external time, when they happened is crucial.[1]

Exercise: Writing your main personal events

Identify ten key events that are specific to your personal chronology. Either list them or present them in chart or map form. If you draw a chart like a family tree you could show the events as being as significant as people (put the dates in brackets). If you draw a map, you may want to treat these events/times as continents or seas.

Later, take one event at a time and write about it using Bernard Selling's popular technique of writing in the voice and style of the person you were at the time.[2] It can be difficult to speak as simply as you did then, so usually it takes two or three goes. Writing in the form of a letter from you-then can help.

For example, Jane wrote this about losing her virginity in 1969:

First attempt
Dear Friend,
I've just come back from losing my virginity. 11 a.m. Mum and the kids have put the Christmas tree lights up – these innocent celebrations. I feel different in my knickers. The whole of me knows the world in a different way now. *I've* done what *they* do. And it was so much fun. I want to do it again – straight away. And I'm so glad this thing is gone. At last. Good riddance to uncool rubbish. Mum suspects. I feel her disapproval, I avoid her eyes. She knows – and won't say. Do I want to tell her?

Second attempt

I'm 19. It's Christmas Eve. My virginity's gone at last. He's a shit but he served his purpose – now no one will ever know I lost it so late. Even he didn't guess. And I liked it – that thudding, that warmth, wanted it to go on and on. Now I know why people like doing it. Oh I want to carry on and on.

And the other side of it is Mum's eyes knowing – and us both half-avoiding each other's eyes. I know she'll read it in mine. I know, I know, I know. And I'm supposed to be feel bad about being a fallen woman and I don't. I'm proud and relieved. And I want to tell her what it's like. And I can't. I want to tell someone and there's no one – safe. The Christmas tree lights are up. The kids are getting ready. It's supposed to be innocent family pleasure. And I'm supposed to feel dirty. And instead I feel proud, and different in my knickers, and ready for more. What's true?

I feel better about the second attempt. It seems more direct but I still think a couple more attempts would mean I could capture the voice of me then (that never spoke aloud of this event, actually).

The point of doing this exercise is to gain an overview of your key times. When you write in that particular way you are attempting to relive the experience, so that your account of it is the more vivid.

STAGES OF DEVELOPMENT

Autobiographical writing is time-specific because people go through certain developmental stages at certain ages; for example, being able to accept other people's differentness more easily or feeling calmer about your identity. The book of Ecclesiastes talks about life being divided into seasons of concentrated preoccupation, that there is 'a time to every purpose under heaven' – for planting and pulling up, for making love and not making love, for staying silent and talking. Folk singer Pete Seeger set this text to music in 1962 and the US group the Byrds had a hit with it in 1965. The Chinese philosopher Confucius identified six stages: ages 1 to 15 learning, 15 to 29 planting your feet, 30 to 40 no more perplexity, 40 to 60 knowing the bidding of heaven, 60 to 70 hearing with a docile ear, from 70 following the dictates of your own heart. In *As You Like It*, Shakespeare talked about the seven ages of man.[3]

Lifecourse studies and life stage psychology have, since the mid-1960s, become important new areas of research. Many people became familiar with these ideas through Gail Sheehy's popular book *Passages: Predictable Crises of Adult Life*.[4] Her section headings suggest the pattern: 'The Trying Twenties', 'Passage to the Thirties', 'Deadline Decade', 'Renewal'. Her later work, *New Passages*, goes on to argue that becoming 45 is the infancy of a new life, and that old models of adulthood starting at 21 and ending at 65 are out of date because we now actually have a first and a second adulthood.[5]

In the 1970s, 1980s and 1990s women such as Bernice Neugarten and Carol Gilligan have increasingly challenged some of the male approaches based on the ideas of lifecourse pioneers such as Erik Erikson and Daniel Levinson.[6] The latter's work is seen as specific to men, and as generally too prescriptive and static. You might be one of the many who believe women's lives are much more unpredictable than classical male theorists maintain. Psychiatrist Iris Sanguiliano has studied women's lifecourses and believes that things shift and change so rapidly that events are far more important than supposed stages.[7] Psychologist Carol Gilligan argues that women develop through intimacy and attachment, whereas Erik Erikson believes humans develop by exploring the accomplishment of separation, autonomy and independence.[8] Using Carol Gilligan's ideas you might feel that as a woman your life has developed in response to who you are with as much as in response to decisions such as starting a new career.

If you'd like to try the theories out on yourself – and this would be a useful way to gain a broader understanding of your lifehistory – then try the following exercise.

Exercise: Seeing your greatest periods of development

Identify your greatest periods of development. This might mean the times when you changed most, dared most, suffered most. List the dates and give brief details of what happened.

Take one of these periods. Ask yourself what was your goal at that time: intimacy, separation, social power or something else? Who were your companions in this process? How did the climate of the times help you to achieve your goal?

For example Jo, a 35-year-old mother of three, wrote about a period in detail:

Age 10/11 (1961/62): Father left home which meant trying to understand.

Development: this period reinforced feelings of no self-esteem – my fault he had gone! Must be as I was naughty, moody etc ... Father cried and told me how low he was – became parent to him! – had to develop new strategies for coping with new step-parent, being left by Dad, being in charge of younger sister on access visits!

Goal at the time: escape. Everything happening to me was out of my control. Didn't want to be with Mother, step-dad. Wanted Dad to be strong – not dependent on me for strength and support.

Companions: one friend's parents who were very good to me but didn't really understand.

Times: did not reach my goal, legally Dad had no way of getting custody and did not pursue it. Mum moved us away so had to leave all friends etc.

The point of this exercise is to gain a broad outline picture. This knowledge can help you draft a possible structure for your whole autobiography. Each period of development could be a chapter.

Using life stage ideas for you

If it appeals to you, try looking at what developmental psychologists say about life stages and see whether your own stages fit or don't fit. (See the Notes to this chapter for further reading.) Lifecourse studies offer you ideas that you can enjoy diverging from.

Crises and stages

The ways in which we change can sometimes appear to be a series of stages, like going up ladders. Sometimes we arrive at an easy and welcome new dawn. Occasionally the ending of a crucial stage is accompanied by a crisis: loss of familiar routines, a great wrench made after months of self-doubt. Then, whoosh! The new life begins.

Exercise: Crises and stages

Try thinking of the board game Snakes and Ladders. You could even draw a board if you like.

- Identify the snakes (the obstacles that led you to slide back – how far did you slide?).
- Identify the ladders (the bonuses that hoiked you up incredibly fast to a new plateau).
- How many of each have there been? How hard did the snakes bite – or did they only slither? How tall were the ladders and what did you think of where they took you to? How were the crises illuminating and what did you have to learn before the dice of life somehow allowed you to move on?
- Where are you now in relation to the end of the game? What have you left behind and what have you gained?

After doing either (or both) of the previous exercises, think about whether you can use them as ways of organising your whole autobiography. Is it a sequence of stages? Or of swings and roundabouts? Or mists with bridges in between? Or what?

LIFECOURSE STAGE ONE: 0–20 YEARS

You may want to make use of ideas about life stages. Feel free to disagree and notice how your lifestyles differ from these. Explore only as deeply as you want to; you're not required to analyse alone anything that is too difficult to handle without a therapist or guide.

Age up to five years

How far back can you remember? Some women's autobiographies refer to earliest memories when they were only two or three years old. If you can remember such early days, that may be a thrill to you; it can feel appropriate to identify 'this was the very start of me knowing me'. But don't worry about not being able to do this as it may not be relevant to you anyway.

You may want to enhance, explore or elicit memories of your birth or being in the womb or being a toddler. If so, try going to a reliable hypnotherapist, or doing rebirthing (a therapy that enables you to experience a new, better birth in the process of which you may remember some negative aspects of your actual birth). Arthur Janov's *Primal Scream* helped remind Jo of those early times: 'Just reading about others and the process can trigger your own awareness.'

Try reading books about baby development to see if you recognise any of the developments as appropriate to you. Larger bookshops usually have a sub-section in the psychology department called 'developmental psychology', which examines how thoughts and feelings develop at different ages.[9] You may like to browse in those shelves and then order any books that interest you from the library. Remember, such ideas can be best used elliptically and sceptically. The most recent books are far better because they take gender into account, acknowledging that being a girl is not the same as being a boy.

Using ideas from developmental psychology can be dangerous because such books are normative: they tell you what *should* be without taking individual circumstances and differences into account. Put them aside the minute you feel yourself worrying because you did not do the right thing at the right stage. Move on to another less prescriptive topic or to writers who think more generously and permissively. Enjoy who you are and the child you were.

Age five to eight years

By five, you often have very clear ideas about who you are – as well as feeling confused by how others seem to see you. You know what food you like, the people you trust, your waking habits. You are trying out interactions with strangers when playing in the playground. The knowledge you have of who you are and who you are seen to be and who you should be, your values and your concerns, come from parents, family, playgroup, nursery, school, the street community, the baby clinic and all the other situations you have been in. You may want to use those early sets of ideas about you as ways to understand how you developed as you did.

Ask yourself:

- What did I know of me?
- What did I believe in?
- What did I understand?
- What was I passionate about?
- What did I try to escape from and how?

Suffragette leader Emmeline Pankhurst knew very early on about her sense of justice. Her account of her life (1858–1928) begins with a political memory: a huge bazaar in Manchester.

> The object of the bazaar being to raise money to relieve the poverty of the newly emancipated Negro slaves in the United States. My mother took an active part in this effort ... Young though I was – I could not have been older than five years – I knew perfectly well the meaning of the words slavery and emancipation ... runaway slave ... stories [I was told], with the bazaars and relief funds and subscriptions ... I am sure made a permanent impression on my brain and my character. They wakened in me the two sets of sensations to which all my life I have most readily responded: first, admiration for that spirit of fighting and heroic sacrifice by which alone the soul of civilisation is saved; and next after that, appreciation of the gentler spirit which is moved to mend and repair the ravages of war.[10]

Age eight to eleven years

A recent book, *The Girl Within*, argues that girls have a particular moment of peak development at eight.[11] You are at your boldest then, dream dreams, venture, masturbate, know what you want, have great strength. And then you lose that power (the writer Emily Hancock then tells you how to retrieve it). This seems an important idea that, if it's true for you, may affect how you view your subsequent life.

Exercise: Being eight, dreaming of the future

- Write down what were you like at eight: characteristics, clothes, toys, preoccupations. What pleased you? What did you thrive on? What did you do? Who were your friends?

- Invent a recurring dream you might have had then.
- Write a letter from that eight-year-old you, in the words you used then, discussing what your future will be like. (It could be to someone who you trusted to take you seriously.) Work hard at getting the tone and language level right. It usually takes most people several attempts.
- After a couple of weeks, look at the letter. How did your future actually turn out? What were the pragmatic compromises? Reflect on what views you have about the discrepancies between the letter and the reality (including what you want to do about it all now).

The point of this exercise is to help you get in touch with your childhood needs and wisdom, as well as your ambitions and abilities and courage. It helps you to survey your whole life from an early, confident place.

Age eleven to 13 years

Several US psychological studies of adolescent girls found that at around the age of eleven or twelve girls feel vital, real and not masked; they are able to state their views openly and confidently from a basis of feeling that they really know themselves. They sense it's safe to disagree because they feel they won't lose each other's love by disagreeing. They are able to connect closely with each other, and enjoy good friendships intimately.

US researcher Annie G. Rogers and her colleagues found, however, that in adolescence girls are encouraged to disconnect from their own knowledge; to see and hear the world largely as it is seen and spoken about by men.[12] You may like to consider if there was a stage when you felt you no longer knew what you knew, and were unable to say what you used to say. Many girls deal with that crisis by trying to stay connected to that knowledge, to resist repressive conventions about what females should be and to fight for authentic values. But resisters get punished by classmates and schools, so many capitulate, muffle their voices and go psychically underground. Did you?

When a girl goes undercover, what happens? When she loses her non-feminine parts of herself, such as her exuberance, what happens to her? Do such parts drop away for ever, or turn sour through neglect or do they remain stored, ready to emerge in later life under the right circumstances? What masks do you think you adopted? (You could paint them now if you like and speak through them, or speak through the mask of your bolder early self.) If you feel some of those ideas might be true for you, try the following exercise.

Exercise: Your strong feelings at eleven or twelve

- Make a list of the things you felt strongly about at eleven or twelve – for example, which friends you loved and hated. Visualise that feeling (not the person, but *your* feeling). What colour and strength were the feeling? If it was music, how would it sound – like clashing cymbals or a passionate concerto? Paint it or write it down in the most visual way you can.
- Now think about that feeling as a separate part of you. Did it carry on growing like a sturdy plant? Did it somehow drop away, like the discarded skin of an animal that had grown a new coat? Did 'the music of it' change?
- Reflect: where are those strong feelings in you today? How do they get expressed – or strengthened – now? How have they coloured your life over the years?

The point of this exercise is to explore the freedom with which you could feel your feelings then and so show in your lifestory some of the passions that may have since become latent.

Early teens

In writing lifestory work about your early teens you may find yourself writing about passionate emotions, their force, their denial, their expression. You dealt – perhaps feeling a mixture of wild confidence and terror – with the challenges of a new school, new friends, menstruating, dating, changed attitudes to you as a young woman, thoughts about your future career and relationships and children. Some US feminist developmental psychologists studying girls have found that when many girls move into adolescence they experience distress and feelings of vulnerability. There is often a sharp increase in periods of depression. Girls start to put down their bodies, to develop eating disorders. They also feel less secure about their view of their academic achievements. Their self-esteem and confidence drop.[13] This may or may not have been true for you. If you want to explore the struggles you had – or that your friends and sisters had – try the following exercise.

Exercise: The girl's struggle

Imagine yourself to be at some significant point between eleven and 15. Reflect thoroughly. At this stage you may want to list things that might help you remember better, especially visual aids such as girls' fashion magazines, as this is a time of concern with self-image. Playing music from the period will help too.

Reflect as long as you like; it could take several days. Write responses to the following questions in list form. Write as if you are you-then, in the present tense. Act in role. Ask yourself:

- What has been the best and worst time in my life so far? If I kept a diary what would I say in it?
- What are the five deepest, truest, most unsayable things I can say about me?
- What things am I worried about? Who do I share those worries with? When are they actually expressions of something else? How do they get resolved?
- Whose bodies do I admire? How do I feel about my own body? How do I treat it?
- By what standards do I evaluate myself?

Now, as your adult self looking back, ask yourself did the sadnesses, struggles, joys and rages have any particular cycle? What factors triggered them? What means did you find for dealing with them?

Use this exercise to reflect on how you developed and learned to cope over the years. It should help you get an overview of the ways you tackle difficulties and experience pleasures.

Late teens

In your late teens the things that might have preoccupied you include leaving home, dating more, and understanding your very specific requirements in lovers. You may have done a lot of travelling, including backpacking in foreign countries. You may have learned to drive. You may have become more embedded in a career path and wondered about whether you had chosen appropriately. You may have faced the realities of unemployment and the world of work. You'll probably have met other adults very different from your parents.

Exercise: Tributaries and rivers of your teens

List all the new things you did in your late teens. Take one or two key experiences. Draw or write a diagrammatic history of the rivers and streams that fed that pool, that particular experience. Then draw where the wide rivers went on to, in later years, once you'd left that particular experience. How did they feed into the pool of your future?

Use this exercise to understand how you are a product of particular early influences. You can use this exercise to explore many different trails in your life. Indeed, each chapter could be about a river or trail of experiences from source to sea. Not only can this exercise help illuminate decision-making, it will keep your lifestory more clearly conceptualised.

LIFECOURSE STAGE TWO: 20–45 YEARS

Early twenties

Psychologist Jane Loevinger believes that by our twenties we have learned to accept inner conflicts, paradoxes and contradictions as normal in life.[14] This is an important step. How about you? The recognition of ways you achieved this acceptance will affect the way you write about adulthood in your lifestory. The following exercise will help you to explore further.

Exercise: Learning to accept conflict and paradox

Try listing your conflicts, for example to travel or settle, to do socially useful or profitable work, to look to children more than career. If the conflicts are binary, that is, if they seem like a pair of opposites, write them down as that. If a middle way or an extra factor occurs to you, write that down too. It is always very illuminating to work at thinking of a third element in the conflict – somehow calmness and wisdom seem to come in. For example, Jess chose: 'Independence vs relationship vs the adult ability to feel independent within the relationship.'

Now identify the different dates/times when it occurred to you that you could actually cope with the conflicts and contradictions.

From your wiser position as you-now, write a letter to you-then at one of those times of conflict, offering congratulations and recognising what it cost to tackle that conflict.

The aim of this exercise is not only to understand your past conflicts clearly and generously, it's also to enable you to be so knowledgeable about them that you can weave them into your story of your past and future selves.

Late twenties and thirties

Lifecourse theorists argue that our late twenties and early thirties can be a time when we recognise the limitations of autonomy, enjoy personal relationships more and accept the autonomy of others. One of our tasks is looking for partners, finding one who will do and adjusting to living with them, trusting and learning to love. The other task is the struggle for autonomy. Erik Erikson argues that people not only struggle to find intimacy but to succour the need for isolation, to balance the desire to share with someone with the ability still to enjoy the very new sense of independence we have. This may or may not be true for you as a woman: many women still marry for economic security, for example. What do you think?

Mid-adulthood

Erik Erikson believes that our preoccupation in mid-adulthood is the care of the next generation – generativity.[15] It's a time not only of creativity and productivity but about exploring what makes you a human being – establishing and guiding the next generation. The focus is by no means only on your own flesh-and-blood children but also on adopted and fostered and neighbourhood children. It means not only parenting but helping in clinics, teaching, career guidance and being a generous mentor. The preoccupation is rooted in the need to be needed, because we all have a need to care for as well as *be* cared for. It helps us fulfil ourselves (and it's hard to be happily concerned with generativity if we ourselves haven't been cared for by somebody trustworthy and empathetic).

Children leave home

Writer Lillian Rubin believes that life stages are not age-bound and that the most important event for a woman is when her children leave home; it may be the first time in her life that she can attend to her own needs.[16] It may be also that this is a time in your middle years when you ditch some of the conditioning to be selfless.

I've tried to design the next exercise to include both mothers and non-mothers.

Exercise: Attending to your own needs

Sit down quietly, perhaps in front of some snaps of you-then or with the clothes you wore then (drape them round you). Do your hair as you did then. Surround yourself with symbols of the demands made on you which meant you couldn't attend to your needs – for example, bank statements indicating you absolutely had to work, children's toys to indicate childrearing priorities. Now surround yourself with symbols of what you didn't do – such as names of courses you didn't go on, slips of paper representing refused invitations. Get into that you-then.
   Ask yourself:

- What needs were on hold?
- Score them one to ten as to how much they were met. (This will vary over time.)
- When did you realise this, and what did you do about it?
- What enabled you to start recognising your needs?
- What difference did it then make to your time and self-view?

Write down what (including children) led to those needs being neglected, if they were. Write a letter to the most untended need, explaining what happened.

The aim of this exercise is to help you evaluate how you've handled your needs and their fulfilment. Using such a perspective may help you write a lifestory that appraises your achievements and successes as well as comprehends your objective difficulties and possibilities for growth.

LIFECOURSE STAGE THREE: 45 ONWARDS

Reappraisal time

The period when you are aged 45 to 60 can be a time for creative reappraisal of what you are doing in life and why. For example, people make moves that other people consider irrational: wives leave husbands, adults behave like teenagers. You start to say you are of the older generation now. You may begin to parent your parents (even more!). You have a heightened sense of mortality. You re-examine your beliefs about yourself, others and the world. Some of the responses include joy, relief, wonder, bitterness, grief and freedom. The big external modifications include choosing to live abroad, divorce, change jobs. Changes can also be internal.

Lifecourse experts suggest that most of us look at the dream of the future we thought we were going to have and realise it will probably not be fulfilled. Some of us then reduce the dream's tyranny and begin to lead a more pragmatic life using the wisdom gained. You may not consciously know the dream – it may not be clearly formulated – but it affects your actions nevertheless. Knowing the dream on which you've based so many decisions helps.

Exercise: Knowing the dream

What has been the dream that has led you to live life in a particular way? Where did it come from? Try to describe its components, as if it were a nightdream that you were recounting to a wise friend who did not interrupt. What do you look like in it? What material objects do you have? What do you survive on? Why is the dreamed-of you such a happy one? How much did you expect its fulfilment and how did that matter? In what ways didn't you go for it? What has been going on in the mean time?

Use this exercise to understand what you have done on the side, accidentally as it were. Also use it to consider if the dream was also a cover story to get out of doing something else.

Age 60 onwards

This post-60 period in our society is supposed to be a time of reduced expectations and increased pragmatism. Women used to have to retire from employment at this point. That reduced version of life has been challenged by women who take part in Growing Old Disgracefully workshops, the Older Feminist Network,[17] and grey power campaigns; these are women who give the concept of crone and tribal elder a new meaning. Simone de Beauvoir may have called the fourth volume of her autobiography *All Said and Done* but actually she went on to do a lot more saying and doing.[18]

If you're lucky, wisdom grows faster than health problems and maturity increases as mobility decreases. You may move or consider moving to somewhere more suited to your needs. You endure – and challenge – the ageist stereotypes of our society. Getting closer to death can mean gaining great insights about the nature of your life.[19]

If you are writing this lifestory in your later years you may be in a period of serious evaluation. Your long-term memory may be improving and your willingness to challenge all the more strong because you have – in some ways – less to lose. You have the privilege of having more to re-vision than younger women and thereby a greater opportunity to reflect on a bigger picture. A recent British anthology of interviews, *Sixty Years On: Women Talk about Old Age*, illuminates 14 women's views of aging.[20] You may like to look at it and ask yourself some of the questions the interviewers ask the older women, or try looking at some of the professional texts about reminiscence which explore what remembering in later life can mean – including the difficulty of not being able to find a narrative that works, a way to tell the story.[21] Feel free to write now what you couldn't say in earlier times. May Sarton's *Journal of a Solitude*, which she wrote when she was old, is a diary rather than a lifestory but it attempts to be evaluative of her whole life by deliberately setting out to be an account that includes the anger – including her anger as a lesbian – which she somehow omitted from her other writing.[22]

Exercise: Looking back and seeing patterns

Take a good chunk of time off, say a few hours. Use it as time to muse on the following questions:

- Looking back, what stereotypes do you now see you have conformed to that have damaged you?
- If you evaded them, what enabled you to do so?
- With hindsight, what should you have done and what would you have liked to do?
- Can you characterise certain periods of your life in certain ways? (For example, a decade of rashness, a seven-year season of plenitude?)
- What do you leave out – and gain – if you do this kind of totalising?
- What have you omitted? (Anger, like May Sarton?)

Start writing when you're ready – lists and diagrams might be a good way of not getting bogged down in such a big overview. Use precise images at all times, especially of clothes, landscape and the language used then. This exercise may well take several days. It will require much reflecting and remembering. Perhaps you may need to do it twice: once off the top of your head and once with the evidence of 'the facts' to hand.

The aim of this exercise is to suggest some ways of creating an evaluative overview. It is only a first push – and you will certainly come up with much better questions for yourself.

It happened to me then

This chapter is the third and final one that focuses on time: it is, in a sense, a synthesis of the other two. In it I suggest ways to think about the impact of particular public events at particular times in our lives. We remember certain things most potently because of the particular life stage we were at when it happened. A clear example of this is the way the songs we heard in our early teens are usually far more important to us than songs we heard later (except those that evoke exceptional experiences such as the birth of a romance). Similarly, different aspects of the women's liberation movement (WLM) were found to be important to different US women because of the particular stages of development that they were at. For example, Carla experienced self-validation from the WLM because she was an older teenager going through the identity formation stage of late adolescence. The sense of community and similarity was the most important gain for Nina, who was at the early adult stage at which she needed connection with the community. Sarah was in midlife when the WLM affected her and her chief gain was the acquisition of a useful explanation framework at a stage when she needed a renewed sense of meaning.[1]

You may like to use some of the ideas in this chapter to explore the impact of events experienced as a teenager, or in middle and later life. Try the exercises to help you write about why particular events are retained in your memory.

EVENTS THAT OCCUR WHEN WE ARE TEENAGERS

The Vietnam War turned a whole generation of teenagers into protesters. Why was this? US professor Abigail J. Stewart has found that social-historical events (such as the Vietnam War) which are experienced in late adolescence are likely to have deeper and more long-lasting effects on us than if we experience them later or earlier in our lives. She talked to 61 women in the USA who had been born during the Second World War and asked them which ten public events they saw as most and least meaningful. Most of these occurred in their late teens and early twenties. Over 30 per cent rated the women's movement highest, with the Vietnam War and civil rights movement next, the Second World War and Kennedy's presidency next, then the Korean War and the impact of black rights activist Martin Luther King.[2]

This is significant in two ways for lifestory writing. First, it means that you will probably write more about the public events that happened in your teens than in any other period. Second, when you are sharing autobiographical stories with people of a different age, you need to bear in mind that they won't have experienced an event's significance in the same way as you did. You may find your readers disagreeing with you about an event or phenomenon.

Exercise: Understanding the different significance of events for different people

- Make a list of key public events which happened in your adolescence – say when you were aged 14 to 18. Now select one of them. Make sure it is an event that you *think* others will have had the same feelings about. Write down your view of that event and its impact on you.
- Now ask someone at least six years older and someone six years younger than you to write a little about that event or to talk about it. Try people as different from you as possible. Three lines will do. Or if you like, show them what you have written. Compare the versions.
- As a result of what they say, go back and make notes as to how you can work up your account to show the impact of the event on you. Allow your knowledge of the mismatch to affect how you polish your autobiography for others to read.

This exercise shows why it's always necessary to explain and illustrate the significance *for you* of the events in your autobiography. If people so near you in age experienced an event so differently, then how might readers from other cultures and in the future misunderstand your point?

It's different from anything that's ever happened before

Abigail Stewart writes about teenagers:

> If events occur that are radically discrepant with their life experience to date those events may have enormous power in shaping the newly-developing personal identity of the adolescent. Thus young men and women raised in turn of the century England were faced suddenly, in 1914, with international conflict and violence on a massive scale. Many in this generation grounded their identity formation in their experiences of World War One – an experience utterly discrepant with the period before.[3]

Exercise: Working on the impact of something very different happening

Think about some of the people in your class in your last years at school. Name them to yourself. Look at a class photo, if you have one, to remind you of that existence. Now consider what mass movement or social event – that had never before happened in the world – affected your generation. It could be a new kind of music or a political event.

Try and describe its impact on five of your classmates – just in note form. Now consider how you specifically were affected. What would you (each) have been like if it hadn't happened? If you are still in touch with them you might even ask them these questions.

The aim of this exercise is to comprehend, through looking at your peers, the impact of a period on your adolescent self. Use it in your lifestory to talk about your social context. US lesbian activist and writer Sarah Schulman talks about this fruitful interlinking: 'When I came out in the 1970s, I came out into a feminist movement of lesbians and heterosexual women working together for women's liberation. Abortion was legalised in this country when I was 15 years old. And my first real activist commitment was to keep abortion safe, legal and funded.'[4]

Changes in basic ideas because of social events

People in mature adulthood seldom change their identity, values and expectations specifically because of social events. Such events, says Abigail Stewart, 'may affect adults' behaviour – what they actually do – but *not* how they understand or think about what they're doing'.[5] Basic beliefs and identity remain impervious to outside events. As evidence of this she quotes a surprising US survey which found that young, middle-class, white mothers returned to the labour force in the late 1950s and 1960s because of a climate of opinion that had affected their identities while they were in their twenties in wartime. They believed that they were still being good wives and mothers by doing so. By working for their children's schooling and for holidays, they were behaving according to a set of values instilled in their earlier days.[6] If you are over 30 you may like to consider what beliefs and elements of your identity that you developed in your teens, through social events, have remained unchanged.

Exercise: Seeing how beliefs stay even if behaviour changes

Sit down undisturbed. Close your eyes. Think, 'I am 16, it is 19—. What I believe in includes ... I see myself as ...' Try and think, in an image-filled way, what you looked/felt like.

Now write notes on this, widely spaced. Then tear those notes into pieces with an idea on each piece. Arrange these pieces in order of significance to you now. Consider what you have recently done that illustrates how unchanged (or not) your identity and beliefs still are. Reflect on where the ideas came from and what other events have affected your life.

The aim of this exercise is to explore how those early social events and movements have had an enduring effect on the older you. You can use it in your lifestory to create a more coherent overview of your development.

Changing our minds

Despite the fact that we tend to retain basic beliefs acquired at a young age, it is of course *possible* to change our minds about certain things.

We can radically revise our beliefs and identities when we're faced with significant social events and this is more likely to happen when we are in our forties and fifties.[7] For example, some older middle-class British women involved in the 1990s port blockades against veal exports commented that they had never laid down in the road in front of lorries in their lives before, never been in mass protests before, and that their trust in the police had been shattered for ever. The veal exports – and the women's concern – created a whole new set of ideas about the way it was possible to behave and the nature of justice in Britain. Similarly, women who raised their kids in the 1950s were affected by the 1970s women's movement, and reconsidered their lives. They returned to education and took up careers. Such flexibility comes about either because things happen in life suddenly that don't fit in at all with our earlier perspectives and identities or because of some strong but mysterious push inside us.

ENDURING MEMORIES OF EVENTS

Significant events shape you and remain in your consciousness. You use them to help you develop your own personality. So you may like to ask yourself why you have retained memories of particular events. Why do they linger? What aspect of your personality is it helping you develop?

Exercise: Using lingering memories of events

Look back over the last two chapters at how many times you thought of or listed certain events. Consider both the public events in Chapter 7 and the private events in Chapter 8. Now write a separate list of the ways your personality has developed; for example, how have you become stronger/more touchy/less fragile, more brave?

Go back to the earlier list. By the side of the events, write how they might have helped someone – not you – to develop. Now put the lists in front of you and see how they help you appraise the process of your development.

The aim of this exercise is to help you clarify why some memories remain, and their role. It will help you to give them appropriate weight in your lifestory.

You may also want to think about smaller uses of time, such as rituals in your life at a particular time – for example, the weekly ritual of double maths on Fridays and fish for lunch; annual rituals such as a visit to a grave or summer holidays. How about the way you use time – filling every moment or enjoying a deliberate pace? And how about saying something about how you handle thoughts of the future?

You may also want to think about occasions when you have experienced timelessness. Or have there been occasions when you have felt that you time-travelled or experienced déjà-vu or foreknowledge? Perhaps intimations of the future have been given to you by the Tarot or a fortune-teller. Experiences of the past may be gained by dressing in old clothes or lingering in haunted places. Perhaps you have experienced a sense of dislocation about time – such as you might get when resting during an illness, when using a time-distorting drug such as LSD or if you have suffered traumatic memory loss. All these things can give you special insights about time in your life.

Use whatever ideas you feel are appropriate when telling the period-specific story of this long and peculiar accumulation of seconds and hours and weeks: your life, private and public, as a woman, and as part of the history of the world.

Who shall I include?

This chapter is about who to include in your lifestory and offers ideas for ways to write about them. You will find yourself not only describing them but exploring your relationships with them. This chapter is about people in general; Chapter 11 talks about ways to write about specific people such as mothers and lovers, friends and relations.

WHO ARE THEY?

There will probably be many people you want to write about. The main people in most western women's lives are:

- **Usually intimates:**
  parents
  honorary parents (those you adopt in order to get the parenting you need)
  lovers
  siblings
  close friends
  children you care for
- **Usually less intimate people:**
  cousins
  aunts and uncles
  grandparents
  ancestors
  neighbours
  colleagues

- **People who are usually more distant:**
  heroines (for example, movie stars, great forerunners in your field)
  mentors
  leaders (for example, Brown Owl, bosses, political leaders)
  rivals
  significant strangers – glimpsed in passing/known briefly
  people in books
  health professionals

They don't all have to appear – only the ones that have meaning for you. There's no obligation to do a family roll call.

WHY INCLUDE OTHER PEOPLE?

The first question in thinking about who to include is: 'Why include anyone else?' Why not be selfish – you surely deserve to be for a while – and just go on about you? Why not, indeed? It is your story. Nevertheless, there will have to be other people in it because you don't live an unpopulated life.

There are two main reasons to write about other people. First, they are part of your story and, as such, deserve to be there in their own right. You will probably want to show how other people have contributed to the rich picture of your life. You may want to show their effects on you, your relationships with them and their separate existences. You may even want them there metaphorically as companions in the creative process of building your lifestory; helpful ghosts sitting on the computer, or lounging in the room behind you as you write.

Second, they can be used in your lifestory as a way to tell your readers (including you, the discoverer) about you. In this sense, you are using them for your purposes, consciously or unconsciously. For example, in anthropologist Margaret Mead's autobiography *Blackberry Winter*, she writes about her daughter but in doing so reveals more about herself.[1] Indeed, writing about others may be the best way of understanding yourself – as if by proxy. Sally Cole, an anthropologist who has studied Portuguese coastal women and Inuit teenagers, believes that some ethnographers 'study and write about others in order to reach a higher stage of understanding of their own lives and society

– the comprehension of the Self through the detour of the other. We "encounter Aborigines" in order to encounter ourselves.'[2]

Using women

Women autobiographers have used fictional or mythologised other women as the peg for their own lifestory – sometimes deliberately and sometimes unconsciously. For example, Canadian lesbian writer/artist/ornithologist Mary Meigs used Lily Briscoe, the fictional painter in Virginia Woolf's novel *To the Lighthouse*, and called her autobiography *Lily Briscoe: A Self-Portrait*.[3]

Perhaps the most famous example of this strategy is Gertrude Stein's use of Alice B. Toklas, her real-life lover/amanuensis, as a way to write about herself, in *The Autobiography of Alice B. Toklas*.[4] It is 'Alice' who reports on Gertrude in this book: and the book's whole raison d'être is Gertrude not Alice. Other women have written about themselves using someone else's lifestory. For example, Lilian Faderman wrote substantially about herself as a lesbian and explorer/historian when she wrote *Scotch Verdict*, a book about two early twentieth-century Edinburgh teachers accused of lesbianism.[5] She separates the auto-biographical and biographical chapters. The recent auto/biography movement has helped us to recognise that writing someone else's biography, however short, is a means of exploring ourselves.[6]

Exercise: Exploring yourself through other women

- It may help to start by listing all the women who are nothing like you.
- Then write about one of them – the one you least identify with, the one you think could reveal absolutely nothing about you. List all her characteristics.
- Have a dialogue with her about how she can help you write about yourself. If you were her, what would you say about you?

The point of this exercise is to find new ways to speak about you. It could be used as the focus for the entire autobiography.

For example, Debbie said:

I was very new to creative writing and felt I was just practising writing by doing lifestorying. I'm nothing like Mary Queen of Scots. In fact, I know sod all about her. Just a woman in tartan, who I see in glorifying pictures, but I wrote:

> Mary Queen of Scots says about herself: 'I am tired of being an exile, tired of being looked after, shielded, imprisoned, living in others' houses, I want to live in my own safe place. I don't care about thrones or rights or dispossession or about "leading my people", I just want to settle and rest. Stuff everything.'

Well, it shocked me to write that. Because that's exactly where I am at. I'm split between a very uneasy home life and a professional life 150 miles away, a polite tenant in someone else's split-pine life. So, I don't know whether or not I have accurately reflected Mary Queen of Scots' feelings but I know I've got me down, to a T. And these are things I wouldn't have recognised if I was writing directly about myself.

Using men

Writing about a man can be useful as a distorting mirror; he is a '*not me*'. Using men when reflecting on lifestory can help you to think about gender and how women are constructed by this society to be in opposition to men; they are positioned as 'it' and women are, using Simone de Beauvoir's term, 'the second sex'. Women are sometimes able to explore themselves obliquely in writing about men. For example Elizabeth Barrett Browning does so in *Sonnets from the Portuguese*. When US writer H.D. (Hilda Doolittle) writes about her analyst in *Tribute to Freud*, she also shows us quite a lot about herself.[7] Simone de Beauvoir classically reveals many aspects of her character as she writes about her lover, the philosopher Jean-Paul Sartre, in her four-volume autobiography. US writer Jane Lazarre offers insight after insight into herself as she discusses her relationships with men in *On Loving Men*.[8]

You may like to write as if you were a man and discover the insights that this offers. Try writing about an incident from the point of view of a man who is your exact opposite. Look at similarities as well as differences for the deepest possible view. Sometimes writing yourself through a man happens in very subtle ways: your unconscious does the work. One of the earliest introspective autobiographers, Margaret Cavendish, Duchess of Newcastle (1623–73), wrote two books simultaneously. One was a biography of her husband and the other was a utopian fantasy that revealed much about her inner view of herself as both Duchess of Newcastle and as 'Empress of the Blazing World'.[9] She may have written about herself in fiction to get round the idea that a woman should not write at length about herself, certainly that she should not write a lifestory as long as her husband's. In this way she showed her readers a woman who had authority as a warrior and leader (masculine roles) who became the Empress's favourite companion. Cavendish played with the idea of herself as a powerful man as well as a woman who preferred women's company.

Exercise: Writing with a man as shield/mirror/other

Briefly, try imagining which man's biography you might write as a shield or cover story. What kind of man would he have to be: related to you or nothing like you or like one element of you?

What fantasy or free expression of you would you then, like Margaret Cavendish, be enabled to write? How does the whole exercise work for you as a way to explore your most grandiose fantasies under a safe cover? Or have you experienced men as less powerful by contrast to your own sense of freedom and power? How is this affected by our cultural stereotypes?

Use this exercise as a way to loosen up and reveal any 'immodest' and 'unladylike' desires and let them permeate your lifestory. Or try listing the kind of man you would like to be, noting the similarities and differences with the person that you think you are. Also, you could use it as a way to explore the real male characters in your lifestory.

WAYS TO HANDLE WRITING ABOUT OTHER PEOPLE

The people you love are not only hard to write about because they are so much a part of who you are; they are hard to write about because most people want to be loyal to their loved ones (especially if the loved ones are going to read about themselves). Lovers and parents are far more difficult to write about than enemies. Self-censorship is strong. Fear of being accused of disloyalty can lead to silence. Re-read Chapter 3 on speaking out appropriately. Talk with others who can advise you realistically about the level of loyalty that is necessary.

Julia, writing about friends who'd been involved in the former Yugoslavia, found it quite a balancing act. At times she was deliberately reticent, respecting their friendship more than her own academic quest, and at other times experienced 'periods of emotional over-involvement as I compared my situation, my quest for a therapeutic outcome with their very different reactions to their own situations'. It is a difficult balance to achieve but many women have done it.

Invented details

Some people will be so dimly remembered that you may decide eventually to omit them or to invent details about them. For example, my great-grandfather, a ship's barber, had a second family in Southampton as well as his 'legitimate' family in Liverpool. There's very little I can find out about the history of that 'wife', Mrs Fisk, and the daughter Honor Fisk/Quinn, so I'm inventing possible stories about Honor, based on the lives of other women of her age and type in Southampton and other seaports at that time.

Invented characters

In other cases, you may want to invent an entire character, as a way to talk about things that cannot otherwise be talked about. For example, when Drusilla Modjeska wrote *Poppy*, which was largely a biography of her mother, she invented a fictional sister, Lalage, as a way to talk about some events from a necessary distance. So Drusilla the author spoke as Lalage, and not as Drusilla; she spoke as a fourth sister who didn't really exist.[10]

HOW TO WRITE ABOUT OTHER PEOPLE

Showing through metaphor

Your job in writing your lifestory is to show not tell. One of the best ways you can do this is by using metaphor. The most enjoyable way of gearing up for this is to play a metaphor game that evolved from the Dada movement in 1920s Paris. It can be done while musing on a bus, aloud with children as a guessing game, or on paper. The metaphors illustrate rapidly what the person is like. Ask the following questions:

- If this person was a car, what kind of car would s/he be?
- If this person was a flower, what kind of flower would s/he be?
- If this person was an animal, what kind of animal would s/he be?
- If this person was a type of weather, what type of weather would s/he be?
- If this person was a piece of furniture, what piece of furniture would s/he be?
- If this person was a house, what kind of house would s/he be?

Main things about a person

Some of the main things to ask yourself about any person include the following:

Category one: How can I sum them up?

- What did they look like?
- What did they smell like?
- What did they sound like?
- Who did they mix with?
- What did they care about?
- What did they leave behind?
- Where did they visit?

Debbie wrote:

My friend Tina from school was five feet four inches tall, she was a size 10 at the time when size 10s barely existed. She had long black hair with split ends and red highlights (natural) and size 5½ shoes. She smelt of the TCP she put on her spots and some 4711 she'd nicked from Woolworth. She sounded like a nutmeg being grated when she laughed but when she moved it sounded like a brook. She swished rather than plonking her feet down on the ground. She cared about

Neil Sedaka and the size of her spots and the existence of her little sisters and whether anyone would marry her before she had to get an awful job. Her gift to the school was six or so issues of a magazine she founded before it got banned. And she left me with a love of Zelda Fitzgerald and Tagore's poetry and Greek dancing and the courage to wear daring clothes. The places she went – at that time – were Prestatyn holiday camp with her family and the only secondhand bookshop in town and fancy makeup counters and the doctor for her spots.

Category two: What was going on underneath for them?

- Imagine/paint the person as an iceberg (in the sense that most of her/him is under water, not in the sense that s/he is cold). What were the submerged nine-tenths like? Why were those parts submerged?
- Whose standards did s/he live up to – and how did s/he cope with moral dilemmas?
- What hidden and unacknowledged fears and needs did s/he have?
- What fairy-tale characters might s/he have modelled her/himself on and who/what were the companions/props in this fantasy?
- If s/he didn't exist, how would the world be different? What would people have had to invent someone like her/him for?
- What would s/he have liked to have done?
- Where did s/he hold back, and why?
- Were the outer and inner selves mismatched or collaborative or mutually useful?
- Did s/he have elements you would call 'feminine' and 'masculine'? Where were the gaps and where was the fit?
- What has punctuated her/his life; for example illness, travel?
- What do you suspect/intuit about her/him?
- What is everybody supposed to know about her/him, indubitably?
- What is her/his most illogically shaming secret?
- What did s/he gaze upon? What did s/he gain from certain others' gaze?

Taking that list of questions, Debbie wrote:

The most useful idea for me was about fairy-tale characters. I was thinking about my friend Babs who always behaved like Beauty in

Beauty and the Beast, except all her beasts never turned into handsome princes who rewarded her. She modelled herself on this rescuing Beauty, and I think it was to compensate her for life absolutely not being under her control; she kept finding people who were so horrible that it seemed obvious they could be transformed. I mean they couldn't stay like that – you'd think. But they did. Oh God, they did; fat men in undersized loons, a hoodlum, two alcoholics. And everyone said, Why does she do it? And she sailed on, smiling beatifically. What she meant to me, I suppose, was an example to me of what I didn't want to do. The person I feared I might become if I didn't watch out for myself far more than she did.

Many books on how to write fiction contain excellent advice about creating characters; you could consult them for your lifestory as a way to bring your significant people to life. Obviously, you will use their speech. Make sure you really 'hear' and convey their speaking voice by speaking aloud in their tones and accents as you write. On the assumption that they won't be around to collaborate with you, I include the following suggestions as a way to show their full character and their significance to you.

Dialogue with them

As preparation, you could try the exercise of writing down dialogues with them as in a play. Try not to get into a 'You did, You didn't' rut, but have a genuine exploratory talk. Who are you? What matters to you? If you are going to ask your characters challenging questions in your head, do so warmly, so that you don't 'frighten them off'. These will probably be rough notes rather than material to include in the finished text.

Be them

Try being that person. It's a bit like method acting. Try wearing a mask and acting out their life. You can make a mask by enlarging a photograph on the photocopier, cutting it out and blue-tacking it to your face as you walk around the house. Write in front of a mirror.

Exercise: Being them

Close your eyes and conjure up an image of the person you want to write about in a typical place s/he likes to be, for example the bingo hall. What is s/he wearing? How is s/he feeling? What is it that s/he gets out of this place? Try to speak to yourself in writing as the other person.

The point of this exercise is to show your characters as deeply as possible.

Ask their help

If these characters are not working for you, then stop. Dialogue with the character in your imagination. The pattern should go something like this:

- Hello (character's name).
- Thank you for agreeing to give me your wisdom.
- Why am I having trouble with you?
- What do I need to give you so you will be fuller/happier in this story? Would you be happier to go away/be given a pseudonym/left till another day/mood?
- Thank you for telling me this.

Love them as you write

One of the key things fiction handbooks insist on is that you should love the characters you create, otherwise no one will want to read about them. This can be hard – any frank autobiography will contain people who have angered you. If you want to do this as part of your process then one possibility is somehow to find a way to love them as well as hate them. One way to do that is to forgive them. This can be a difficult process, with beneficial long-term repercussions.

YOUR RELATIONSHIPS WITH OTHER PEOPLE

Questions for exploring your relationship with the people who are important enough to be in your lifestory include:

- What did they mean to me?
- What difference did they make to my life?
- How am I like them?
- How am I unlike them?
- How do I feel about that?
- What impact did they have on others around me (for example, siblings, classmates)?
- Did they have the same impact on others as they had on me?
- What is their legacy – and how have I rejected/accepted it?
- Who was the I who received their impact at the time?

I was trying to write about Judy, someone I knew at art school; a woman who seemed much older and had a lover in Paris at the Ecole Polytechnique, which was prestigious. The question that worked for me was: 'Who was the I who received her impact at the time?'

The answer is that I was 18 in 1967, and totally inexperienced in the ways of passionate, determined, non-mealy-mouthed women. I didn't know anyone else who had a foreign boyfriend. I didn't know anyone else who wore all black. I didn't know anyone else who listened to the World Service news as if the international news mattered and as if she had a responsibility to hear it. I didn't know anyone so uncowed; she even made a feature of her thick legs and her large knickers. She taught me a lot about taking your power.

Use stereotypes to make fresh contrasts

There are stereotypes about most kinds of relationship: friends are traditionally described as fickle, fair-weather, loyal, cosily from childhood or new and thrilling. Think of an old friend and see how much the stereotype *doesn't* fit. For example, how you see your friend struggling to be loyal despite being torn by her own dilemmas; how she fights against her fickleness; or how you love her fickleness because it's a proof of her liveliness and discriminating tastes; how the very oldness of the friendship thrills you because of its roots in your childhood.

Using social psychology

On the other hand, you may like to use ideas from social psychology to explore your relationships.[11] For example, some relationships are described as being narcissist–complementary narcissist, in which one person applauds while the other performs. Thinking in terms of opposites is a useful way of starting to think about relationships with other people. Some pairings include:

educative – limiting
reciprocal – abusive
angry – tolerant
coercive – cooperative
deficient – satisfying
intimate – estranged
flourishing – moribund
dependent – independent

For example, if a relationship is coercive rather than collaborative, one partner bullies and there is no respectful sharing. However, these descriptive pairings never fully work, because such polar opposites reduce complexity. It's better to think in threes, for your next stage. Thalia said:

I looked at some of those pairings and I thought, that's the story of my life – *deficient* bloody relationships. Especially with Philippa, and with quite a lot of my friends in the early years. Never *satisfying*. But then I thought about my inability to recognise satisfying elements, out of fear of intimacy. I remembered some people have accused me of being deficient. Thinking that made me take more responsibility so I'd say of that pairing it could be a threesome of 'deficient – fearful – satisfying'.

Implicit deals and needs affect who does what in a relationship. You may like to identify these, along with the elements that cause it to founder or soar. For example, Cathy knew that in the 1970s her relationship with Keith, her mentor/lecturer as a mature student, was based on the fact that he knew the ropes and she didn't. He helped her in return for feeling superior, and she had known this at the time. But in writing her lifestory she started to see it was also true of other relationships; it was a pattern followed by many women, and not something she should take individual blame for:

I ended up writing a list of about six men, and then tracing the pattern with my mum and nan, and with my friends. We all got a lot out of that bit of my autobiography. Having letters from Keith in front of me helped, too. With hindsight I could see what he'd been up to. Now I'd call it abusive.

HOW MUCH TO INCLUDE OTHER PEOPLE

Remember not to get bogged down in writing about other people. This is your autobiography, rather than the family history. While it is obviously important to acknowledge the people who loved you, reared you, socialised you, they are secondary characters. *You* are the principal actor and you can have them on stage with you as little or as much as you want.

If you are writing an autobiography for publication then *you* may be the selling point and others may be comparatively irrelevant. On the other hand, a writer who has already published a lot, such as May Sarton or Rebecca West, has many readers wanting to know about all aspects of her life, including what she thinks of people she knows. May Sarton has written a whole volume of essays about people she's met. Rebecca West's *Family Memories* is about just that. Of the 254 pages, only 30 are about herself ('Cissie'), while the others are divided into three sections: the Campbell Mackenzies (her maternal line, including Highland pipers); the Fairfields (her Anglo-Irish paternal line); and Isabel (her mother).[12]

Why do they mean something to you?

Victoria Hughes, who worked as a women's lavatory attendant on the Bristol downs, has written a potentially satisfying lifestory. In *The Ladies Mile* she describes a period between 1929 and the 1960s where she meets mainly prostitutes (plying their trade on the downs) but also women tramps: women called Buggy, Weeping Mary, Doris and Running Mary.[13] However, it does not work as well as it might because she writes too superficially about the 'colourful characters' who dropped in for a chat as they spent a penny. Conversely, she doesn't explain why she feels such affection for them.

If your lifestory is based on all the interesting characters you have met, then it pays to ask: Why do I want to write about this character? What can I see that goes beyond me being an observer? What use has s/he in my lifestory?

Writing about other people can be one of the most enjoyable and challenging experiences in writing lifestory. The next chapter suggests ways to talk about people connected to you in specific roles, such as lovers, mothers, friends, fathers. The principles stated in this chapter can also be applied, of course.

Writing about specific people

This chapter builds on Chapter 10 by talking about ways to write about specific people; those we usually know intimately, those we usually know a little less intimately, and those we might be quite distant from, or know only fleetingly.

PEOPLE WE MAY KNOW INTIMATELY

Mothers

Mothers are the main figures written about by women autobiographers. Their impact on us is colossal. French novelist Colette famously begins her autobiographical novel, *Break of Day*, with a letter from her mother.[1] She says she won't visit Colette because her precious cactus is about to do its rare flowering and she wants to see it before her death. This immediately illuminates the tension in Colette between the child's desire for her mother and the adult's recognition that her mother has her own agenda, which Colette, as a person who also loves plants, understands.

How can relationships with mothers (including step-mothers and primary care-givers) be other than complex, when these women are not only our nurturers but also our positive and negative role models, our 'm/others'? In most cases they reared us, so they know a lot about our histories – and we know a lot about them. In any event, we carry their genetic patterns and their behavioural traits whether we lived with them or not.

At some point in writing about your mother you may like to read some of the best recent autobiographies (and autobiographical fiction) which focus almost entirely on mothers: Vivian Gornick's *Fierce Attachments*, Carolyn Steedman's *Landscape for a Good Woman*, Kim Chernin's *In My Mother's House* and *My Mother, My Self* by Nancy Friday[2] are illuminatingly frank about difficulties with mothers and the challenging complexity of the bond, especially 'the feminist daughter's enabling and disabling ambivalence to the mother'.[3] In Judith Arcana's anthology, *Our Mothers' Daughters*, 120 women talk about passions and conflicts, expectations and the potential for enlightening change in mother–daughter relationships.[4] *Between Ourselves: Letters between Mothers and Daughters* contains correspondence from as early as 1750 which may give you an extra dimension when thinking about your bond with your mother.[5] Tillie Olsen's *Mother to Daughter, Daughter to Mother: A Reader and Diary* offers you space to write your thoughts as you read.[6]

Exercise: Words you associate with your mother

Set a timer for five minutes and then write every word that comes into your head about your mother. Don't stop. Don't make sentences. Then go back and see which words should be highlighted.

Reflect on what you have learned, what you missed out. Use this is a basis for further writings about her.

Mother's body

Your mother's body, unless you've been separated at birth, is the one you know best, earliest. You've been physically connected, which is why some women's autobiographical writing starts with the umbilical cord and the severing of it which marks the start of your separate existence. From your mother's smells and maybe her very vibrations you probably recognised her from yards away. Her touch was the first significant touch and it could bring you all the comfort in the world. Growing up means growing away from that body and losing such deep knowledge of it. This playground of flesh with which you once made so free becomes private and something which you have only complicated access to. You may not have seen her naked body at all in later life, perhaps not until her laying out. What does that disconnection mean for you – liberty, loss, predictable rhythms of changing rapport?

Exercise: Mothers' bodies

List the feel, smell and sound of various parts of your mother's body. In brackets note the emotions you attach to each. Which of these do you want to convey in your autobiography?

Describe the different touches: their pressure, scope, the parts of you that were touched by her and the parts of her you touched. What did/do the different touches say? What didn't they say that you wanted to hear? What impact has their lessening had on your bond now?

This exercise can work as a fast way to comprehend the deep places of your relationship. It's for background rather than for putting directly into the lifestory and may well bring up strong feelings.

Mother tongue

Your mother's voice is usually the first voice you heard and you almost certainly got to know her through her voice. Her words are the first you tried to make sense of. From her you learned language. And through her you learned the systems of meaning in your society – she prepared you for what it means to live.

Her language is your first language. It's not forgotten although you may have stopped using it and started using the tongue that is used by most of the people around you. Amina, a Pakistani research student, experimented with this and wrote in her mother-tongue, Urdu. She found significant insights 'because of the articulation of gender, and because of the change in who one is writing to and for'. You may want to write paragraphs in your first and second language, at least at the experimental stage, to convey this complex history of your connection with another culture.

Exercise: Remembering mothers' speech and language

Set up a private time for yourself when you can reflect in peace. Close your eyes. Think of the common words your mother used when you were little. Say them aloud to yourself in her tones, if you can.

What are those words? What happens when someone says them today? Which of them do you use when you talk to young people? How has the meaning and personal history of the words and sounds affected the way you see the world?

Use your notes from this exercise as background. The exercise can remind you of early emotions and the forming of concepts. To make the lifestory rich you could reproduce your mother's speech rhythms. (You may want to go on to explore what it means to sound like someone of such a different time.)

Mothers' rhythms

Many women are shocked to find just how many of their mother's rhythms and patterns they reproduce in their own lives. For example, you might be in the habit of celebrating the changing seasons by putting up summer curtains on 1 June and winter ones on 1 October because this was what your mother did. You may respond to others' questions in the same manner as she did. You may walk with her gait and at her pace.

Exercise: Seeing similar rhythms

Try listing the rhythms you regard as characteristic of your mother. Tick the ones you think you reproduce. Then try listing an imaginary mother and daughter's similar rhythms. Put the two lists together. What is true for you?

Use this exercise for background notes. The point is to get beneath old habits of thinking to explore how similar/dissimilar you are.

Mothers' history

Many autobiographers explore their own mothers' histories, especially experiences of work, love, childrearing and migration. Maxine Hong Kingston, for example, in *The Woman Warrior: Memoirs of a Girlhood among Ghosts*, focuses on growing up in the USA reared by an emigrant mother who struggles to keep the culture of her native China alive and to pass it on.[7] You may like to try exploring your own mother's history both through interviewing her and researching official records or histories of women similar to her. (See Chapter 14 for ways to get background information.) Some women gain a lot by doing this with their mothers as a collaborative project (but it can become tricky if you disagree about interpretation).

One of the difficulties of writing about mothers is to see them as separate from you. It can be so easy to forget that your mother has her own existence and her own needs.

Exercise: Seeing your mother as separate

Suppose she'd never had you (though perhaps she had someone like you). Stand back. How would you – in your non-daughter role – describe her? What are her characteristics and her pleasures? If she'd written an agenda for her life, what would it contain, in order of importance? Who mattered to her (in this story in which 'you' are absent)?

Use this exercise for background information. The point is to give you greater clarity of vision about your mother, as if you were not in the picture. It can help establish a different way of seeing her.

In Penelope Mortimer's autobiography of her early years, *About Time*, she describes her mother's intimate relationships with women, that may or may not have been lesbian:

She had many loyal and affectionate lady friends, my unrelated aunts, and when she was with them she had always seemed like a stranger. Sometimes I preferred this stranger to my mother, particularly when her face flushed and crumpled into paroxysms of laughter.[8]

Fathers

For many women, fathers are usually harder to write about than mothers. They offer less material (which sometimes can be a blessing), fewer aspects to identify with and often less specific information. As mysterious figures, they can be more intriguing. Germaine Greer's bestselling partial autobiography, *Daddy, We Hardly Knew You*, describes her quest to get to know this distant figure. It moved many people who had a similar desire to uncover this significant but so elusive parent.[9] Other women find fathers easier to write about than mothers because they excite less ambivalent and intense feelings.

Don't worry if in writing about your father you find that it's a story of absence. Say so. Say what you missed, where you would have liked him to have been, what you imagine. Do research on him if you want. Or try doing the brainstorming exercise, fast, writing down any word that comes into your head when you think of him.

How does the world see him?

Carolyn Steedman writes that 'working-class autobiography frequently presents, as a moment of narrative revelation, a child's surprise at the humility of a domestic tyrant witnessed at his workplace, out in the world'.[10] You may like to use this in thinking about your own father, grandfather or significant male authority figure.

Exercise: Seeing fathers in a public context

Think of some places your father took you to – preferably just you and him, so that the memory will be more personal and intense. His work? The pub? To see your mum in hospital when a sibling was born? To school when she couldn't come? How did he behave? How did others treat him? What surprised you about how he was seen by others? What had you already suspected? How was he different from the way he behaved at home? List some of the scenes you witnessed there and see if they have any meanings for your overall lifestory.

Honorary parents

Some of us adopt honorary parents in later life, however temporarily, to supplement what our parents cannot give us. This is particularly the case for people making major transitions into areas where their birth parents can't follow. This transition might be to a different country, a different class, a different philosophical viewpoint such as a religious cult or political party. These honorary parents could be a tutor and her lover, an experienced activist and his wife or some sort of guru who includes you in her/his family.

Exercise: Thinking about honorary parents

In what situation(s) did you feel you had left your birth parent(s) behind? What did you need that they could not give you? Who did you find, however briefly, who could take their place in that situation? Make a diagram of your life that somehow shows the significance of these honorary parents or the bridges they helped to create between your worlds.

Use this exercise for background information on your formative influences.

Sisters and brothers

Sisters and brothers are often the first people with whom you explore the world, once out of your parents' hands. They can be the people with whom you test your power and equality. They also provide good ways for understanding at one remove your relationship to your parents. This goes for step-siblings and foster-siblings as well, although the complexity of their relationship is very different.

In writing about your sisters and brothers the basic things you may want to show are what they meant to you, the tidal pulls of intimacy and hostility, your use to each other and the ways you could/not get along together.

Exercise: What your siblings showed you about you

Make a calm space to sit down for a private hour and reflect. Ask yourself: what did my sister/brothers implicitly show me about myself? You may like to draw or paint this. Did s/he show you how like or unlike your parents you were, how many qualities you shared? How was s/he like and unlike you? What did and didn't you do together that determined how you – differently – handled life?

Use this exercise for background information. Its point is to help you explore any family connection or lack of connection that you might want to make explicit for your lifestory.

When Carolyn Steedman was young she worried that her sister was not baptised because it meant she couldn't enter the kingdom of heaven. When Steedman voiced this to her mother (who had both children illegitimately, and had baptised neither) she received another kind of information:

> this revealed distance ... permitted my growing recognition that we represented different stages of endeavour to my mother, that my sister was a disappointment in the way I wasn't. It was a genuine shock to [later] ... discover that I wasn't the privileged elder daughter after all.[11]

Significant relationships

Significant relationships with non-family members come in many shapes and sizes and have many different impacts on our lives. Judy Hill Nelson (or her publishers) clearly rated her relationship with tennis star Martina Navratilova as being of such importance that her memoir, *Choices*, was subtitled: 'My Journey after Leaving My Husband for Martina and a Lesbian Life'.[12]

Try making a list of the most significant relationships in your life, including names, dates and roughly who you were at that time. File it and move on for now. This is just so that you have some sense of the scale of the scene you are surveying.

You may find it easier to write about elements and essences of a person, woman or man, rather than attempt to sum up the person or the relationship. Don't worry if you find yourself writing about the relationship and yourself rather than about the beloved; after all, it's your autobiography. The point of including the other person is to show what s/he meant to you.

If it seems as if the story of this person and your relationship with them is turning out to be really *too* much about yourself alone, try thinking about who s/he would have been without you. Proximity is a catalyst. You can no longer see the person that s/he was before you reacted upon each other.

Exercise: Seeing significant friends objectively

Look at your list of significant people and imagine that they have never met you. How would a stranger describe this person whom chance later made into your special friend? Speak as someone dispassionate and objective. Now imagine that the stranger sees you entering the picture; how do they now view your beloved?

Why were you close?

You may find it does not pay to ask yourself questions about why the relationship did or didn't work. The effect is often to rationalise and sum up intellectually what actually works better when implied or symbolised. It's said that usually no one can answer the question 'Why did your relationship end?' On the other hand, most people can answer 'What first attracted you to this person?'

Uprights and horizontals

You may like to consider a relationship visually, as something woven or built. What would the main pillars/towers/ladders be? What would be the horizontal threads/waves/lines that intersect those uprights?

Paula wrote in her essays on relationships:

I loved Fran for our shared interests: cats, walking with a women ramblers group, decorating. Those shared interests were the uprights. And the threads that ran across were: our complementary jobs – each of us coming in with gossip and input, overlapping sometimes; the ordinary housework; sex of course, this huge fat warm wave of a thing lapping the struts of the pier that was our outside life; and I suppose our different ways of seeing – telling each other what our eyes saw and enjoying the difference in our two visions of the same sight. We weren't tightly woven, but we were woven, and it was beautiful, what we made.

If you want to explore the question of why you were together, some questions that might work for you include the following:

Context: What was the context of your coming together? Include material things like 'the youth club' but also spiritual dimensions such as 'I was having a hard time with my form teacher and needed a companion who showed they really really liked me.'

Expectations: What expectations did you both come with? What baggage (try thinking of a full suitcase) did you bring from your previous relationship? How were these expectations met/unmet and how did that affect you both?

The nature of the relationship: You may also like to ask yourself these questions as a way to explore the nature of some of these relationships. Do note if the same thing is true of several relationships. You might want to explore the origins of that pattern and its evolution.

Magic: If this person had been sent to earth by a higher being, just for you, in order to help you learn some profound lesson about life, what would that lesson be?

Forbidden: If your love was a forbidden love (too old, too young, wrong sex, wrong colour), what did that teach you about your respective cultures and their values?

Alter-ego: What aspects of you – especially hidden ones – does this loved one illuminate? How are they like a secret you, one you won't admit to?

Irritations (and inspirations): What did they do that you hated, that felt like a fork being rasped over your raw skin? What made you metaphorically sing? What did they do that helped you love the others around you all the more?

Support: What couldn't you have achieved without their assistance?

Their view of you: How would they describe you and why would they be right/wrong?

Obstructions: What got in the way of being as you wanted to be together?

Happy chances: What part did serendipity play?

The deal: What implicit contract was involved between you? You would do/be what? In return what would they be for you?

Exercise: Assembling the elements of a significant person

Reflect on the person and your relationship with them. What symbols always remind you of that person and how s/he was to you? If you could collect together a basket of elements/symbols, what would you choose? List them. Don't make sentences. Paint them if you like. Visualise them. Feel free to make them not only material objects but also songs or feelings.

Now, imagine what would the basket be: supermarket mesh or cosy wicker lined with flannelette; a bike basket or something woven from African raffia? And who is the person carrying it, offering it, burying it, discarding it? This is metaphorical, of course.

The point of doing this exercise is to use illustration to show yourself and others something about the relationship. Do use detail.

Vivian Gornick does this really well when she writes about her (married) lover:

> He said that the point is to make as much world as possible in whatever small clearing is allotted one ... He never stopped delivering life to me, at me, for me ... We had champagne in bed, oysters in mid-town, surprise trips to the ocean. He bought me books I needed, sent me clippings daily ... our emotional life was an absorbing one for me and became one for him as well.[13]

Your children

The children we have borne are often much more absent from auto-biographies than might be expected, given the significance they actually have in mothers' lives. Annie said: 'I was surprised to find I didn't feel like writing about them much – this was *my* space. But also I felt I had no right to expose them – I was protecting them.'

Mothering and step-mothering and mother-in-lawing are incredibly complex and emotional sets of tasks, so you will need to find the right time – maybe years ahead – to articulate the process and the people involved. Jane Lazarre in *The Mother Knot* and Adrienne Rich in the first chapter of *Of Woman Born* offer useful examples of profound ways to write about the violent and contradictory feelings they had as birth mothers.[14]

In writing about the children who mean something deep to you, you could include your godchildren, children you never had, children whom you co-parent but did not actually bear. You may want to describe both who they are and what that means to you, and talk about how they are different and similar to you.

Exercise: Writing about your children from a useful distance

Take at least an hour off. Think about how your children might describe you if you weren't their mother but just a woman they knew. In order to avoid feelings of blame and responsibility, just write a list. Or draw how they might see you. It's fine to make this exercise time-specific, about a particular time in both your lives. Reflect on what 'they said' of you. How does that connect with the woman you experience yourself as being? Now write about the children who could write that account of you. What qualities do they have that enabled them to see what they saw?

Use this as warm-up material for writing about children more fully. The point of this exercise is to enable you to proceed obliquely towards the task of describing who your children are.

Exercise: Landmarks

Write a list of significant times you spent together; for example, family holidays, crises. List these 'landmarks' (together with the date) down the middle of a big piece of paper. Then on one side of that central column write who you were at that time, and on the other side write about the children.

For example, Annie wrote:

Holiday in Cornwall, 1987

Me	The kids
fraught, fractious	joyous at the cliffs and surf
scared I was pregnant	Ben protected me in his dad's
worried about redundancy	absence
reading old Muriel Spark novels	Caro's periods started
	wrote a rock opera about rocks!

The point of this exercise is to get some sense of the different perceptions of the same event, in case you want to use the contrasts and similarities in writing your lifestory. By concentrating on some events that stand out you can write in a more grounded and specific way.

Imaginary children

As well as real children, you may want to write about your imaginary children – be they dolls, pets or invented characters. Carolyn Steedman's invented daughters were Joanna and Maureen. They lived behind the mangle. She writes in her autobiography that she believes they evidenced her ability to wish for a child, 'which is the wish to see oneself reproduced and multiplied'.[15] Such fantasy children can be an implicit affirmation that you have had good enough mothering to be able to pass it on. So the presence of imaginary children in an autobiography can be a proof of how loved you felt in your earliest times.

Friends

The friends we choose, and that life puts in our orbit, are important in autobiography. This is because they illuminate what we wanted, what we thought we were and what kinds of people were attainable to us at any one time.

Exercise: Exploring friends

Head a page for each five years of your life. In reverse chronological order, starting with today, write down the friends you had in that time. Note the key ones and the continuity between periods. Note in brackets what those friends were for. Take one that stands out. Draw them, and you in relation to them, if you can. Try and remember the quality of their voice, their smell. What did you do together? Where did you first meet and why did you stick together or break up? What made them dear to you or distant? What impact did they have on your future development?

Use this exercise – repeating as many times as necessary – for background. The point of reverse chronological order is that it can be liberating.

PEOPLE WE MAY KNOW LESS INTIMATELY

Grandparents

Conventionally, grandparents are the elders who give you the unconditional love that parents may find harder to give. Their role is not usually to discipline; they can even spoil you. Of course, they are actually complex people with their own needs and histories and roles. Their chief value in your autobiography will probably be that they are usefully like/unlike your parents and that they know your parents almost as well as you do (but differently) and therefore can give you insights into your own upbringing. Second, they are people who have lived in a very different period, and so can help you understand how your particular family deals with changing times. Interview them if you can, bearing those two points in mind. Grandparents are usually much more complex people than they seem when we are young.

Exercise: Understanding your grandparents

Photocopy a picture of your chosen grandparent when young and a picture of you. Cut out your face carefully, and position it on his/her body. Gaze at it for a while.

Note the year – say 1909. Then write a list of all the things you might have been concerned about if you were their age living then. Then see if there's any useful way you can write it up.

The point of this exercise is to empathise with your grandparents' circumstances. If we understand people's early lives we can often write better about their later lives. It can help with the hard task of understanding someone very much older than ourselves.

Cousins

Today when families tend to be far-flung, many western people's relations with their cousins are distant or are a part of their early life. So your writing about your cousins may well peter out after you reach your late teens. Think about what connects you to your cousins today and in the past. How has their existence affected your life? Don't feel obliged to put them all in your autobiography. Many lifestories mention just two or three cousins in passing, no more than a page, unless they were more like sisters and brothers than cousins. Try imagining them in a wall mural of your life, or on a pair of scales: what weight and size and prominence do they merit?

Cousins can be useful in autobiography because they are a way of exploring how different the products of grandparents can be.

Exercise: Cousins' different inheritances

Think about some cousins. List their characteristics. With different coloured pens underline which personality inheritances came from which grandparents. Use an extra colour for 'don't know'.

Then list your own characteristics, briefly. Which do you now think came from your grandparents and which from your parents or 'don't know' sources?

You could use this exercise as background material to ponder on what has been genetically, culturally and differently passed on to you and your generation.

Aunts and uncles

Aunts and uncles can be reminders of an old life no longer lived, severed by geography and cultural differences. They are familiar 'parents' and yet not *your* parents.

Exercise: Using aunts and uncles

Think of a characteristic interaction between your mother or father and their brothers or sisters (of the opposite sex, preferably). List the traits you see in common and by contrast. Take a short break. Reflect on what this shows you about your mother or father. You may also want to consider the impact of this on you, if any.

Vivian Gornick's autobiography describes how she watches her aunt Sarah and her mother: 'The two sisters were always together and always bickering. Ordinary conversation between them was entertaining aggression ... I always enjoyed a visit from [my aunt].'[16]

Ancestors

If you're interested in your family history, you may want to use a family tree. The things we know about great-great-grandparents, alleged

Genogram by Jo

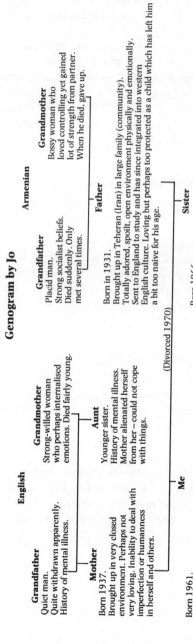
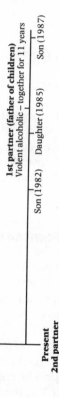

Armenian

Grandmother
Bossy woman who loved controlling yet gained lot of strength from partner. When he died, gave up.

Grandfather
Placid man. Strong socialist beliefs. Died suddenly. Only met several times.

Father
Born in 1931. Brought up in Teheran (Iran) in large family (community). Totally adored, spoilt, open environment physically and emotionally. Sent to England to study and has since integrated into western English culture. Loving but perhaps too protected as a child which has left him a bit too naive for his age.

Sister
Born 1966. A good baby! Quiet, undemanding, fitted in. Favoured by mother until later in life questioned this situation. Also affected by divorce of parents but perhaps too young to understand, until much later. Over-protection as child makes it difficult for her to cope sometimes with reality. Only became close as sisters in recent years.

1st partner (father of children)
Violent alcoholic – together for 11 years

Son (1982)　　Daughter (1985)　　Son (1987)

English

Grandfather
Quiet man. Quite withdrawn apparently. History of mental illness.

Grandmother
Strong-willed woman who perhaps internalised emotions. Died fairly young.

Aunt
Younger sister. History of mental illness. Mother alienated herself from her – could not cope with things.

Mother
Born 1937. Brought up in very closed environment. Perhaps not very loving. Inability to deal with imperfection or humanness in herself and others.

(Divorced 1970)

Me
Born 1961.
Spent 30 years trying to resolve feelings of distance from mother. Spent childhood parenting my parents. Felt my appearance out of place, not English, felt more Armenian. Always wanted 'ordinary' childhood, not liberal, intellectual parents of early 1960s, too absorbed in own pursuits. Craved security. Fairly extrovert on surface. In later life, certain crises forced changes and ability to deal with and resolve many issues. (Divorce affected me deeply as father major support in childhood.)

Present 2nd partner
Soulmate, could have only worked if met when we did – both been through hard times but he is my rock (security). Caring, independent and not much baggage. We complement each other. Loves children and vice versa.

founders of the family, will usually be limited to a few bare facts about birth and death dates. Any colourful details will be based on others' stories about them, often second, third and fourth hand. There may be the odd photo or relic.

The point of including in your lifestory someone so indirectly known is that they stand for something that interests you so passionately that you are prepared to deal with the problem of dodgy information. You will need to show why that interest is so great. You may like to try making a genogram (like the example on page 149). This is a map used by psychologists and social workers in order to understand inherited family patterns, especially emotional behaviour.

PEOPLE WHO ARE USUALLY MORE DISTANT

Enemies

It's useful to spend some time thinking about enemies because the reason for the enmity often illustrates something quite profound about you. An enemy can represent the antithesis of all you hold dear. Or they can be someone who embodies traits that you can't bear to know you have. There are many reasons for enmity, including rivalry, betrayal, fear.

Significant strangers

People met in passing can act almost like messengers from another planet, illuminating what you need or want to know. US feminist activist Sarah Schulman understood her Jewish identity the better for a casual contact:

> The tailor sewing in the window across the street had a number on his arm. We bought our clothing in a store in Brooklyn run by people who had all been in the same concentration camp. I was only size 6X so the numbers on their forearms were eye-level for me.[17]

Teachers

Teachers, both formal and informal, can be the people who give you key equipment for handling life. Some may have been important to you, especially if you had a personal relationship with them as well as a learning relationship. Teachers are important people to include in lifestory writing because they show us in the process of struggling to move forward.

Draw a picture of them if you can to help you remember how they looked, or use a photo or recollect some fabric that they wore or the sound of their voice. Carrie said:

> I had a particular secondary school teacher, Mrs Forbes, and I loathed her for years. It was only reading about negative role models that I understand she stood for all I never wanted to be, as a middle-aged woman. I hated her shape, I hated her gabbling speech, I hated her always going on to us girls about her two eligible sons. They were boys no-one in their right mind would go out with. She was frivolous, ungrounded.
>
> Later when I came across the term *mensch* – Yiddish for person who has really lived – I saw she was the antithesis of that, or at least so I thought then. So she helped me see by negative example and through social behaviour not through teaching what I actually did want to be: a heavy woman with gravitas. That's me now. That's her legacy.

Leaders and mentors

A leader is someone with more authority than you, often older, under whose aegis you may well commit acts you would not otherwise do. A mentor guides you, usually on a course you have chosen. Include them in your lifestory if the changes you made under their guidance feel worth including.

People in books

Sometimes, especially if you are imaginative or feeling isolated, people in books or on TV may be as important to you as people in real life. Safer than real people – they can be switched on and off at will – they can become companions. Are there any characters from books or television to whom you have been attached?

Doctors, nurses, health workers

These are sometimes key people in women's lives. You speak through your body (see Chapter 6) and so your relations with health professionals are crucial to how freely you speak and are listened to or how much you are silenced. Write about any encounters that have meaning in your overall lifestory.

Gangs and groups

You may want to write about gangs not just individuals. For example, college peer groups, school gangs, evening classes, teams and organisations may well have been important to how you came to be who you are now. It can be very hard to paint a good overall picture of a crowd or group. So the best strategy (used in fiction, too; think of Mary McCarthy's *The Group*) is to describe individual people and individual activities or moments, as examples of the broader group.

Think of what the group meant to you. List or draw the main people and their relationships to each other. Working diagrammatically is a good idea. Show who had power, who was picked on, who was the cementing force, who the trouble-maker.

This chapter has taken the various kinds of relationships most of us have and has suggested ways to write about them – the intimates, the less-familiar people, the people who are almost strangers. Feel free to include other people only to the extent you want. Any life lived will probably have a cast of scores, if not thousands, but there's no need to include them all as major characters. Let some have walk-on parts or even be absent. This lifestory does not have to be an encyclopaedic summing up of everyone you've encountered. The point is just to show their significance in the course of your life. Also, your readers' pleasure may well be in seeing the unconventional, quirky and contradictory relations you have with these people. Feel free to say whatever you want rather than the customary or anodyne things that people are *supposed* to say about their mums, sisters, lovers, kids and so on. Politeness and correctness are not obligatory here.

Writing about place and space

Where have you come from? What was/is it like there? What did you think of it? Where are you now? How are you different here/now from the you who was there/then? How does the 'place'/location you're in change your perception of yourself? How do different places make you feel?

These are some of the key 'where' questions that you can explore in making a well-situated, rich autobiography that works for you and for others. The various places that you have lived in and the landscapes that you know affect both how you see your lifestory and how you tell it. In writing of place you may need first of all to understand what 'place' means to you. Then you will be able to understand what it may mean to those who read or hear your story and you can learn how to convey the meanings you intend.

This chapter is about what it means to be (and not be) in particular places in your life. You can use your awareness of its impact as a way to explore the needs, desires and feelings that aspects of a place bring to consciousness. If you want to explore ideas about women's use of space and place, you may like to read books on feminist geography, a genre that has been emerging over the past decade.[1] Also look at accounts by women immigrants, travellers or tourism sociologists; these will give you fresh insights into what you can say about place.

MY PLACE(S)

I'm using 'place' here to mean material space, a particular definite situation we know through having occupied it for a length of time.

Phrases associated with the word 'place' are my place, place of refuge, woman's place, place of sanctuary, place of abode, place of last resort, place of lodging, place in the world, place in the scheme of things.

'My place' is the place where you feel you belong. You may not own it but it is the place that you feel somehow in charge of – and there may have been many such places in your life. It may only be a room, a shed, an allotment, a temporarily known haven. Very often it is called 'home'. Elizabeth Bowen wrote a whole book on her beloved family home in Ireland, *Bowen's Court*. For Virginia Woolf, the crucial thing was a safe space in which to write creatively: 'a room of one's own'.

Where particular importance is given to ancestral grounds and tribal territory, such as in Australia, Africa and New Zealand, subsequent generations have a great sense of attachment and responsibility. You may want to think about which land, if any, feels as if it could or should be your ancestral land if this culture was different. What bit of the earth do you feel entitled to by usage, allotment or right?

If in your lifestory you are writing about 'your place', you will need to convey what it meant or means to you, by describing it and stating your responses to it. The deeper question you may want to address is: 'By what means do I know it was my place?'

Exercise: Writing about 'my place' or 'home'

Take at least an hour and a half off. Reflect on the following questions:
- What did it mean to me?
- What did it look like from the outside? Draw it, many times, if you like.
- What did it feel like from the inside?
- What was the general climate in the house, the relationship between the others who lived there (especially between parents)?
- What was beneath it? For example, the kind of earth it was built on.
- What 'framed' it? For example, fences, steps, yard, gardens, etc.
- How much land did it encompass?
- By what smells and sounds and images would you recognise it?
- What happened in the room that interests you most – who did that room 'belong' to, mainly?
- When you feel you've envisaged it properly, write a brief list of the key things that happened to you in it.

The point of this exercise is to understand what it was that made the place so magical for you so that you can convey it to others.

Mapping

If you want to contextualise this important place you can do so by mapping. Draw or model a map of your place and its location with your key elements in it (for example your school, Brownie headquarters, hospital, aunt's house, friend's house). Don't worry about getting things in proportion. The key elements can be of any size and significance that you choose. You may well need to do this several times as new items of significance occur to you. Keep the earlier versions for reference. You could create a 3-D effect using plasticine, modelling clay or papier mâché made from old magazines of that time, or fragments of old clothes you wore then. A map could certainly become a patchwork quilt or a collage. If you're making a model but can't save it then take a photograph of it.

The point of doing something visually (even better if it's in 3-D) is that it's a good way to get to know your deep feelings about the place. Later it will enable you to write it up better.

Where am I from?

One of the key things you will want to say is where you are from. Certainly your readers will want to know. It is one of the first questions that we ask of strangers: Where are you from? Where do you live? Where have you come from today?

Knowing where someone is or has been located helps us to make all sorts of (sometimes erroneous) assumptions about them based on stereotypes (such as friendly northerners, romantic Hungarians, lively Irish). To interest your readers, you may have to paint that location vividly. You may also have to disabuse them of any stereotyped ideas about it. Show them the place that is *yours* through *your* eyes. They are visitors privileged to be allowed on this intimate tour.

Make sure you highlight what your place of origin means to you. For example, are you proud or ashamed of it, confused by it, still re-visiting it in order to fathom it out? How did it make you what you are – if it did? What does coming from there, especially then, mean to others?

PLACES THAT HAVE MATTERED

The wild landscapes you saw, the polluted or country air you breathed, the amount of space you had, your connections with distant seas, Gothic towers or concrete slabs, all these are an important part of how you came to be who you are and the way you think about yourself. Sometimes places matter so much that they are used for the title of an autobiography; for example, Elspeth Huxley's *The Flame Trees of Thika*.

The places that matter enough to you to be included in your lifestory may be places of outstanding significance, or places that you felt totally alien in, or particularly disliked. Nevertheless, they had an enduring effect. For example, the place where you lived as a child and the things you saw every day on your way to school. The house, the street, the neighbourhood, the borough, the county, the country: all have played a part in constructing you and the lives you have lived. You also construct that place, to a lesser extent. You may want to think about the extent to which other people's ideas about a place (how it was constructed in their minds) influenced its impact on you.

Ways to begin

- Flip through an atlas or map book and see what places leap out at you as significant.
- Look at your guidebooks or holiday souvenirs and note the places that have mattered to you (though be warned, writing about holidays often leads to a dead end).
- Bring in ideas from a guided fantasy (a daydream whose structure is organised in advance for you) about landscapes that have been significant to you.
- Think of some key moments in your life and note down your immediate responses.
- Make a list of all the places you have lived in or visited, adding the length of time you were there and your age.

It's a good idea to leave a lot of space between lines and around this list, or to make several copies of it. There will be things you want to add; for example, places you'd forgotten, and refinings/re-findings.

After writing the first list Annie felt she wanted to write in more detail and so she added:

Belfast 1961–72 (aged 0–11); Kenny born 1963, Maeve born 1967, extension built (year?)
Kilburn 1972–80 (aged 11–18)
Leeds 1980–84 (aged 18–23). Chapeltown, Willow Road then Casey Street
Harrogate 1984–96 (aged 23–35), but commuting daily, 1987–89 to Ripley. Sense of not really having moved, settled

After making your skeleton list, take a separate sheet of paper for each location and head it with the place and the dates. Go into that place in detail, using the following questions to help you. Feel free to answer as many or as few as you like; they are just prompts.

The building

- What did it mean to you?
- Use any questions from the exercise 'Writing about "my place" or "home"'.
- What impact did the previous inhabitants have?
- What impact did co-tenants, neighbours have?

The street/road/lane

- What did it mean to you?
- How old/new/mixed in age was it, especially your part of it?
- How long/short and what key things did it connect to?
- What other streets was it like?
- By what means did you go along it and how did that change your view of it? (For example, the difference between walking/ biking/driving along it.)
- By what smells and sounds would you still know it?
- Which other houses did you like/avoid and why?
- Pavements and road surfaces: wide/tarmac/marl/concrete/ pitted/well-kept?
- What debris? (For example, old gas-lamp mantles, crisps from football matches.)

- The best/worst/most scary/most educative things that happened to me in it?
- Trees/flowerbeds/grass verges?
- What were the main buildings in it?
- What was it once? (For example, the route to the well, the turnpike.)
- What did some of the people in it think of other neighbouring streets and what did the neighbouring streets think of it/use it for?
- Was it ever in the media? Why? Did this change it?
- What did the people who lived there talk to each other about? What were their common interests?

The village/neighbourhood/town/borough

- What did it mean to you?
- Was it open/dense space, established or newly built?
- What was it called and how has this changed and why?
- What do you know about its history and imagine of its future? (For example, population statistics, new roads, dying shopping precinct, landscaping of old slag heaps, blue plaques.)
- What did it mean to other people? (For example, the posh part, the MP's safe bit of the constituency, the 'wrong side of the tracks'.)
- Which area is it twinned with, if any, and why, and what effect has this had on you?
- What are the key buildings in it, for you and for others? (For example, the mental hospital that people refer to fearfully, the town hall that you protested outside/got married in, the baths where your kids learned to swim.)
- How near is it to other significant sites? (For example, the sea, the capital, common land.)
- Did the land once belong to a local squire or factory and what impact has that had?
- Who owns it now?
- How is it like/unlike other places?
- What does it do to/for the people in it?
- What do you know about it that perhaps others don't? (For example, the underground stream, the six kinds of mushroom in the churchyard.)

- List the flora and fauna of the area.
- How might architects, developers, local historians describe the area?

The county

- What did it mean to you?
- Was it well known for anything in particular? (For example, pottery, cheese, cider, hops.)
- How have its boundaries changed and what impact has this had on you and those around you?
- Are there any personal associations, such as representing the county at a sport or belonging the county ladies' darts' team? What do they mean to you now?
- What did it look like in the papers/on TV/on maps?
- How far did it extend?
- What do people you know from outside think of it?
- Is this different to your experiences of it?

Counties had never mattered very much to Del, until she married someone who was cricket mad:

He wanted me to have all my children born over the border in Yorkshire so that if they were boys they would be able to play for the Yorkshire team. For the last two months of every pregnancy – in case the baby came early – he wanted me to leave my home and go the 40 miles to stay with his mum in Yorkshire. You can imagine the inconvenience this caused – especially when I had to lug the kids up there too. I lost my continuity with the doctor and the hospital. And when this future Yorkshire champion turned out to be a daughter it felt like a lot of futile moving round at a bad time! I had no county loyalty but I did want some tranquillity. I'm just deciding whether to call my autobiography *No Borders* or *Tranquillity* or *Staying Put*!

The country

- What did it/does it mean to you?
- Do you feel national pride, shame, etc? In what circumstances and why?

- How could this have changed your life?
- Have you lived in any other countries and how does your life there compare to this?
- What changes have you seen?
- Which bits arouse which emotions in you?
- What national and international organisations do you belong to and how does this affect your view of the country?

Virginia Woolf famously wrote: 'As a woman, I have no country. As a woman I want no country. As a woman my country is the whole world.'[2] You may want to reflect on this. Perhaps continents on the whole planet are more significant to you than individual countries. If you have changed languages you may want to explore the significance of this, as did Polish-born American writer Eva Hoffman, who entitled her autobiography *Lost in Translation*.

WAYS TO WRITE

Meaning

Bear in mind the question at the start of the previous sections. What did it mean to you? This should help you ensure that you are conveying the deepest possible meanings about your subject. Pure description can become tedious for the reader and it can overwhelm you if you haven't worked out *why* you are describing something. Check with yourself. Why does it matter? Why should the reader be interested? How can you embellish/expand on your description so that the reader can share your experience?

Don't discard the weird thoughts

Include (in brackets if you like) the odd or unusual things that come into your mind as you work. They may be useful later. Put your odd thoughts in your notebook.

Absence

If you don't have any feelings about a place that you've been in for a long time, then you may want to note that too. The absence may be significant. Perhaps it's a sign of feeling excluded, or it could be that your feelings are too deep to recognise.

Go there

Go there – perhaps with people who were significant to you then – and make notes, take photos or even talk into a tape recorder. Don't go lightly as it may have a deep impact on you. Be prepared for the area to have changed radically.

Wait and see

Leave a piece of paper, headed with the place name you have in mind, somewhere prominent for three days. Dwell on it but restrain yourself from drawing or writing anything about the place for a few days (I'd say ideally no less than two, no more than four). See what work your unconscious will do then and draw or write whatever comes out. The point of doing this particular kind of non-coercive focusing is that you may uncover deeper responses.

Contrasting others' versions

Glance at records of the place; for example, in your family album or a gazetteer. Note down the discrepancies and similarities in the way you feel about it from the inside and the way others describe it. Explore the contrast between public and private representations of it.

DISLOCATION AND REMOVAL

Since the nineteenth century, people in the western world have moved as never before. It is no longer probable that you will live on the same street as your mother and grandmother and be known by the descendants of all the women they know and have known. Married women often have their location determined by their spouse and economic decisions. Such changes, which can be forced on you by the need for a job or training or the hunger for big city glamour, can be a blessing or a curse. You may want to write about the complexity of your removals and travels.

The experience of going to another place, or somehow feeling dislocated, perhaps because our usual place has changed, can be an important ingredient in writing a lifestory because of the way our context suggests key things to us about our identity.

The meaning of moving

If you are thinking about the meaning of moving, try the following questions:

- What did it mean to you?
- Why did you move there?
- How did you feel about it?
- Who moved with you?
- What did they feel/say/not say about the move?
- What did you leave behind? (Positive and negative things.)
- How did the move change your views of the world/the family/yourself?
- If an exile has different eyes, different feelings, what has exile done for you?
- How much were you encouraged to be located?

Denise came from Georgetown in Guyana to Hackney in 1957 when she was 23:

I was shocked at the greyness in London. The mean, mean gardens here! In my home street we had breadfruit trees and sugar-apple orchards. I started doing the autobiography by just writing long captions in an album for my grandchildren. The pictures came from Tourist Board leaflets, postcards and things I cut out from Guyanan magazines, as well as family snaps. After doing a class on autobiography, the things I started thinking about were: How do I see Guyana after being here? What differences does it make that Guyana was British Guiana then and so I came to the 'mother country', finding that things were run the same way, we spoke the same language, yet it was so different? How did my roots there affect what I did here? My nursing qualifications weren't good enough for England, so I had to retrain or just be an auxiliary. If I hadn't left the West Indies, what would I be there now? What would I need to help me go back and live there now?

Seeing as strangers and travellers

Sometimes you only know the meaning of a place after you have left it. When American poet Adrienne Rich visited Nicaragua after the revolutionary Sandinista government had been in power for four years she discovered what it meant to be an American citizen, 'to be part of that raised boot of power, that shadow we cast everywhere to the South'. You may like to ask yourself how you now see your old place, having been distanced from it. Old diaries can be useful reference material here. You could even try writing on this subject in postcard or letter form, now that you are free to sum it up to no one but yourself. You don't need to use actual postcards or airmail paper but it can help. Write as directly as you would have written then but use the benefits of hindsight. Angela Carter deliberately sought out a non-Christian country, Japan, as a place to stay in for six months in order to view England from a different perspective.[3] Try putting yourself – in a metaphorical sense at least – somewhere else in order to see and understand the you who was in some of the places you will be describing in your lifestory.

Exercise: Writing from another place

Take two hours off to be reflective. Imagine being in a place from where you can see anything and everything. First, write a little about the place you are looking from. Then write about seeing a place or thing which is usually inaccessible.

The point of this exercise is to warm you up for writing with fresh eyes about a location that matters to you.

The meaning of staying

If you are thinking about what it means to stay, try the following questions:

- What did it mean to you?
- What was it like, staying in that place for that long?
- What did you feel about staying there?
- Why did you stay there? (Be aware that deep desires can be masked by economic necessity.)
- What other memories do you have of staying anywhere?
- What associations do you have with the word 'stay'?
- Was it 'home' or 'place' or 'location'?
- Were you passive/active there?
- Are your memories passive/active?
- How did it affect your identity?

Jean said:

I feel rather embarrassed at being someone who stayed all her life in the same house, the same village. But I like it so much I don't even particularly like to go away on holiday. In my autobiography, I made a virtue out of staying put by writing about all the changes I'd witnessed. I celebrated it in a rather lyrical epic manner, an *Under Milk Wood*-kind of way. In my autobiography I'm like a witness, a fascinated recorder of mutation.

SPACES

Burgundian novelist Colette stayed in a small sunless room in the Rue Jacob, Paris, in which her husband Willy ordered her to write the memoirs that, spiced up, later became the *Claudine* quartet. Colette had consolations: Kiki-le doucette, her Angora cat, sweets and plants.[4] She did not break down the door with a sledgehammer nor shoulder her way out of her prison – not least because she was economically and emotionally dependent on this older man who knew the city as she did not. It was only later, once successful and independent, that she travelled and lived where she chose.

The room you have to manoeuvre, the space you have in particular locations, affect your life. You may want to write about how the spaces (and juxtapositions) have affected you. A woman's place and space are not the same as a man's. Women are traditionally allocated different sites (the ladies waiting room, the kitchen) and occupy different spaces; consider the way men spread out their legs in trains and bulldoze their splashy way in swimming pools, in contrast to the more cautious body language of most women. Writer Walter Benjamin talked about the *flâneur*, the man who knows a city's life by strolling its pavements, hanging round its cafes; women have discussed the ways women can/not be a *flâneuse*. Elizabeth Wilson, in *The Sphinx in the City*, talks about women's use of public space and how women out in public were often seen as bad, or as being prostitutes.[5] Some women seek places separate from men – the cosy gossip-filled kitchen rather than outer space, the local council's sports centre jacuzzi rather than the noisy pub or the football stadium. That very different experience of place and space may be something you want to reflect on in your lifestory, in order to highlight specific locations and perhaps your actions. What spaces have/haven't you felt you possessed and why? What have public spaces meant to you? Which domestic spaces have and haven't worked for you and how could you/others tell?

Exercise: Thinking about how you use space

List any ten places that come to your mind – places that you use or have used. Now consider what space you chose or were allocated in them. Take one or two key places and draw diagrams of the amount of space you actually had, including proximity to others. Then identify the amount of space you would have liked, or perhaps what space a man might have taken up. Draw this. Try applying this kind of thinking to some of the other sites in your life.

The point of the exercise is to understand something about the room we have taken up, our spatial opportunism, and perhaps how this has contrasted with our desires and needs during our lifecourse.

WHAT CAN HELP

You may want to supplement your knowledge with extra information about your place, or to verify an intuition, or to stimulate your imagination with pictures when you're tired of words.

Maps

It is worthwhile looking at all sorts of maps, including schematic maps showing population density, agricultural usage, geological formation, industry, rainfall, voting patterns. Local history sections in libraries have maps, as do borough planning offices. Aerial photographs are also illuminating. Books on social, human and political geography contain maps and graphs that can show you patterns that you never suspected and can explain the physical and social causes of something you took to be individual to you.

You may want to photocopy one (or more) and then draw on it, highlighting your key routes, or stick photos of yourself and people who matter to you on it. Generally insert yourself, visually, in this chosen map or diagram.

Plans

You can see and sometimes buy or copy plans of your area or even of your home. Ask your library's local history department or the borough planning offices. These can show you the way your house used to look – for example, before it had a bathroom – or the way the builder had completed only part of the street before the war.

Old photographs

Old photographs – especially when examined with fresh eyes and a magnifying glass – can suggest entirely new ways to think about a place that once was familiar to you. Sources of old photos include: your family; the library; illustrated local history books with nostalgic titles such as *Harrogate as It Was*. These can be particularly enjoyable if you disrupt the nostalgia by photocopying and blowing up key pictures and then drawing in what you think should be there or adding speech bubbles and irreverent captions to undercut the message in the image.

Others' eyes

It can be salutary to ask other people who know the place what they remember, and what they think of what you think. Chapter 14 shows that there are many accessible books for people wanting to study local history, including guides for beginners on how to use archives, histories and records.

Books discussing future planning strategies for the place you have in mind – say, those written by conservationists, town-planners, feminists or green campaigners – may offer you new insights into your particular site. A fresh view can trigger new understandings of what the old place meant.

Including deeper thoughts

What will you include in your lifestory? As well as events, people and places, you may want to include more nebulous but equally crucial things: feelings, dreams, ideas and beliefs that have shaped your thinking. If you were building a house, this is the chapter that would help you with design concepts, the cement, and the connecting devices holding all the bricks together in the particular shape of your enterprise. I am assuming you will not be writing in self-defence or to lay blame (because these reduce the beauty and freedom with which you explore and write), nor will you want to be ignorant of what you are doing. This chapter will help with that.

FEELINGS

The lifestory you write will probably be full of feelings, both implicit and explicit. These will include the huge emotions felt and expressed overtly, such as joy, rage, frustration, jealousy, grief, terror, as well as the feelings that have a quiet, background effect. The latter include feelings or intuitions that you may have consciously denied or never even noticed because they were taken for granted, or put aside as somehow irrelevant. Pleasure, boredom, interest, confusion, for example. All these feelings are an important part of your lifestory. Your autobiography will be the richer if such feelings are acknowledged, respected and given the status they deserve.

Exercise: Feelings

List the *most powerful* feelings you have. Write down three occasions, with dates and details, on which those feelings occurred. What instigated them? Who else was involved? What connections do you see with similar feelings within your birth family? How and why did your feelings go? Put that list aside. It is probably something you will go back to later.

Now make a list of the *little* feelings you have. For example, the stirrings that are barely there but which are somehow important. In doing this you may like to act as an outsider and make a list of evidence of 'her' feelings: what visible things (hair, clothes, behaviour) show you that there is something going on in 'her'? This is a way to bypass your denials.

Now write a list of all the feelings you *never* have. You may like to reflect why you don't, and what it means if other people who are significant to you have those feelings all the time.

With all this data try making a chart of your life. Divide a sheet of paper (squared or plain) vertically into periods, for example decades. Now give powerful feeling, little feeling and feeling-you-never-have a colour each. Take felt pens or crayons and draw the progress of those feelings (those colours) across the decades of your life. It should look a bit like the temperature graph clipped to the end of a hospital bed. It indicates the patterns of your life.

Because there will be so many feelings, your chart may well look messy. You may want to do one chart for each of the three different groups of feelings. Or you may prefer to use three layers of transparent paper. Some women find that certain years or even months are so volatile that they require a chart of their own.

Whatever you want to do is fine – the only constraint is that you are trying to achieve clarity so you can't afford to let a chart become too dense with colour. It's better to have ten readable graphs than one over-done graph. Don't throw draft versions away. The process is as important as the outcome.

The point of this exercise, which can be profoundly stimulating, is to give you an overview of your emotional life and its impact. The charts themselves are not for inclusion in your finished book/presentation but they are a useful aid to writing.

Cathy drew a chart about her loneliness (see page 170). Later she thought she would have done better if she had divided it according to when she lived in different countries rather than by age.

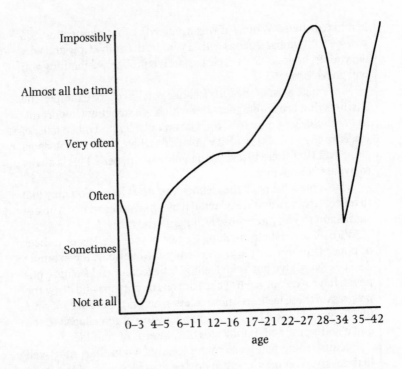

DREAMS

Your dreams, by day and night, are important illuminations of your internal world and its arrangements. If dreams are the landscape of the unconscious, then you may well want to materialise that landscape in words, pictures and 'maps'. The continents or high peaks might be what you see in recurrent nightmares; the meadows might be the sense of peace and ability you get in dreams. You may want to bring into the open the principal characters who people your dreams, so that your lifestory shows what is important to your unconscious mind as well as your conscious one.

As a standard-length autobiography has limited space, you may decide not to recount many whole dreams in your lifestory (summaries of a couple of key dreams could go in an appendix), but there could be one or two dreams or even nightmares that you see as vital in that they led you to do something or they symbolised some important elements of yourself. Sometimes when women begin working on their lifestories they keep dream diaries and go to dream groups. You may find it a useful adjunct to your more conscious work of lifestory-telling.

Exercise: Dreams

To explore your overall dream landscape, I suggest you write down brief descriptions of recurrent dreams or nightmares, assigning them titles. What do you think they were telling you about you? How did they end? Could you change them? Did you act on them? What was your key feeling?

Once you have an overview of this territory, your dream life, you may like to investigate some significant dreams in depth. Here are some ways to do that:

- write the dream out in full in the present tense
- get different elements of the dream to speak for themselves and to dialogue with each other, as if they were separate entities (doing Gestalt work on dreams helps you to acknowledge divided aspects of yourself, so that you can create a fuller picture)
- use dream dictionaries

The main interpreters of dreams are two of the founding fathers of psychoanalysis, Sigmund Freud and Carl Jung.[1] Each has a different approach and many women prefer Jung's flexibility and his ideas about archetypal figures such as the Terrible Witch and the Beneficent Goddess-Mother. The primary use of such dream interpretations may well be to provide you with fresh ideas or something to react against. By being wrong, some interpretations will help you to reach what you feel is right for you. Take notice of the interpretations you are inclined to dismiss quickly, in case you are missing out on something important by being defensive.

More recently, personal development therapists, especially in the USA, have written about dreams and how to use them. In 1995, Lucy Goodison produced the first popular book in Britain specifically about women's dreams. Although not arranged for easy reference like a dream dictionary, it offers a new view on women's dreams and is invaluable for this kind of exploration.[2]

If you want to work on your more conscious fantasies and day-dreams, then think about their key elements and characters, and especially what desires of yours they express.[3] Then dialogue with elements of them or ask them what they want. It can be particularly instructive to look over your old diaries and letters and identify what you yearned for in the past. Desires are so often clues to our deepest selves. There's a useful formula you may want to apply: 'If there's a fantasy then there's a need. If there's a need, then there's an absence of something that matters. What is it?'

IDEAS AND BELIEFS

Much of the rest of this chapter deals with exploring those ideas – formulated by the intellect – that you carry along with you. These conceptual underpinnings should be exposed, and examining them will help you structure your autobiography more clearly. A concept can be defined as a 'general notion' or the 'idea of class of objects'; it's the way you organise your thinking. And, of course, your thinking and your ideas have been influenced by many different forces, not least by ideas about what women should be. If you want to read further, some useful starting places include feminist texts on philosophy such as those by Morwenna Griffiths and on psychology by Carol Gilligan, Dorothy Dinnerstein and Nancy Chodorow.[4]

To get started, try thinking about how you formulated ideas on the following and how this has influenced your life's course:

- what you think is moral (right, correct) and immoral (wrong, unethical, unfair, unjust)
- what you value (including how you evaluate yourself)
- what you believe in (and what you lie and fudge about)
- what you do (and what you don't do or you say you do), what you think (secretly and aloud)

Try exploring the tensions and spaces in between such key ideas in your life as:

- the relationship between free will and determinism (how much say have you truly had over your life, who has had power, and what pulls have you been aware of accepting and resisting?)
- being bewitched/enthralled and freedom/extreme rational critical awareness

- tolerance and intolerance/refusal
- authority and submission/acceptance and challenge/resistance
- respectability and a lifestyle chosen for maximum self-expression
- appearances and 'realities' (how much you seemed to others to be one thing, but you actually felt differently, perhaps without knowing it)

For example, Carol found that in writing her lifestory:

it was an account in which I described myself repeatedly as someone who always looked successful and dynamic but actually I usually just went home to sleep and cried most nights after work. Writing the story helped me see the pattern, the synthesis, and the contradictions between persona and 'true self' and the compromise person in between.

These explorations will also be of interest to others, because we all want to know how other people manage their lives – not least for guidance and for making comparisons. For me, as a reader of lifestories, any (optional) blueprint is welcome in the struggle to figure out what my life is/has been/will be about.

Responses to these ideas

There are many forces that have shaped you, from your background, society at large and your specific culture. Your autobiography will be the richer if you write about your many and various responses to the forces that determined (or, for most women, *over*-determined) your life. Feminist lifestory theorist Marlene Kadar argues that certain kinds of lifewriting and reading (roughly, the kinds of suggestions I am making throughout this book) can emancipate us from being an over-determined 'subject'.[5] That is, through taking a variety of different views or thinking positions about how you have determined yourself and been determined by others, you can learn to tell your lifestory as the complex person you are. Writing as a multi-faceted being you can create a lifestory as your sometimes-influenced, sometimes-resisting self. This is much better than feeling like a pawn whom other people make decisions about. While that is partly true of all of us, how you escaped others' ideas and constructed better ones is the truly interesting story.

Bringing beliefs into the light

Like everyone else, you have ideas, beliefs and ways of explaining the world that structure how you handle it and how you see yourself. Exploring and exposing these can help you write a lifestory that is deeply satisfying. Many of your structuring ideas will have come from the state and its agencies, such as church, school, family. Often a belief is associated with a whole culture. Tereska Torres indicates how important this was for her in the very title of her autobiography, *The Converts*, referring to her Jewish parents' secret conversion to Catholicism and the family wrench that came with the exposure of that secret.[6] Some belief changes come as a result of exposure to ideas that teach you a new way of ordering your life patterns. For example, recent feminist interest in mythology and ancient matriarchies has enabled many to think of themselves as part of a very long tradition of powerful women.[7]

Exercise: Ideas that affected your life

Make a list of the ideas or sets of ideas that shaped you. You might like to use umbrella terms like 'Anglican values', or you might like to think of family ideas of behaviour embodied in maxims such as 'Do as you would be done by', or 'Always look on the bright side', or 'Nobody's better than us'. Then write down where you learned them. Assign them a number in order of importance to your later life. Think about which ones you ditched and which ones you still adhere to. Ask yourself where you might be today without any of these ideas.

For example, Alison Halford, the former Merseyside assistant chief constable who brought a famous sex discrimination case over her lack of promotion, sees ideas about justice as crucial to her life. She felt that her education from 1945 at Notre Dame convent school in Norwich may have affected her later career:

I think I have a heightened sense of justice ... there must be a connection between ... a very good education with proper standards and wanting to come into a job which is all about treating people fairly and being decent to the community that you serve.[8]

The point of the following exercise is to get to know your own thinking. You could use such knowledge by storing the list in an appendix at the back of your lifestory binder and referring to it as you revise.

Exercise: Beliefs that have structured you

When you were younger, who or what did you think had the power to make your life better or worse? God? Fate? Krishna? The universe? Only yourself? Or were different forces/gods responsible for different areas of your life? Were you perhaps structured by non-Christian beliefs, including myths, Marxist philosophy, spiritualism?

Now explore the periods in your life in which those beliefs held sway. Where did they come from? You might like to draw a 'family tree', showing which idea married which, and when, and what their offspring was.

When you have finished tracing their genesis, take a fresh piece of paper. Consider what changed these ideas, modifying or even displacing them. Do you still find yourself making irrational deals with fate, such as not treading on cracks in paving stones or touching wood?

Consider what superstitions and beliefs affect your current and past daily behaviour and how you take responsibility for organising your life.

You may like to try this exercise again when you are reading to revise. It can make sense of what had hitherto seemed random. Its aim is to help you see the underpinning holding your thinking together.

Katie Boyle early learned to haggle with higher powers in order to get what she wanted:

I have often bargained with the Madonna saying 'Now look, if I am a good girl and I really do this, I will swap if you do that for me.' I know one serious one was when my stepmother was told she had cancer and that she had to have her breast removed. I said 'Look, if I don't touch butter for the whole of this term ... will you please get her well ...' She died five or six years later but I felt I had pleaded and done something for Jesus ... If I fell down I used to say I am not going to cry because if I don't it will help a soul in purgatory.[9]

ABSENCES

Sometimes what is *not there* says more about you and your life than what *is* there. I am talking about several kinds of absences. First, there are the things you never did, never knew, never said. (Why not?) Second, there are the absences of information; things you can't include in your story for one reason or another. It might be a certificate that got lost in a house move or a secret that has to be withheld. Third, there are the absences, discontinuities and gaps that you may discover during the writing process. With hindsight, these are the things that are remarkable. They are enabling absences; the gaps you need between yourself and the world, between where you fit into context and where you don't. Gail Scott, in a collection of essays, *Spaces Like Stairs*, talks about these climbing spaces between the stairs, these fissures, these places of temporary 'nothingness' in which we grow and learn.[10]

Exercise: Using the stairs

Imagine a flight of open-tread stairs. Draw them, allowing lots of space between each stair. Then look down the steps. Label each step, going down, with a particular landmark you have reached (for example, finally getting the job you wanted). Then, when you have labelled all the steps, go back. Look at them in whatever order you like and reflect on the huge gap in between. What didn't you know, then? What discoveries could you only have made because of that empty place between where you were coming from and where you were going to? It's like a stretch of water that has to be crossed even though you have no boat. This gap is the place that enabled you to make discoveries, even if it was against your will. This patch of 'not-knowing' or non-achieving or absolute mystery enabled you to reach the next place.

List any useful thoughts that come out of this process. They can fuel later work.

The aim of this exercise is to create an awareness of the crucial impact of breathing space on our development. You could use it as a way to structure your book – a chapter for each gap – or simply as a way to give weight to the 'non-events' as well as the events.

SCRIPTS

Many people sense they were predestined to do certain things in life – as a result of family plans or inherited traits or because society dictates certain courses of action. Sometimes it's a mystical destiny, based on astrology or the lines in the palm of your hand. One of the strongest shaping forces is the plan your family had for you, however unconsciously, even before you were born: the pre-natal script. Whoever the new child was, she was expected to be certain things, such as a comfort for grannie, mum's little helper, dad's pal. The script may have been thought out in quite some detail. You may like to consider the script that you were born to speak.

Exercise: Finding your script

Think about what script your family had for the child who became you. What were the acts, who were the stars? Was it a tragedy, a comedy or what? Sometimes you can detect it just by listing the things commonly said to you, injunctions, instructions and homilies.

Then look at how much and how little you have diverged from that script – and why and how.[11] This exercise can be a good one to do aloud, even lightheartedly, with siblings, then with parents. Their insights and contradictions and contrasts can be illuminating.

Scripts from books or the 'novel-tie'

Another way we can receive an early script is through the lasting influence of a first influential book we read or had read to us as a child.

Mine was *The Water Babies* by Charles Kingsley, and it left me with the idea that I had to suffer in life, be shoved up chimneys and beaten by wicked men in order finally to get to swim with the happy pure little water babies in the river.

Exercise: Detecting your lifescript

What's the earliest book that comes into your mind? Write a description of the main characters, and what they did, how they handled life. What was their scenario, their goal, their pleasure, their connection with others? Now compare the plot and the character outline with your early life. Make notes on your discoveries.

Use this exercise both during revision, as you study your overview, and as part of the story of your early development.

Names

Sometimes the 'script' that affects how you handle your life consists of just one word: your name. Ziddah, a Palestinian who went to Calgary in 1971 as a young bride, wrote:

> Like my name says, 'life is struggle' – that is what my name means. It is funny – that I should get that name. I appreciate what I am now because before, I wasn't what I am now. We don't know these things when we are down and lonely.[12]

A number of African-American women changed their names to reclaim their African heritage: Marguerite Johnson became Maya Angelou, Paulette Williams became Ntozake Shange. Some of us change our names in order to be less like our early selves. If you re-named yourself, explore the circumstances surrounding that refusal of old values which re-naming implies.

Exercise: The meaning of naming

Think about your name. What does it mean to you? What does it mean to those who named you, and to others? Look it up in a name book to find its traditional meaning. Think of some names you *might* have been called or that you would like to have been called. Take one that seems significant to you. Write for five minutes about how your life would have been different if this had been your name.

Use this knowledge in writing your lifestory as a way to understand one of the things that determined you and as a way to understand how others see you.

This chapter has suggested ways to go underneath the obvious things you would include in an autobiography by using feelings, dreams, fantasies, ideas and philosophical beliefs – things that have structured the way you have lived your life. The aim is to help you be aware of the nature and origins of the knowledge that has shaped your life.

This is the last of the chapters dealing with the basics of who, what, where and when. There will be no more probing questions. Chapter 14 looks at how to get background information so that you can write a thorough and contextualised lifestory if you want.

Getting background information

Your memory may be wonderful, your ideas brilliant, your overall story thrilling, your diaries full of information. Good. Nevertheless, you may need a bit of extra help in getting background information. This is information that you either don't know or can't remember. If you find yourself saying at this point, 'I don't need any reminders,' then take care. This is a sign that you want to tell a very particular story that already exists in your head, rather than bother with other people's material. You may not want additional information to accompany your writing, or not just yet. Fine, do it when you are ready. But it is a good idea at least to consider background information.

Three pieces of advice can help you to handle the information you need:

1. Be prepared for the facts to be at variance with your memory. Relish any discrepancies and utilise them; don't ignore them. Give your memory's inventions as much respect as the 'facts'. Both are useful to you.

2. Don't over-research. When you start feeling bogged down, stop. You can go too far and stifle your creativity. Stop too soon rather than too late.

3. Play with facts. Feel free to use fiction but indicate that you have done so. Tell the reader that this is fiction as well as autobiography.

Bearing these three points in mind, you can have a good time in this new stage of the process; adding other people's stories to yours (which are, of course, unconsciously created in conjunction with other people's stories anyway).

USING YOUR OWN RESOURCES

Diaries

Diaries, your own and other people's, can be a great help in your lifestory writing. Even the sparsely used diaries will remind you of dates and events. Old address books, too, can be handy in reminding you not just of the people who were part of your life at different times but also the places (their homes) you visited that were once part of your familiar landscape. If you have been in the habit of writing about your life, you will come to lifehistory writing armed with a useful set of skills. The information you have already amassed will be invaluable.

Diaries differ from autobiography. First, a diary is private. When Sarah Gristwood was looking at women's diaries she found that many were implicitly saying: 'Keep out trespassers.'[1] An autobiography, on the other hand, is saying: 'Here I am. Look at me.' Diaries are micro-statements and they come very much from the inside. Often they are not designed to be read or explain anything to others.

Second, a diary entry is usually written immediately after an event, sometimes in haste. Your lifestory is the product of much reflection and sums up a whole lifetime. For example, your diary may describe a wedding you have just been to and record your immediate impressions and feelings. Only a rare diary would compare it with other weddings in your life, and reflect on their meaning in the lives of women in general. That would be the task of autobiography. Your central organising thought in lifestory writing is: 'How does this all add up?' That is not necessarily a diary writer's preoccupation – she is usually concerned with recording the here and now.

What do diaries show?
Some diaries will show you a mass of overlooked data about your old selves, including forgotten fragments of feelings, overlooked little twists, adventures and realisations. In many cases, when you re-read them you are immediately aware of what they don't say. You could almost go back and write them again, this time acknowledging what you didn't admit to at the time. Do read against the grain as well as with it.

Diaries can be a bit shocking, so be prepared. Often mine has dented my pride: did I really write so often in those early days 'Went to park/friends/pictures' and include details such as hair washing? Yes

I did, but I also wrote some good descriptions of encounters and one of my chief thoughts, as I read old diaries, is: 'I knew so much even then. This stuff is wise. So why the hell do I still mess up my life?' Diaries can remind us to love, respect and not condescend to our earlier selves.

Don't be distressed if your diary tells you a version of an event that does not match what you remember. It's often the case.

Ways diaries can be used

A diary is a piece of verbatim evidence from your past, though of course it may not be 'true'. It is your on-the-spot story of what happened/what you felt/what you thought at the time. As such, it will often contradict your memory. This discrepancy can be very very useful. Historians working on other's lifehistories – for example, Alessandro Portelli – are fascinated by the gap between the story people tell later of what happened and what 'actually' happened.[2] It reveals the way people construct something convenient from what is painful and thereby shows what hurts/what is acceptable/what others may have wanted them to do and say.

Reading your diaries will show you the you who was writing/living then. It will enable you, through tone of voice and everyday details, not only to understand your earlier self a bit better but to convey a flavour of the times to your readers. It will help to authenticate and contextualise your account.

Extracts from your diary (a maximum of 70 words a time will probably be sufficient) can be interspersed in the text of your lifestory. Written in a different style, they will add texture. You might want to use a fragment at the head of every chapter (as some people use a line or two of poetry; an epigraph) as a way to say something profound in a slightly different voice. It can be your keynote statement for the whole chapter.

You may even decide that you want to create a volume simply of diary entries. Why not? Such volumes, Virginia Woolf's *A Writer's Diary*, for example, are riveting.[3] They are also usually selected and edited by others, sometimes posthumously. You may benefit from using a friend as your editor. However, this is not the kind of lifestory that I'm talking about in this book. An alternative is to create two parallel 'books': a lifestory and a collection of diary entries. So be it. The point of this process is to satisfy you. If you are primarily writing for commercial publication then you should discuss policy on unusual forms with your editor before you proceed.

Diaries are a precious resource, and reading them for the purposes of lifestory writing can take up a lot of time. I have therefore drawn up some rules to help you use them.

1. Don't let your diaries bog you down. Don't even open them during your first draft. Use them for the second draft.

2. Let the stories they tell co-exist with the story you are telling now. Don't let their evidence cancel out your more recent version. Use both if you wish.

3. Don't read your diary while you are writing, or are in writing mode. It will skew your ability to do the overall appraisal. Make notes from the diary at another time and use those notes to assist you instead.

4. Confine yourself to reading the diaries for a limited period that feels right for you, for example just for an hour or a whole holiday. The feelings they provoke may well be overwhelming and raw and you might need to deal with them slowly before you can use them as part of your lifestory.

Beginning diary writing

You may decide that you want to take up diary writing or change your approach to it (perhaps for a second volume of lifestory or simply for your own pleasure). It is never too late. There are three essential books to read, two of them by Marion Milner: *A Life of One's Own* and *Eternity's Sunrise: A Way of Keeping a Diary*.[4] Thousands of women in the last decade have raved over her techniques, including the notion of writing 'beads': intense gems of memory which can be strung on to a 'necklace', a longer account of a time. The other book is about the 'Creative Journal' technique devised by Ira Progroff and written up in *The New Journal* by Tristine Rainer.[5] Since the early 1980s many women have gained insight – and produced wonderful illustrated journals – using this exciting Jungian-based approach which includes evaluations and images. Creative journalling techniques enables you to reflect as you go along, which makes the eventual work of writing the lifestory much easier. You are already prepared.

Therapy notes

Some people who write their lifestories are interested in doing substantial personal exploration which may include some sort of psychotherapy. This is often a place where they try out the telling of deep lifestories.

So therapy sessions can be a good rehearsal for lifestory writing, although others might feel that such personal exploration is inappropriate in a piece of published work.

Should the contents of therapy sessions and your old therapy notes or tapes be included in lifestories? Yes, if they're relevant. That deep knowledge, so hard won, is important. Other people will benefit from it. For example, many women I know have indirectly learned a lot about how to handle themselves from Anais Nin's accounts of her therapies in her diaries. US feminist theorist/psychologist Kim Chernin has brought out a book of her interactions with her therapist, *Differential Levels of Listening*.[6] A number of women have gone further and created important autobiographies based wholly or partly on their experience of psychiatric hospitals, for example New Zealand writer Janet Frame with *An Angel at My Table*, or Kate Millet's *The Loony Bin Trip*.[7]

However, like diaries, therapy sessions are private, and are usually places for working things out rather than for creating a finished product. What gets said in therapy can be so raw and immediate that you may want to write several versions of it or summarise it rather than replicating it directly. You may also want to protect yourself from such public vulnerability. Only reveal what you want to; a lifestory is not synonymous with a total confession.

Sometimes people think they should transcribe all their therapy session notes before they start their lifestory. But is this wise? Transcribing is so time-consuming (and therapy sessions are often repetitive); not all of it will need to be transcribed. Discuss with a friend whether you feel it's worth your time, or worth the money and exposure if someone else types it up for you. (If you speak at 120 words a minute, then you will have spoken 6,000 words in your 50-minute session. A whole chapter in fact. A skilled audio typist may charge £5 per 1,000 words. Is the summary of each and every session worth £30? Multiply this by the number of sessions. If you have 40 sessions a year that comes to £1,200.

You may find it works better to include just fragments of your sessions – a page or half a page in appropriate places. One of the most acclaimed writers of oral history, Ronald Fraser, devoted nearly a quarter of his early lifestory to reported dialogue with his analyst, P. It is dovetailed in an exemplary way with his own account and with interviews with those close to him in *In Search of a Past: The Manor House, Amnersfield, 1933–1945*.[8] Fraser's first page deals with his (never fully exposed) analyst and another 40 pages report verbatim but piecemeal therapeutic conversations with P., interspersed with fragments of Fraser remembering. He focuses on the process of what he remembers and how and what can be deduced from the recalling of those particular memories.

Photographs

The easiest way to remind yourself of people and events and earlier versions of yourself is to play around with old photographs. Annette Kuhn did this effectively in her photo-based collection of autobiographical essays, *Family Secrets*, and Jo Spence famously did it in *Putting Myself in the Picture.*[9] Your snaps and your family albums – and the family albums of people similar to you – are an invaluable resource. Use a magnifying glass; detail can be constructively surprising.

Useful questions to ask about any photograph are:

- Who in it is significant to you?
- What are the people in the picture doing?
- Where are they?
- What was the person taking the picture trying to say?
- Where are/aren't you in all this?
- What clues do you get from clothes, body language, who is near to whom?
- What doesn't the picture show?
- What isn't there?
- What images did the people in it have of themselves? Why?
- What did they look like in standard photos? How did they hold themselves?
- What does their response to the camera show of what think about themselves?
- What pictures were never taken of them? Why not?
- What would an outsider make of these pictures?

You could even try talking to the people in the pictures as if they were still alive or draw speech bubbles and get them to 'speak' on their own behalf.

Bet, for example, looked at everyone significant in her school photo, blew it up, cut the significant people out, rearranged them and then got them to 'say' something about her:

I wrote out something that they often said to me and something that they never actually said to me but I expected they wanted to say. It only took about 20 minutes, for all eight of them. Boy was it rude stuff! I did think of going round in real life and asking them if I was right, but decided not to. But as an exercise, it worked as a way to instantly remember what it was like in that class, and understand why I did and did not trust certain people.

Exercise: Writing about a photograph for your readers

Try describing the contents of any significant photograph as if you were someone from outer space. You have never seen this lot before or any other creatures like them. What do you think is going on? Make rough notes of what you'd say.

This exercise is something to do in rough as preparation, rather than as a set piece of work. Use it to understand worlds and people you have forgotten or do not know much about. For further ideas about playing with photographs read Jo Spence's books or any volumes on phototherapy.[10] You may then decide to try a phototherapy workshop.

Letters

Letters, both from you and from other people, can help to remind you not only of what has happened but of the person you were when you wrote and received them.

Take note not only of the contents but also of the writing paper and the handwriting, the postmarks and stamps, the place of origin and the place of receiving, the conditions in which the letters have been kept. What do these things say?

What do letters show?
Old love letters can give you clarity about old ways of relating. Most of us remember our relationships in quite a partisan way: 'It was all wonderful, that affair – not like this now'; 'She was always telling me what to do'; 'He could be so sweet – when he was away.' Using letters

to illustrate the complex and usually contradictory dimensions of a situation can add richness and telling detail.

Letters from friends can illustrate pleasures and pain shared. Notes from family can reveal unexpected elements of the bond. Even business or medical correspondence can illuminate both private concerns and public handling of life situations.

Ways letters can be used

Use letters both as text, quoting directly, and as information that you will take into account when shaping your overview. In general, it is best not to quote more than 100 words from a letter in any one part of your account. Lifestories containing lengthy extracts from letters can become tedious and have a self-serving feel to them. I skip. You may disagree, and of course this is your account so you can do what you like. You may also decide that you like the epistolary form so much that you want to write your lifestory as one long letter, as a collection of letters (invented or real), or as a mixture of diary and letters. Two autobiographies which use letters (and diaries) are Cynthia Koestler's joint autobiography with Arthur Koestler, *Stranger on the Square*, and Barbara Pym's *A Very Private Eye: An Autobiography in Letters and Diaries*.[11] Both these books were edited posthumously, but Cynthia Koestler deliberately used quotes from letters in the chapters she had written, whereas it was Barbara Pym's editors who used her letters to give snatches of her voice.

Letters you have written to others (and sent)

If you've been thorough or were aware of the value of your writing, you may have been keeping copies of your letters for years, or you may like to start keeping duplicates now. If someone has died or had a big clear-out, you may have been able to retrieve your letters from them. Enjoy this process. It can be salutary to see the discrepancies and connections between yourself then and now, and to see how you feel the letter relates to you, having been in someone else's possession. You can see now, for example, how they could have mistaken meanings that you thought were self-evident.

Letters from you will reveal: factual information (what you were doing, thinking, feeling, planning); your tone then, who you were then and how you spoke/wrote, including the colloquialisms of the time; and what you were and weren't saying in your relationship with that person.

Retrieving letters that you have written to others may be quite a complicated process and may revive a closeness, or even distance, with that person. It is more than likely that other people will not have kept the letters. This will have more to do with a lack of storage space and habits of throwing things away than with a lack of esteem for you. One solution is to invent the missing letters with your recipient's help. This could be a highly enjoyable process.

The recipient may not want you to use the letters. Ask if you can just read them and offer to do so under whatever conditions they impose.

Letters others have written to you

You are more likely to have letters that people have written to you than copies of what you have written to them. Letters to you from others will reveal factual information, how others saw you and related to you, and the way some people spoke/wrote then. They may also reveal the writers' projections and their expectations of you and may prove quite illuminating. There can be a healing aspect to this process, as well as the assistance it gives to your account.

You must get permission to quote from the letters people have written to you. It's both an ethical and a legal requirement. You own only the letter, not the copyright. Your publisher will help you on this. Their letters were private gifts to you. Try to track down the writers and ask if it's OK to quote. They may want to know the context in which they are being quoted, so there may be a two- or three-stage process:

1. Getting the permission in principle.

2. Showing them the context of how you think you'll use their letters.

3. Showing them again when you've made your final revisions.

Theses, essays and other academic work

Chances are that you have written about yourself in indirect ways in academic work such as essays, projects and theses. Re-read anything that seems appropriate. You probably won't want to use any parts verbatim but it will certainly help you to think differently about yourself reading through these particular eyes. You may find that some of the quotations and statistics you've used will add depth or even poignancy to your lifestory.

USING RESOURCES FROM OUTSIDE

This section is about resources in the world outside your own home to back up your writing. It will particularly help anyone who wants to bring a little social and family history into autobiography.

You may already have been making notes as you go along about things you would like to look up. Or you may not yet know what kinds of things you want to find.

Here are some reminders of the things people research:

- When things happened. Dates. When did that song top the charts? When was what's-her-name born?
- Whether things happened as you thought they did. Detailed other versions of occasions that matter to you.
- What happened when you weren't there. Events in others' lives that had an impact on yours.

Checking facts

As you work, keep a list of things you need to look up in dictionaries and directories at the local reference library, such as dates and minor details. Use encyclopaedias, chronologies and gazetteers rather than distracting yourself by reading whole tomes on your topic.

This is not to say you shouldn't browse. Scan the reference shelves to get an idea of the range of information on offer and the way it is ordered. Incidental discoveries can be fun and useful. There are also subject dictionaries you may never have imagined – from saints to psychoanalysis. They can help to clarify the significance of an event.

Many public libraries also have videos of every year since the 1940s. These compilations of popular songs and newsreels are an instant reminder of what the outside world was doing in one particular year.

Interviews

You can't remember everything, so get others to help you. And you can't know the whole story, so hear other versions. It can be surprisingly productive to ask people what they remember, and it's often healing, too, to get this new light on the past.

At its best, an interview is like being told a story but it's much more complicated than that – not least because you will be dealing with competing versions of 'the truth' and considering which one fits your needs. Battles can ensue over whose 'truth' is 'the truth'. There are some useful handbooks about the process of oral history that discuss the merits of sticking to questionnaires and explain the ethics of story-taking. Others are more discursive, arguing, for example, that ways of speaking, Freudian slips, hesitations and the stories people construct are useful in understanding the underlying needs and viewpoints of the story-teller. 'Lies' and absences are as revealing as the 'facts'.[12]

Taping

You may decide to have informal chats or prefer a relatively formal taped interview. Make it clear at the very start how you intend to proceed. If the interview is to be taped, have exploratory chats before you use a tape recorder. Use a machine with which you are familiar and happy, so that you can approach the whole session in a relaxed way, forgetting about the technology. Always carry extra batteries and tapes.

As a woman, you may find you are trusted more readily than a man. You may also find that some women interviewees are more frank and able to remember telling details than most men. But if you know the person reasonably well, you may find that tape recording creates formality and inhibitions.

Tensions

Interviewing people is a complex process and can be particularly tricky with relatives and friends, who are often simultaneously trying to please you while keeping you away from particular areas. They may be trying to sell you the authorised version of a powerful story. While interviewing can elicit much unexpected information it can also cause such upset within a family that you feel under pressure not to question further. Sometimes I've felt so daunted by conflicting versions that I don't know who to listen to or how to continue. In that case, it helps me to discuss it with an outsider and also to remember that I am writing *my* version of *my* history.

Julia was using her own and other women's lifestories to write *Excluded from Liberty*, a 6,000-word academic project about four women affected by the war in former Yugoslavia. She found:

> Being dependent on contributions from other people did add to the pressure and in two cases I was very conscious of creating an extra burden for people with on-going heath problems and anxieties about accommodation and relationships. In the end ... they both commented on the therapeutic outcome for them in completing the exercise.
>
> The project ... developed gradually but spontaneously as a result of increased contact with my three women friends and sharing individual dilemmas at a critical phase in the Yugoslav conflict. The final spur was the discovery that each of them would celebrate their fiftieth birthdays in 1994 and was willing to contribute by writing.

Interpretation

When it comes to interpreting others' words, the issues can become more tricky. Julia found:

> In my own case there were long established friendships at stake. I was unwilling to compromise or jeopardise them. Had this not been the case, I might have taken more risks, challenging statements rather than accepting them, demanding more rather than making the most of what was supplied willingly. My advice to other women who are relying on collaboration from others is, let people know that you value their experience, respect their right to confidentiality and if you interpret their writing, take the trouble to provide them with feedback before you go into print. In this way, even if you stick to your own original conclusions, you can anticipate the problem areas.

Balance your interviews

Stop doing interviews the minute you feel overwhelmed. Choose your timing carefully, so that you are doing interviews at the right stage. Interviewing before you have written anything can lead to confusion about the points you want to make and the course you want to follow. Interviewing after you have got your version of events sewn up may mean you can't be bothered unpicking it to include new insights.

Interviews are not the only way of getting help from others. Try asking them to talk you through photo albums or to accompany you on walks in significant places.

Newspapers

You may want to refer to newspapers and magazines from various points in your life. The obvious one is the paper from the day you were born, whether you choose *The Times* or the local rag. All national papers and many papers from other countries are available at the British Newspaper Library. Newspapers at the end of each year often contain a summary of the entire year. By looking at the 29 to 31 December editions you can identify which events of particular years are relevant to you.

You can also add to the colour of what you are writing with magazines from your girlhood – I've found *Girl*, *Jackie*, *Boyfriend* and *Honey* useful. Back copies of music papers such as *New Musical Express* will show the songs that were being played in the period in question. The Radio Four programme *On These Days* summarises some of the recorded public events that happened in a specific week in the past. You could read the professional journals for the early days of your career or the movie fanzines your mum read when she was carrying you. If you were involved in a public event – be it as local May Queen or as political demonstrator – you can look up the way it was reported and compare it with the way you remember it.

All these papers and magazines can be consulted free of charge, for as long as you like, at the British Newspaper Library in Colindale Avenue, London NW9 5AG (tel: 0171 412 7353; fax: 0171 412 7379). Some of the newspapers are in bound volumes, some are loose and some are on microfilm. You can get photocopies, although these are quite expensive. And of course this is another source for pictures if you want to illustrate your work. The library does have a postal service (minimum charge £12), if you know the exact date of the article you require.

The British Newspaper Library also has Keesings directories and other reference books that tell you what happened on a particular day. You can look up both the dates and the public events that interest you and then look up the newspaper for that day.

Another arm of the British Library is the National Sound Archive, which collects and makes available, free, all sorts of recorded radio programmes, speeches, lifestories and music from the past. Going there and hearing the accents and sounds of a time can immediately bring back memories. Appointments are necessary so contact them at the British Library National Sound Archive, 96 Euston Road NW1 2DB (tel: 0171 412 7440).

Newsletters and reunions

Other sources of information include the newsletter specific to your interests or history. For example, some occupations and most trades unions not only have regular journals (back copies can be consulted at head office), they usually also have an archive and a research officer. You can look up records there or find out where the records are now deposited – often at the Modern Record Centre at the University of Warwick, Coventry CV4 7AL (tel: 01203 524219) and available free to all comers.

I recently went to a school reunion and found it instructive and healing – a follow-up newsletter would be even better. The school secretary will tell you if there is a bulletin or any way to meet up with 'old girls' (and old boys) from your time there. You may even want to organise a reunion yourself. Most universities' publicity departments are now developing alumni associations, so if you want to get in touch with people you studied with, place an advertisement or article in the newsletter. Include a photo (decent, sharply defined). This is a sure-fire way of getting published because journals are always looking for more images to brighten up the text.

Family history sources

Depending on how much you want to make this the story of you in your family context, you may like to research some family history. This is not obligatory but it is deeply enjoyable and many people become addicted to it. It may pay you to make an agreement with yourself, such as 'I'll only spend 20 days on family history research,' or 'I'll write a maximum of 20 pages in total about my family's past.'

There are so many good books on how to research family history that I am going to mention only a few points here.[13]

1. One of the best ways to begin is to look at the journal *Family History*. The advertisements alone are invaluable because they indicate the kind

of help available to you and the sort of things other family historians do. It is often found in local history libraries.

2. Find out if anyone in your extended family has already created a family tree you can use. In the past, people drew family trees in the family Bible. There may be someone in your family – almost always a woman – who is a repository of family lore. Even a birthday book can be useful.

Contact your local family history society through Mrs P. Saul at the Federation of Family History Societies, c/o Benson Room, Birmingham and Midland Institute, Margaret Street, Birmingham B3 3BS (no telephone). The Federation also publishes pamphlets, including *Beginning Your Family Tree*. Send an SAE when you write.

3. Investigate the family surname through the relevant 'one-name' society (there are hundreds of these).

4. Get everyone you can to talk you through the family photo albums. Track down home movies, which can be a vital source of information. You may want to convert the film to video or even use clips to illustrate your lifestory.

Libraries
Every borough has a local history library, staffed by librarians well used to family history researchers and adept at explaining whatever you need to know in an accessible and friendly way. Sometimes they supply a free users' guide to help you find your way round the system. They usually have parish records on microfilm, old newspapers, books and pamphlets, maps, and sometimes scrapbooks and other archive material. Some even have family rooms so that you can collaborate with another family member during the research process without disturbing the other library users.

Britain's Public Record Offices (PRO)
The records of many aspects of British and colonial life are kept at the Public Record Offices in Chancery Lane, London WC2A 1LR and at Ruskin Avenue, Kew, Surrey TW9 4DU. The telephone number for both is 0181 876 3444. They issue a number of free leaflets on how to research various aspects of family history – for example, if you want to trace a relative who worked in a public service such as the armed forces or as a nurse. Read leaflet no. 14, *Family History in England and Wales: Guidance for Beginners*, or leaflet no. 39, *Records of Births, Marriages and Deaths*. It is quite a challenge to learn your way

around the PRO so prepare as much as you can in advance. An introductory video will help you when you arrive. The bookshop is also worth visiting for its publications on how to use PRO sources such as *Tracing Your West Indian Ancestors* or *Maps for Family History*. If you can't go yourself there are professional researchers who can be hired for about £120 a day. The PRO has a list of them.

For Scottish history, try the Scottish Record Office, HM General Register House, Edinburgh EH1 3YY (tel: 0131 556 6585). For explorations of Welsh family history, try the National Library of Wales, Aberystwyth, Dyfed SY23 3BU (tel: 01970 623816). The Northern Ireland Public Record Office is at 66 Balmoral Avenue, Belfast BT1 6DU (tel: 01232 235211).

International Genealogical Index (IGI)

The main resource for researching your family way back is the IGI, which is available on CD-rom. The IGI will show you baptisms, marriages and deaths of people whose name you know arranged in chronological order nationally. So, for example, if the earliest known woman in your family is Sarah Welsch, and she was born around 1650, the index will offer you a range of Sarah Welsches, Sara Welshes and S Walshes from all over the country. And you can skim the years before and after 1650 as you choose, in case the birth date is drastically wrong.

The information is easy to use, and is available at some major public libraries. In London, the printed books department at the Guildhall Library in the City is the main place to use the IGI. It's at Aldermanbury, London EC2P 2EJ (tel: 0171 332 1868/1870). The Guildhall Library is a haven for family historians with its *Who's Who*, its gazetteers and chronologies and thousands of other reference books. It also carries the periodicals of the main national and local historical societies.

Genealogy

Genealogy is the more formal branch of family history. The Society of Genealogists has a library you can use for a fee and publishes a quarterly journal, *The Genealogist Magazine.* Inquire at 14 Charterhouse Buildings, Goswell Road, London EC1M 7BA (tel: 0171 251 8799).

The Institute of Heraldic and Genealogical Studies runs courses on researching family history. The five-day residential beginners' course costs £190, but there are some bursaries for those who can't afford that much. The Institute also organises weekend courses and a correspondence course and has a calendar listing the events and courses nationwide of interest to family historians. The Institute of Heraldic and Genealogical Studies is at 79–82 Northgate, Canterbury, Kent CT1 1BA (tel: 01227 768664; fax: 01227 765617).

Books

If you are writing about a particular British location, there are some books with a good overview that can help you explore a larger context. They also have thorough bibliographies to help you to intensify your research. I've chosen illustrated books as much as possible, as photographs can stimulate memories. The best book to start with is Deirdre Beddoe's *Discovering Women's History*. It is full of useful addresses and practical ideas for starting off.[14]

Books about different places

J. Aaron, Teresa Rees, Sandra Bells and Moira Vincintelli (eds), *Our Sisters' Land: The Changing Identities of Women in Wales*, University of Wales Press, Cardiff, 1994.

Esther Breitenbach and Eleanor Gordon (eds), *Out of Bounds: Women in Scottish Society 1800–1945*, Edinburgh University Press, 1992.

Rosalind K. Marshall, *Virgins and Viragos: A History of Women in Scotland 1090–1980*, Collins, London, 1983.

Roger Swyer, *We Are but Women: Women in Ireland's History*, Routledge, London, 1993.

Books about different times

Duncan Crow, *The Victorian Woman*, Allen and Unwin, London, 1971.

Eric J. Evans and Jeffrey Richards, *A Social History of Britain in Postcards 1870–1930*, Longman, Harlow, 1980.

Colin Ford and Brian Harris, *A Hundred Years Ago: Britain in the 1880s in Words and Postcards*, Allen Lane, London, 1983.

Memory Lane: A Photographic Album of Daily Life in Britain 1930–1953, introduced by James Cameron, Dent, London, 1980.

Sybil Oldfield (ed.), *This Working-Day World: Women's Lives and Culture(s) in Britain, 1914–45*, Taylor and Francis, London, 1994.

Paul Thompson, *The Edwardians: The Remaking of British Society*, Routledge, London, 1990.

Those Were the Days 1919–39: A Photographic Album of Daily Life in Britain, introduced by Francis Donaldson, Dent, London, 1983.

If you want to write about the effect of the two world wars try:
Gail Braybon and Penny Summerfield (eds), *Out of the Cage: Women's Experiences in Two World Wars*, Pandora, London, 1987.
Norman Longmate, *How We Lived Then: A History of Everyday Life during the Second World War*, Hutchinson, London, 1971.

How to get these books

Many of these are popular books which can be found on the general history shelves of a public library. Remember that every borough has a local history library, usually based at the central library. The local history society may be worth joining for its newsletter and contacts. The community librarian or local history librarian will be able to give you the society's address. A useful source for books on women's history is the Feminist Library, 5a Westminster Bridge Road, London SE1 7XW (tel: 0171 928 7789). Phone first as it has very limited opening hours. Or try the Glasgow Women's Library, 109 Trongate, Glasgow G1 5HD (tel: 0141 552 8345).

Silver Moon, Europe's largest feminist bookstore, stocks women's history, autobiography and biography. Silver Moon has a mail order service: 68 Charing Cross Road, London WC2H 0BB (tel: 0171 836 7906). New Beacon Books, 76 Stroud Green Road, London N4 3EN (tel: 0171 272 4889) has books on Black British, African, Afro-European, Afro-American culture and history and women's lives (mail order and free catalogue). Green Ink is an Irish bookshop which has women's and history sections: 8 Archway Mall, London N19 5RG (tel and fax: 0171 263 4748). It has a mail order and catalogue service. In Edinburgh, a women's bookshop, Word Power, offers mail order and specialist subject lists: 43 West Nicholson Street, Edinburgh EH8 9DB (tel: 0131 662 9112).

Most major universities have local studies departments with an archive or library you can use for reference. They may also hold newspapers on CD-rom and indexes of recent magazine and periodical articles which you can look up using key words, for example 'lesbian history' or 'Dublin, women nineteenth century'. If the university teaches women's studies, the library should be very useful.

The best way to take advantage of university resources (and remember, you pay the taxes that keep them going, so you have rights) is to contact the library in the holidays and ask if you can go in and use it for reference. Only rarely will books be loaned to non-students. During the summer break is the best time because then most of the books will be back from loan. Write rather than phone, initially, because in big institutions it can take some time to contact the right person.

Enjoy your research and remember not to overdo it. Too much information can be daunting. Getting the right sort and using it in the right quantity will ensure that your lifestory and the lifestorying process are jam-packed with stimulating ideas.

Section III

Shaping and finishing

Pulling it into shape

This section of the book assumes that you have now written a fair amount of autobiographical fragments, perhaps stimulated by the exercises in Section II or you may have material you have been writing for a long time anyway. The writing stage may have taken months or years. It will almost inevitably involve some useful chaos which has to be explored.

A stage will come when you feel the need to put your fragments in some kind of order. Presenting your life in a way that makes sense is actually most people's key reason for writing a lifestory: you want to see what you add up to, what shape your life makes, what meaning and design and style it has.[1] This is the stage where you are trying to survey your whole story/life.

Shaping is the part of autobiography that some people long to do and others dread. You accumulate so much stuff as you go along – by now you may have a whole dossier on almost every event in your life – that you may fear it will never be put into order. Like a room full of junk, it now has to be tidied up.

There are two pieces of good news. The first is that you will find much of the material is already in shape in your mind. It may be a rough shape but it is distinct. That's partly because the brain has to impose some sort of order when so much information needs storing. You will certainly already have sections and sub-sections even if they only follow the chapter headings in Section II of this book, such as place, people, time, your body, your ideas. You may have something more subtle and personal than that: your own story emerging. Indeed, the whole process so far has been about letting various stories emerge, affect each other and become one.

The second piece of good news is that you can do the tidying up or structuring in a very organic way. *Your* shaping does not have to conform to anyone else's standards of tidiness. It does not have be a smooth narrative in which every chapter is the same length and written in the same style. That may kill *your* creativity – or not. The key thing for now is to let it be uneven and disunified; you may want it to stay that way for good.

Next, you should disabuse yourself of any mystique you feel surrounds the word 'book'. For the purposes of these next stages 'book' simply means a coherent collection of pages, just a sheaf of papers, some of which will be grouped together. No mystique. No notions of 'properness'. Your job for now is not to think about publication, or grammar, or how other people will react, but simply to consider the arrangement. Like a sculptor alone in her studio contemplating starting to work on a big piece of rock, you need to be free and alone with your material, in a lump, in order to understand how you'll work on it. Now is the time for you metaphorically to circle it, sniff it, measure its circumference, taste it on your tongue, see how it reacts to chisels and cotton buds, hammers and fine sandpaper, heavy rasps and types of varnish.

Don't feel you have to go through this process for anyone other than yourself – certainly not at this stage. This stage is for you.

ONE WAY TO START SHAPING

I am assuming that you are at the stage of having a lot of papers – perhaps 150 or 200 sheets, typed or untyped – and some pictures and objects. I'm assuming some of it is in order, either in ring-binders or box-files. You may have got further than this, or not quite as far. That's no problem.

There are many ways to start shaping a lifestory and you may gradually evolve your own plan but this is the best way that I know. It involves a kind of day off in which you are free to see fully the scale of the future book. Read Chapter 16 a few days before you start, so that you have some idea of the different structures available to you.

Step one
Set aside a period up to seven hours long. Allow plenty of time. No phone. Prepare sandwiches or even a cold feast – but make sure you will not be diverted by cooking or any other of your usual jobs.

Arrange to have a clear floor in a very large room. Perhaps you can borrow the flat of a friend who is away, or it may be worth staying in a (big) hotel room or hiring a community hall for a day for the purpose (the latter can cost as little as £3). Do make it very clear that you don't want to be interrupted. I find I need an absolutely safe space for this stage of the process. Take all your writings there (forgotten bits can turn out to be irritatingly important). If you really can't bear to take all that material away from home then at least unplug the phone and insist on complete seclusion.

Step two

Arrange the papers in front of you. Make sure they're loose enough to be accessible but not spread so wide as to be demoralising.

Take up the ones that appeal to you and glance through them (this is not a stage for deep reading – just skim).

Place them on the floor with a label on them – a 'Post-it' works fine – indicating the topic in one word, such as 'sex', 'my birth', 'parents', '1985' and so on.

As you pick up more, see if they have a theme in common with other bits you've already looked at. If so put them together. Go on doing this, creating clusters. Do it reflectively, for this is an important process and may fix your story in a very particular shape which is hard to break later. Do it slowly and well.

If you have any clusters already, from your ring-binder or box-files, put each of them on the floor in front of you with labels for each category. Or, if it feels right, disrupt the categories and strew the papers wide, then gather them together in a new way (for example, if they were chronological before now make them thematic).

After a while, you'll have a number of unwieldy bundles of paper. You may like to place the growing clusters on (rather than, at this stage, put them into) folders made of a piece of card or paper; or clip them together with a very large bulldog clip (they cost about 50p); or have a box for each of them. Greengrocers' trays for tomatoes work very well for this purpose; they're good and roomy and the sides aren't too high.

The main problems are usually that you can't decide where to put something (try keeping a 'don't know yet' box) or that you think things should go in several places (in that case, put a photocopy in each place). You may want to write a brief diary of this process; and

such a record can be very useful later, if you find you forget why you
initially made a particular decision.

Step three
I'd recommend a maximum of seven hours. Put each cluster away in
its separate labelled folder, file or box. Don't worry if it is not completed
to your liking. It is temporary, a start. Make notes about anything you
need to remember about each cluster. Then put them all away ready
for working on next time.

Expect to be tired. Congratulations. You have completed a major
piece of work. Allow yourself to do this initial sorting process several
times if necessary.

FIRMING IT UP

The next stage can also be done in your big room or anywhere else
you think suitable. This is the time to start thinking about the clusters
as chapters, and their relationship to each other.

Connect clusters

When you have collected bits into some clusters that seem to make
sense, start to think about the way each cluster might connect with
another. Does the one follow the other? Do they overlap? Are they about
a similar theme? Is there a link you can't quite formulate?

Again it is best to do this on a big floor so that you can mess around
in plenty of space. Place clusters together with other clusters that
seem related to them. You may want to make several clusters connect,
and do a lot of rearranging. This is a time for experimenting. You may
want to chalk arrows on the floor to connect several piles.

Sequence

Now, if these clusters are chapters, what is their sequence? Is there
an opening cluster/chapter? Is there a closing one? Try and let the
sequence occur to you through reflection rather than organising it.
This is a bottom-up rather than a top-down process.

Links

If there are sections you haven't yet tackled, you can use lists and jottings to remind you of what is still to come. For example, Helen found:

> I'd written quite a lot of fragments – between half a page and seven pages long. Most of it by hand. And I imagined that I had covered most areas of my life by now – because I'd thought about them so much while I was writing the rest. But actually they were only implicit, only in my head.
>
> So I took some sheets of turquoise A4 paper, which I treated as what I called 'sign sheets'. I just wrote on each of them two or three lines about what I would write about later. I thought by having another colour I could just go towards the pile – yeah, that's what I call my lifestory at the moment, the pile, the heap – whenever I had a free moment and fish out a blue sheet and write a bit on that topic. It worked – and I didn't have the overwhelming number of blue sheets that I'd anticipated – about 35 in the end.

Numbers

It may help you at this stage to think about numbers. There's no 'correct' number of chapters in a book. To start with, choose a number – it could be ten or 40 – that feels right. Experiment. (Remember, they don't have to be the same length.)

Write each chapter number on a separate sheet of paper – a simple exercise to encourage you to see the structure emerging.

At this stage additional ideas may emerge that you don't want to number in yet. They may be two or three pages long and may grow into full chapters, or become part of a chapter that does not yet exist.

Don't think that your lifestory has to have, say, 30 pages for every decade you've lived or 20 pages to each cluster/chapter. Different periods and topics will a have differing significance for you. You are certain to write more about your formative years and your adventurous years than about some of your more run-of-the-mill years. The older you are, the more likely you are to write about your youth because access to your long-term memory will be improving.

OTHER PARTS OF THE BOOK

Now that your collection of writings is taking on the form of a book, you will be thinking of other parts such as the title, a preface, an introduction and appendices. These things can be worked on as and when appropriate. The ideas below are to suggest ways to start thinking about them.

Title

You may not know your title yet, or it may have always been in your mind. Having a title – which is another label – can help you in this 'making sense of me' process, so jot down possible titles as they occur to you. Pat Arrowsmith's title, *I Should Have Been a Hornby Train*, reflects how much she is aware that her life was shaped by being a disappointment to her brother (who wanted a train not a sister). Marie Christine Ridgeway's autobiography is called *No Place for a Woman*, thus stating the basic premise of her story: pioneering in the Highlands was unusual for a woman.

If no title occurs to you, don't worry. Titles are wonderful creatures: they turn up on your doorstep, in dreams, in overheard conversations, they leap out of other people's books, they are given to you by casual friends, they are found lying within your own text, shining and winking. One will come eventually. Working titles such as *My Story* or *Cathy's Tale* are fine too but a name may help consolidate the book idea. This is still a private stage in the process so there is no need to worry about a title being 'attractive' to publishers.

Preface

Not all books have a preface, those first few pages after the contents list. It's a kind of pre-introduction and is not essential. Some lifestories contain an introduction or a preface, or both, or neither.

A preface is usually a personal account of the book as process and product. Some contain acknowledgements of the people who have helped you: friends, relatives, librarians and so on. If the book is for publication, this can also be where you thank publishers who have given you permission to use photographs or extracts from other books. If you have a lot of acknowledgements create a separate 'chapter' for them under that heading.

I've noticed that when I am writing something big, I spend a few weeks or months scribbling odd bits and then I start to type a preface and acknowledgements. It's a sign to myself that says: 'This is going to be a proper book. It is more than just a lot of fragments that will be gathered into a file. It's something substantial with its own identity and reason for existing. It is a valid thing to be respected.' And from having drafted that preface I can then call the thing 'a book' and feel it will eventually have a life of its own.

Foreword

This is a preface written by someone else, commending your book. You do not need to do anything about it at this stage but you may like to bear it in mind.

Introduction

Sometimes a preface contains what other people put in an introduction. It is just a different label. It can be an extended version of the way you would answer a friend's question: 'What are you writing your lifestory for?'

You may want to paint the background picture of the times and places you are writing about for readers unfamiliar with them and who might need to be ushered into the book a little. It is your welcome to others, written very much in an explanatory mode and therefore with great consciousness of your readers.

Sometimes an introduction can be a riposte. For example, former domestic servant Margaret Powell said in her second autobiography, *Climbing the Stairs*, that people had written to her complaining that they had never treated their servants as badly as she described being treated in *Upstairs, Downstairs*. In her introduction she replied: 'Yes, I agree. Perhaps they didn't. But they still looked on their servants as possessions.'[2]

Appendix

An appendix is where you put additional material that supplements your main text. It is by no means a standard part of an autobiography, though some contain several appendices.

For example, you might want to use your marriage certificate as an appendix to prove that the momentous event had happened; or an appendix could contain suggestions for useful background reading; or might contain a brief chronological summary of your life events – especially useful if your autobiography is non-chronological.

An appendix can be useful during the writing process as a repository for material that you think you might not use but don't yet want to discard. It allows you to remain undecided for as long as you need.

I've found that a number of women new to lifewriting are not sure they will be believed and want to create lengthy appendices from other sources to back up what they themselves have written in the main text. For example, Jane said:

> I love my appendices, they reassured me that I was right to portray my ex-husband as abusive. I could use quotes from what the judge said at the hearing. And I included whole paragraphs that I'd valued from feminist writers on wife-battering who had confirmed that what I experienced conformed to certain well-known patterns – it wasn't my imagination. It was an extra way of saying, 'Look I was right.' 'Look, it wasn't my imagination.' 'Look, I'm not abnormal.'

It seems reasonable to me that you should write your lifestory exactly as you choose, with as many appendices as you like. Later they can be excised, but material laid aside – to hand and yet separate – often has a very important function during the writing process.

Illustrations

As you are thinking in such a broad way at this stage, take a little time to consider whether or not you going to use pictures in your book. If so, how many and what sort?

Most published autobiographies have up to 20 photographs, captioned by the author. Usually they include photos of parents and grandparents, and the author at various ages. In later life the author is shown with friends, husbands, lovers, famous people, children. Inevitably the photographic conventions of the time dictate the background. You can be as unconventional as you like in your choice. Look at published lifestories to get some ideas.

OTHER CONSIDERATIONS AT THIS STAGE

Feelings

Some people experience a crisis of confidence when they look at the book as a whole. These feelings can include:

- Why on earth should I waste any more time on this? It's already taken up months/years.
- I hate my life. I want to chuck all evidence of it away.
- I can't say/publish any of this – it's all rubbish/too private.
- There isn't enough material.
- There's too much material.
- It's nothing like other people's autobiographies (so it must be wrong).
- I can't see how it'll ever be other than a rag-bag of bits.
- Who'd want to read any of this?

The answer to these questions lie with you, but they are usually about temporary loss of heart. It passes. Whatever happens, **don't throw away all your good work**. You will almost certainly regret it and others may regret it too.

Stop. Wait. Put the pages away for now or give them to someone you trust to keep them safe.

Your work is never as imperfect/awful/daunting as you think. Never. In fact, it may even be wonderful. Or it may be not good enough yet; that can be remedied. It simply can't be bad enough to reject entirely. You are a human being who has lived and who has passion (why else would you be struggling to tell your story?), therefore what you have written will be interesting to someone else. Leave it for a week or two, a month, even longer. You will see its value when you've gained a fresh perspective on it.

Facing the size and nature of it

This may be the stage when you face for the first time the overall scale and nature of your project. Let it be any size you want. Let it be messy if you want. Let it be like nothing else. **It does not have to be a proper book**.

A slim volume

While most published autobiographies are around 250 pages in length, with 250 words to a page, you do not have to conform unless you want to be published. Indeed, slim accounts can be easier for both writers and readers to handle. If you are worried that it may be too sparse, think how elegant and eloquent short poems can be.

You may find that you are interested in writing about only one theme. You're not alone. Many women have written slim books about one aspect of their lives, and still readers have loved the work. Jane Lazarre (*The Mother Knot*) and Louise Erdrich (*The Blue Jay's Dance*) wrote solely about being a mother.[3] Others have chosen to write about one time in their lives, for example Lucy Irvine's story *Castaway*, which she wrote about being on a desert island (later made into a film). In *Ordeal*, Linda Lovelace wrote largely about the time in her life when she was recruited to perform oral sex for the porn movie *Deep Throat*.[4]

A big book

Sometimes there is so much to say, even after pruning, that you find you are writing a three-volume lifestory. It may be that this is a temporary decision, made in despair at the amount of material there is, or it may be appropriate. You might be someone who always has a lot to say. That's your style. If so, make your decision but treat it as temporary. Make the rough groupings for each volume.

Tina said:

I was proud and appalled – so much stuff. And I thought well, yes, there would be, the way I go for life, and the way I always write a lot. OK. So be it! I was helped by remembering that Simone de Beauvoir had written a four-volume autobiography. And I decided that, like her, I would make them chronological volumes, at least for now: the dutiful daughter, the woman in her prime, the woman who had done and said a lot – but by no means all. It helped enormously to scoop each 'volume' into a plastic bag and label them. Volume this, volume that. I felt like I had some control, some order really. It relieved the pressure.

Publishable?

You may now find that for some reason your lifestory can't be published. That might be because it's too long, too short, too private, not the project you want to spend time on right now. This can be a hard decision. Talk to other people about it in case you're labouring under a misapprehension. Remember two things:

1. All first drafts can be improved. Always. Don't be too quick to judge. Editors exist to shorten texts, to improve style. Different types of publishers have different criteria for length and style. Help is available. Make a fully informed decision on your book's merits – that necessarily means a slower one – when most of the work is done. Hang on for now.

2. Getting published is only one of many things that could happen to this summary of your life. The point may have been just to write this much, this way. You may have done precisely what you needed to do. It just happens that it doesn't conform to current publishers' needs in the current economic climate. See Chapters 20 and 21 on the many ways to make your lifestory public.

Make this evaluation in an informed way. You have probably put in so much work and have such high hopes that any decision at this stage should be made very carefully, in company, and only after taking much advice.

Jointly written?

When you can see your material more clearly you may decide that you want to write with someone else – that it is a joint autobiography. Your partner, or even partners, in this might be your mother or your lover or your children. Many black women have recently preferred a more collective way of writing to express common concerns. Mother and daughter together wrote *Getting Home Alive* (Morales and Morales) and black women migrants describe the impact of arriving in Britain in *Charting the Journey*.[5]

Chapters can be written separately and then interspersed, or you may decide to write half the book each. Collaboration is a tricky business. It can be enjoyable because of the commonalities discovered, but painful because of different expectations, different patterns of work and different power levels in the relationship.

Becky, for example, found:

I tried writing it with Mum – and it hurt. We were both very keen on the idea at first and keen on being frank – we thought it would be great for our relationship. In fact it became quite a miserable process. I let my internal mum – as the person who'd had such power, as the one who raised me – dictate the structuring values. My real mum felt inferior to me because she hadn't had as much formal education. Neither of us knew what was going on over relative power at that point. It got worse because I fell behind the deadlines we had agreed and she got uncomfortable at being ahead. I was appalled at her unreflective approach and lost heart. What was the point in writing a lifestory if you were only going to say anodyne and factual things? We had to drop the project as a joint one, although we have carried on separately.

On the other hand, lovers Sue and Jenny enjoyed creating an autobiography together:

The part that was especially enjoyable was when we looked at set dates and wrote about how different our separate lives had been at those times. Writing an account of the relationship now was harder – but instructive. We wrote it as a short private document – 30 pages – and neatly copied out the other's account: best handwriting. We decorated both copies and had them bound by the binder who'd done Sue's college project. It wouldn't have done at all for publication but it was a good sharing, a good pleasurable activity – like cooking together is when we are getting on well.

I haven't talked about the contents of individual chapters here. This is because knowledge of how to handle them will arise from the understanding gained from this and the following chapter. Chapter 17, on polishing, will help too. For the moment, leave detailed work on the chapters aside.

Ways to arrange the order

This chapter offers you a variety of ways to arrange or structure your autobiography. Try reading this chapter right through once before you adopt a particular form, though the work you have already done in shaping the book will have given you some ideas. When reading this chapter, make notes and lists in general. Detailed re-reading and sorting could be distracting to your planning at this stage.

The main choice is between chronological and non-chronological forms but there are other types of structure too: thematic, encyclopaedic or a collection of unlinked essays.

CHRONOLOGICAL ORDER

The advantages of chronological order are:

- it's easy
- it's orderly
- it's familiar – normal
- it leaves you free to try a more creative order later

The disadvantages are:

- it's too easy – you may find you could think/write a much more exciting and challenging lifestory
- you may find it harder to express your multiplicity of selves and feel obliged to keep creating straightforward, plausible narratives

Some ways to deal with those disadvantages include:

- using footnotes/fragments of others' voices or other types of your writing (letters or diary) to make counter-points.
- writing it freely and only at the very end arranging it in chronological order
- writing several versions of an event, each in a different voice, within each chapter

Your birth

If your lifestory is going to be arranged in chronological order you'll probably begin with your birth or your parents and grandparents, as a way to show what context you were born into. Your *physical* birth isn't necessarily the starting point, as US writer Mary McCarthy shows when she begins the very first page of her account of her formative years with: 'I was born as a mind in 1925, my bodily birth having taken place in 1912.'[1] (Using such a device, you may like to see every chapter as being about birth, in the sense of the emergence of different facets of your life.)

Hilda Bernstein's autobiography, *The World That Was Ours*, is chronological but focuses on just three key years in South Africa, 1963–6.[2] She groups her narrative in four sections:

Prologue: 11 July 1963 (the day her husband was arrested) (7 pages)
Normal lives (9 chapters, 71 pages);
90 days (detention) (3 chapters, 38 pages);
Confrontation (7 chapters, 82 pages)
Escape (5 chapters, 57 pages)

From birth onwards

If your first chapter is about your birth, you may then want to make Chapter 2 about the family, Chapter 3 about your schooling, Chapter 4 about what happened once you left school and so on. If you are really worried about structure then try this straightforward idea for now: agree to yourself that each chapter will cover a fixed five-year period. In such a chronological lifestory you may conclude with the you who just completed her lifestory. While this very organised sequence sounds a bit limited you may find it suits you well, or it may help you to go on to devise a more complicated structure that suits you better.

Flashbacks and flashforwards

You may want to start off with a flashback or flashforward. An example of a flashback might be as far as the first woman, Eve, or about a key woman in your early family history. A flashforward might involve you beginning with the you who is writing now, or a statement by an old you on your deathbed, reflecting on the life. Or it could involve some future descendant of yours – or an imagined reincarnation of you – commenting on the life you have lived.

Playing with the time

Another challenging option, at least as an experiment, is to arrange the events in your life in reverse chronological order. Or to have several sections and arrange each one in chronological order. For example, when political economist and writer Harriet Martineau (1802–76) wrote her autobiography, it had four sections. Each one was taken chronologically: unhappy childhood, early adulthood, 20 years as a successful author, and famous people she had known.[3]

The chronological divisions may reflect events in your personal life or external events. For example, Tina, who was born in the year the first atomic bomb was built, took each major event concerning nuclear weapons as a chapter heading, contrasting the peace and naivety of an individual life with the international political determination to destroy.

NON-CHRONOLOGICAL ORDER

It can be much more liberating to write about ideas. Each chapter could have a theme or a set of motifs, topics and sub-topics. Each could be an essay linked by you as the writer.

Themes

A theme could be a strong human force such as envy or desire, or it could be an intellectual idea. Joyce Johnson called her slim and poignant autobiography *Minor Characters*, and the front cover picture shows her lurking behind beat writer Jack Kerouac, who was her lover.[4] The title refers to her theme – how much women were minor characters in the world of the beat generation in the late 1950s. A number of other contemporary writers have chosen a thematic approach, such as Amryl Johnson, whose *Sequins on a Ragged Hem* studies returning home, and Audre Lorde, whose *The Cancer Journals* explores her illness.[5]

A set of motifs

A set of motifs usually takes one central object and then refers to branches or elements of it. So, for example, if the motif is music you could take the ten or 20 key songs in your life and make each one a chapter. Margaret said:

> One of my main ones was 'We Are Family' by Sister Sledge which I danced to at lesbian gigs when I first came out. Singing along to it – 'We are family. I've got all my sisters and me' gave me a sense of belonging.

Such a song would make a good focus for a chapter on coming out.

Cards

You might choose a deck of cards for your overall structure. Each different chapter heading could use a specific card. Cathy said:

> I've sometimes seen myself over my life sadly as the King of Spades. Endlessly working and taking responsibility and leading. Spade worker. I wanted to write about that aspect of my character as well as the lost two or three of Hearts – the playful loving child in me that I try to keep in touch with. The Joker was a good chapter to write – I enjoyed the freedom of that so much that I had six Joker chapters in the end.

Knots

You could present your lifestory as an account of the different knots you've untied and tied. Like *The Shipping Forecast*, a novel by E. Annie Proulx, you could start every chapter with a particular knot, mentioning its purpose and name.

Windows

You might try thinking about metaphorical windows as a motif: 'These are the different windows I've looked through in my life.' A window allows you to look out and in. It frames a scene, thereby giving it new significance; it excludes wider horizons, thereby intensifying what you do see. For example, Huda Shaarawi wrote in her autobiography that after her wedding day in Egypt: 'The following morning I looked out of the window to cheer myself up with the sight of the large tents with their fine carpets ... that had enchanted me the previous evening' but the wedding tents had gone, as had the trees she had climbed throughout her childhood. The trees had been cut down to make space for the tents. 'I cried for my trees, I cried for my childhood ... and I saw in this barren garden a picture of the life I would live, bereft of all that was comparable and pleasing to me.'[6]

Exercise: Using windows as chapter motifs

Think of some windows you have looked out of, or even into. Write them down quickly, say in two minutes. Then reflect. Is there is an organising idea or theme (for example, looking with relish into someone's calm beautiful home, the landscapes you have loved to look out on to)? Write down six essential things about each scene and try to think about their metaphorical significance as you write. Bear in mind any changes that have happened to that scene and your response to it (like the childhood trees cut down for the wedding).

When it's done, consider whether this principle would work for your whole book. Does it allow you enough freedom, inspiration, poignancy, clarity? Would doorways be a better metaphor?

Other motifs might include:

- flowers that stand for aspects of you or are symbolic of a time in your life

- masks you have metaphorically worn
- milestones/watersheds/crossroads
- sayings or proverbs you have lived by
- cocoons or gaols escaped from
- significant steps
- myths/fables
- landscapes/places you have lived in or loved from a distance
- commandments
- utensils you have used for different activities/jobs at different times
- halfway houses or waiting rooms
- recipes
- sums of money
- archetypes of yourself
- animals
- relationships

Time capsule

Try envisaging your book as a time capsule – the sort that are ceremonially placed beneath the foundations of a new public building. Sealed against damage, time capsules contain objects that sum up the period or the moment. Yours might include a newspaper, a fashionable garment or object, a photo of the blossom on the plum orchard that used to stand where the new building now grows. What would be the objects representing your past that you would seal into a time capsule?

Exercise: Creating a time capsule

Think of ten key objects that sum up ten moments of your life. They don't have to be objects that still exist. Take a fresh piece of paper and write about just one of those objects and what it meant to you. Consider writing the book using each of those key moments/objects (plus some others) as chapter topics.

The point of the exercise is to offer you a way to think visually and historically. Material objects can be useful reminders: they bring us down to earth.

Advent calendar

You may choose to see your lifestory as an advent calendar with its sequence of doors, and notice how crucial it is to open the right door to an element of your life at the right time; or to have the nerve to open the wrong door and deal with what ensues. An advent calendar can be a way of elucidating for yourself what is important, how it can be hidden in covered doorways and how it is affected by the 'neighbours'.

The point of the advent calendar idea is that you see your life as a whole but composed of 20 or so very distinct parts or scenes. It can be very revealing.

Dialectic

Another way to structure your lifestory is to use the idea of dialectic, of two contradictory forces that come together in a synthesis. For example, if you were writing solely about becoming a mother you might show the polarisation of natural and medical models of childbirth. You could, in three different chapters, show:

- what you wanted to happen: an organic, holistic and physically good thing
- what actually happened: imposed medical intervention because of a crisis
- the synthesis: talking about feelings of loss and guilt, as well as praise for how good the hospital was

A subtly used dialectical approach can create a good internal structure for each chapter, as well as for the whole book.

Glossary/encyclopaedia of you

Michèle Roberts wrote a fascinating long short story/autobiographical piece on the basis of a glossary. She pointed out that glossary means 'a list with explanations of abstruse, antiquated, dialectal, or technical terms: a partial dictionary. To gloss: to explain away; to read a different sense into; to veil in specious language; to render bright and glossy.'[7] Her list of terms included 'Absence, Artichauts, Assomption, Beurre, Bonnetière, Brigitte, C-R [cancer], Cadichon, Calvados, Camembert, Caudebec, Caulle, Caux.'

This is a great exercise and one which can go and on. It's an oblique and intriguing way of telling your story. I'd done it myself years before I read her work, and called it 'A Dictionary of Me'. I found that I could spend a lot of time off the point. One word reminded me of another. I could find 20 words for each letter and write a page on my associations with each word. I was so excited a creator that I lost all track of what was relevant and what was feasible to do in one lifetime. To avoid the pitfall of writing too much, decide to choose between three and ten words for each alphabet letter; or even restrict yourself to the letters of your name.

This is both a good warm-up exercise any time you're stuck for a new tack, and a good structure for a book, providing you select your key words carefully.

You in your different roles

You may want to organise your story so that each chapter is about you acting in a different role, perhaps with the heading written in the third person. For example, Adrienne Rich's famous poem 'Snapshots of Daughter-in-law' allows a multiplicity of self-representations. You may decide that in each chapter 'you' will be someone different: the daughter-in-law, the mother, the daughter, the friend, the self, the lesbian, the disabled person, the ex-lover, the guardian. You do not have to use the third person. Instead, examine states of mind rather than roles: my exploring self, my scared self, my vain self, my uppity self, my singing self, my lonely self, my politicking self, my over-working self, my dreaming self, my integrated self, etc.

Within such a structure, which is limiting, you might want to add some linking or discrepant paragraphs and sentences. Keep plenty of spare paper and Post-its by you at this stage; it could generate a lot of ideas. You might need an additional folder labelled 'uncertain' or 'don't know', because inevitably these categories do not adequately include all of you.

Essays on a theme/ structure round pictures

It may be that you need to write a lifestory that is much more disconnected than any of these ideas. You could write a collection of essays on very different topics. In *Family Secrets*, Annette Kuhn's autobiographical essays focus on photographs. The pictures include herself with her dad, in home-made frocks including in a prize-winning fancy dress outfit as 'cinema litter', as well as stills from a 1952 movie that meant a lot to her, *Mandy*. Throughout the book she looks at herself from the outside and the inside. It has no easy sequence of 'first I did this and then I did that'.[8]

A STORY IN SEVERAL PARTS

Because creating an autobiography is such a big job, you may want to break the book down into several parts. You might call these parts 'sections' or 'volumes' or whatever works for you. Do this either for ease of organising material or because you feel your life falls into two or three parts.

When campaigner Annie Besant (1847–1933) wrote her autobiography in her mid-forties, she divided it into two parts. The first, introspective, part is about personal struggles including her childhood, divorce and turn to atheism. The second part deals with her public life as spokesperson on socialism and the occult and atheism; it is much more polemical and includes speeches.[9] I would be interested to know if she wrote both parts at the same time, slipping from one bit of paper to the next. If you try such a split you may want to feel free to be your 'other self' at any time. Using multiple windows on your computer is one good way of doing this.

Tina had a lot of trouble organising her autobiography:

I did it chronologically initially but it sewed up the book's shape too much too soon. It was like I'd wrapped up a baby in tight swaddling bands when it should be free to kick naked in the air. I felt bad and wrong and couldn't sleep. The chronological structure wasn't right.

I finally came up with a solution, through my dreams. The thing was falling into three categories that seemed right: people, places, discoveries. This was daunting. I thought Oh, God, no, I'm going to have to tip out all the carrier bags for each chapter and sort it all out in a new way. I couldn't bear the thought of seeing how much I'd done – and the chaos. But I did it.

Calling the three categories 'volumes' helped. It broke down the tasks. I was able to sort out a chronological order within each of the three volumes. The whole book started to work. And I know it wouldn't have worked if I'd persisted with that first structure with every piece of paper in exact date order. Being ad hoc and flexible was absolutely crucial, at that stage.

Feel free to let the whole book remain ramshackle and fluid for as long as you need it. Structuring a lifestory is a hard task. If no particular structure seems to present itself, then so be it. It may be a relief to opt for the most obvious one for now. Don't feel obliged to be more innovative than you want to be. The next chapter talks about polishing each individual chapter. You can do some of this even if you haven't finalised your structure.

Polishing and fine-tuning

At some stage you will want to polish your individual chapters, paragraphs, sentences and phrases. The time will come to fine-tune your story, which is like finding the precise location on the radio dial to produce the clearest signal.

STRUCTURING CHAPTERS

You will have to refine each bundle of papers into a chapter or essay. If the thought of it it strikes you with horror, then clearly you should wait a bit longer before tackling this. When you are ready, begin to work on the chapter that appeals to you most.

The overall shape

First of all, consider the chapter's overall shape. What will make a good beginning? Will it be witty in style or profound or what? Will it tell a complete story? Will it be chronological? What might make a good title?
  Betty says:

I really enjoyed getting down to polishing my first chapter. It felt as if I had nearly completed the book. At last. A new stage. A very self-respecting stage. This was *my* good work and I was going to give my utmost to it: all the tweaking and stroking and facing up to its strengths and weaknesses that it deserved. It was also a relief to be working on something small at last instead of something macro, huge. Constantly doing the overview can be tiring. Polishing my first chapter (it was actually Chapter 5) was a process of refining and deleting and adding. In doing so I discovered the ways I wanted to polish the other chapters – I found the precise timbre of the voice in which I wanted to speak.

Beginnings

Do you want your beginning to indicate to the reader what the chapter is about? You may like to summarise its contents and your underlying intention. Or you may like to begin with a shock or a trick and then go on in a different way. If you want to lay out the ingredients of a chapter, try asking yourself the following questions. When is it set? What actual events will you be describing? What internal feelings might you be showing?

You may want provisionally to head each chapter with a contents list in italics as some nineteenth-century novels do. For example, Leah wrote:

> *Chapter 19 in which our heroine realises she has got to leave her secure home and try something new. Going to the agency. The Maldives. Leaving. Trying Thailand. The uses of advisers. Making a decision to stick it out. Feeling able to go, at last. Getting on the plane to go home.*

Endings

If you are developing the chapter chronologically, the end will probably show you as someone who has moved on, literally or metaphorically, from the place where you started. You will be older, have different insights, have built on that self you initially described. The beginning and the end of a chapter are intimately related. You may want to write one before the other, or both at the same time.

As Leah's chapter was about a foreign experiment, the ending, she felt, was about booking the plane home, being at the airport and then on the plane, ready to face a new episode:

> It was by reading the journal I'd written in the departure lounge and summarising it for the ending that I realised how I could write

the beginning. The beginning was about restlessness and high hopes and enterprise and wanting to make a leap into the dark. The end was about valuing what I'd learned from that. Sadder but wiser. Browner but more wrinkled. A whopping great hole in my career path on the CV but a whole lot of new knowledge about my capacity for survival.

Middles

You will find it pays to read over the pieces you have written for your chosen chapter several times. If it helps, note the five to eight key things it has to include. (No more, or it will become unwieldy.) Then decide on the order in which to present them.

Leah used her chapter summary for this. The restlessness was the beginning point. Her five key points after that were:

1. The agency: what it offered and showed her about herself and her options.
2. The Maldives: arriving, being there, the job, friends, colleagues, obstacles, realisation that it would not work for her.
3. Making the transition: looking for another job, being more realistic about what she was capable of, going for the interview.
4. Being in Thailand: job, work, friends. Differences when compared with the Maldives experience. Discovering many obstacles. Choosing to stick at it for 18 months.
5. Making the decision to go back to the UK: knowing what she was and wasn't capable of.

Chapter titles

Feel free to play with chapter titles. If you have many more than five alternative titles, that is probably a warning that you need to get your focus more clear, or that you are trying to say too much for one chapter.

Many autobiographies give the chapters numbers only, not titles. Titles are not necessary – although at this stage they can help you keep your goals in mind.

Contents

Not every chapter needs to have the same form as the previous one or the next one. Nor does each chapter have to be written in a uniform way. For example, a chapter may well include any of the following:

- poems
- dialogue (invented or real)
- a bit where you write 'she' or 'you' rather than 'I', or even outright fiction
- fragments of other data such as letters or diaries or recorded dreams
- moments when you address the reader intimately (implicitly as 'thou')
- moments when you are distant
- disjointed fragments such as a quote from a book that you can't intellectually make sense of and yet somehow fits
- sections in another language – Gloria Anzaldúa's *Borderlands/La Frontera* is one example of this.[1]

Divide, sub-divide and sub-divide again. The more you make your work easy to handle, and the more you do it in small chunks, the more in control of it you will feel. Small is beautiful and handy here.

HOW TO SAY IT

The first section of this chapter dealt with ways to organise a chapter's internal structure. Once you have the structure right you can consider the various ways in which you express yourself.

The tone in which you address and attract your readers

Let your readers in, let them really know you. Address them/tell your story with as much generosity and frankness as you want. People love to be let in. Our ears always prick up when we hear someone speaking as if they trust us with their inmost thoughts. Readers of your autobiography assume you will be keeping the pact of telling it all.

Keep the distance that you need, but do reveal as much as you dare – and then some!

Entice your readers to read on – offer them treats and drama. Make this a work of art. Drawing readers in deeper is a very deliberate act, requiring a different approach, fairly (but not entirely) divorced from the self who is (maybe) trying to tell the utmost truth. When I write, I need my first draft to be the most honest and precise account I can make, with no thought of anyone else. Stage two is when I can relax a little and imagine that there is someone else out there who wants to be told a good story well. Now I begin to consider how I want to present it. It's at this stage that I might play a little and become an artist rather than a labourer toiling to put the slabs of my truth in place. Use a dictionary and *Roget's Thesaurus* to help you select precise words to convey your meaning.

Choose the right stage to start creating cliff-hangers, making mouths water and generally contriving responses from your readers. Do it only when you're ready. Think about your role as conjuror now. Do you want to tell it so that their eyes will light up in recognition, so that they'll cry with you, so that they'll write to you and thank you, so that they'll recognise something about themselves through you and change their understanding, maybe even their lives? This is when, if you want it, you can have the magical power of an artist to affect others through your writing.

Detecting your unconscious at work

Your unconscious will have been at work on a thousand places in this lifestory. Look for clichés in case they are clues to something you are fudging. If you have inadvertently used other people's formulations, it can sometimes signal that there is something you are finding it difficult to say. Work on finding your own way of saying it. It repays effort. Go through the text, casually, highlighting the stale words. On another occasion – say, when you can't write – sit down with the dictionary and thesaurus and replace the clichés with something better.

Look at what you've crossed out in the manuscript, or the notes to yourself, such as 'expand on this', that you haven't followed up in this revised version. Notice when you hit a crossroads in writing up your life: do you still want to take the same direction as you took in your first draft?

Relish your Freudian slips as gifts from your unconscious. For example, I often write 'back' instead of 'book', which I take to be a clue about how much I am building a book with my neck, shoulders, spine and muscles – that it's a more bodily expression of me than I think it is. Or I write 'right' instead of 'write', indicating how much writing for me is about putting things in order, creating justice. In lifestory writing, Freudian slips are particularly valuable. Note them on a separate piece of paper and see what clues you get to things that might still need saying. Is there an important buried matter breaking through here?

Showing not telling

This is the basic rule of all creative writing: show don't tell. Don't just inform readers that something happened; illustrate it, so that they can see for themselves. For example, don't say simply 'My mother was an inventive person', but show her inventiveness. Say that she made a vase as big as a pillar box and as exotic as a rainforest, that every summer weekend she took you on mystery tours, that she had designed an umbrella that could withstand gales and had applied for a patent. When you're describing a place, think of it as materially as a stage designer would. Show the overall set, the view out of the back window, the principal items of furniture, the little props, the costumes of the cast, the lighting.

The I who was and the I who writes

It may help to remember something that will let you enjoy this whole process in a relaxed and exploratory way; it's an idea from philosophy and linguistics that most writers on autobiography have commented on.[2] Lifestory writers have to accept that the you who is writing up an event now and the you who lived that event at the time – even if it was only yesterday – are different. There's no need to struggle to replicate precisely what happened because it can't be done – the you who experienced it is not the same you who sums it up in retrospect. The original is always different from the written version.

Using dialogue

You will make this lifestory and the people in it come alive if you show how they speak. Do use dialogue. You don't need to use much, say six exchanges at the most at any one time, but try to convey the precise way people organise their sentences, stress their syllables, choose their vocabulary, salt their speech with sayings or local words and pronunciations. This will not only help you recapture more fully the moment in question but make the book more rich for readers. Remember to respect the rights of those you are reporting. Show it to them but not until you've finished your final draft as their responses may create trouble at this creative stage.

I think it's ethical for you as an artist to invent dialogue people didn't quite say, but only if it's essentially the truth and the people are dead or can no longer be hurt by having words put into their mouths. You should explain what you have done in the preface/introduction.

Use this device judiciously. If you're not sure, try thinking of how you would want *your* words to be treated by someone else in an autobiography.

Why?

Ask yourself: How do I know this? Who told me? With what set of views did I figure it out for myself? Question what produced your knowledge and show that process to readers when appropriate. Be sure you know why you are including an account of something. What is its significance? Why does it have to be in this book, this chapter, this place?

If you're not sure that there is any point in including something, try asking yourself: 'If my best friend was describing this event/thing, what would I think was her underlying point, her rationale?' Or list three things that illustrate why this event/thing should be included, and three things that illustrate why not. The point of including (or not including) the event/thing should emerge.

Humour

Using humour, including irony, may be your style. It was used to popular effect in Sue Limb's comic autobiography *Love Forty: How I Turned over a New Life*.[3] It may be that your particular experience of life is such that it can *only* be written about in comic terms, or indeed that you want to tell an uproarious tale to make your readers laugh. Readers have loved the wit in Mary McCarthy's *Memories of a Catholic Girlhood*, Florence King's *Confessions of a Failed Southern Lady* and Joan Wyndham's *Love Is Blue*. You will need to decide when it's OK to be funny.

Trust yourself and your readers

Don't bother saying the same thing at length or twice. Trust your readers to get your drift and trust yourself to say it clearly the first time. Be sprightly in style – which is not the same as being hasty or ill-considered. It's more about pruning and not indulging yourself. It's about creating the book as an artist and craftswoman, a judicious lover of you and what you've done. You are not going to be able to include your whole life in this autobiography. You have lived at least 365 days of every year and been awake for about 16 hours in most of them. This means that every year you had around 5,840 waking hours. If you are 30, there will have been 175,200 waking hours. If you are writing your book for two hours a day, seven days a week for a year, this means by my calculation that 240 hours (or ten days) of living would have to be summed up in one hour of writing. If you are 60, 20 days' living would have to be written up in one hour. See? That's a lot of summarising and a lot of omissions of boring bits.

What you could leave out:

- things you feel you *should* write; write primarily what you *want* to write
- things you are putting in only for another's sake; feel free of obligation – at least at the early stages
- things that aren't directly relevant; convey your meaning precisely
- superficial decoration; concentrate on substance
- things you feel 'take-it-or-leave-it' about; passionate stuff works better
- things you feel uncomfortable writing about; trust your instincts

Introduce things – show meanings

Be aware that people do not necessarily know what you know. So spell out sets of initials and explain briefly what organisations or trade names stand for. For example, say 'Brasso metal polish' not 'Brasso', or 'the BBC radio's 1950s middlebrow channel, the Home Service' rather than just 'the Home Service'. If readers don't share your culture, then they won't know what you mean when, for example, you joke about the difference between Neasden and Ladbroke Grove. You'd have to show that Neasden is the suburb that *Private Eye* turned into a symbol for all that is tedious, whereas Ladbroke Grove stands for inner London Caribbean culture, Carnival, cosmopolitan and alternative lifestyles.

The narrator

Feel free to leap between saying 'she' and 'I'. There may be parts in the autobiography where you feel you can't face who you are (if something abusive or shaming happened, for example). Or there may be parts where you want to create distance in order to understand a situation more objectively.

It's fine to do this in your early drafts. As a reader, I feel OK about autobiographers switching in this way but how do *you* feel about 'she/I' alternating in the lifestories you have read? If it's easy for you to accept it as a reader, then you'll find it easier to let yourself write it. If you're unsure, ask your friends how they feel about it, in principle. For now, though, it will probably work better for you to keep on polishing your work in your own way. You will need consultants later but not yet; they can pull you off course just as you're trying to find the right voice in which to speak.

Tenses

Decide which is the right tense for your story: past (I did), present (I do), or present continuous (I am doing). For example, Hilda Bernstein switches tenses but mainly uses the present tense in her autobiography of her time in South Africa, *The World That Was Ours*. When writing of her husband's arrest she says:

My life has now become split into separate lives, almost wholly compartmentalised. There is the routine domestic life of home and children, picking up its normal furious tempo as they return from the winter holidays and go back to school. I meet Patrick at the station. 'Patrick, dad's been arrested.' 'I know.'[4]

Writing in the present tense makes a lifestory very vivid, almost as if it is still happening. It's a good way of showing you are reliving the feelings of the time, rather than making up a story after the event. Experiment with tenses to see which is right for the event you are recounting. Work on a spare copy so that you have your original version.

Words, sentences and paragraphs

Consult books on creative writing if you feel unsure about your style. At the same time, consider the probable reading abilities of your audience. This might mean that you decide not to use words your mum or a nominated reader-in-your-head would have to look up in a dictionary; that your sentences will be between 15 and 25 words long; that no paragraph will be longer than half a page; and that no chapter will be longer than 25 pages. Look at other people's autobiographies with these thoughts about form in your mind.

FEELINGS AT THIS STAGE

Polishing a chapter, concentrating on a narrow aspect of yourself, can be thrilling and feel like a homage to yourself. It can be a time when pride grows and you feel you owe it to yourself to make each and every chapter as perfect as possible. Or it can be alarming. You may think: Do I want to be under the microscope this much? Do I deserve this much time and attention? Isn't the whole thing too big an enterprise?

If such anxiety is a problem for you, then try to relax. Anxiety does not enhance creativity. This is often a version of stage fright, though it may include fear about your ability to write well. Deal with the microscope problem by toning down your intense scrutiny. Tackle the time and attention problem by evaluating how much time you think *someone else* in your shoes should spend on a small chapter in what might be their one and only lifestory; I think 48 hours is quite reasonable, for example, but she could take 100 hours if she liked. Then apply that to you. Work on the scale problem by breaking the chapter down into sub-sections of, say, 200 words each, for the time being.

The good news is that you will already know how you want the chapter to be. Your unconscious, again, will have done the work and it may only be a matter of executing what you are ready to do automatically.

Fast finding of what you know already

If you really are stuck or unsure about how the chapter should be shaped and phrased, pre-empt yourself. Get on the fast route to your unconscious mind by drafting a letter as if you were a publisher's reader (someone who assesses manuscripts and makes recommendations for publication) who has just looked at your (brilliant) chapter. She tells her employers:

> Dear editor of Muchmoney Publishing Ltd,
> I have just read — [your name]'s fascinating chapter. On this reading alone I am sure we have found a winner, early stages though it is. Her Chapter — [number] is about [list six main points]. It's set in — [year/place] and draws in material from — and —. Its main strengths are — . Ways it could be made absolutely perfect include —. I highly recommend this book.
>
> Yours sincerely
> Ms. Knowswhatsheistalkingabout

Write this for 20 minutes in your crispest style, as if you're used to sending out succinct summaries. It may sound a silly idea, but it works because it jolts writers out of the deep rut of melancholy. Now go back to the chapter/cluster of papers in question and see how you want to arrange it.

Other ways to handle crises

Other solutions to a crisis about how to write a chapter (normal, I assure you) include the following:

- Take your time. Do not force it. Writing anything is not necessarily easy. It may take an irritatingly long time, but let it if it needs to.
- Set yourself a deadline if you feel you might make too much of a meal of it.
- Tell yourself (and know) that it need not be perfect – certainly by anyone else's standards.
- Do not worry too much about the other chapters at this moment. This one episode in your life deserves all your respectful attention now. The other episodes will receive equally good attention later.
- Leave anxiety out of the process. Self-acceptance and peaceful work at my own pace are what helps me. This bit of lifestory is not just any old bit of writing but something that requires an enormous balancing act, handling my history and my attitude to my past life. I'm thinking important thoughts with possible long-term repercussions as I do this. The story – written and thought – will suffer if it's rushed.
- Accept that there will be bits you can't quite write or understand. Make a note of what you think might be missing and go on. It may come to you later or you may have to live with the fact that some areas can't be tackled
- Give yourself praise and treats for every completed paragraph or page. Some writers think 300 good words a day is an achievement. Therefore completing a chapter or part of a chapter is a coup.

Getting feedback

Now you have reached the stage when building your book is no longer a private process and it starts to become a more public thing. You will find you benefit from other people's help in finishing the writing and shaping of your lifestory. Assistance can be direct or slightly more oblique through example. You may find companions engaged on a similar task.

The impact of finishing your lifestory project and revealing it as a finished item to people you don't know can be profound. It can also come as a great relief. This is the period when your lived history becomes a visible, crafted, public object in whatever manner it is published and distributed.

SHOWING IT TO OTHER PEOPLE

Some people like to read their lifestory out a bit at a time to certain trusted people. Some like to hand the manuscript to someone whose judgement they value and then run away. Others have to have it wrenched off them by someone who knows enough about writers to understand that they may cling to their private draft for ever.

Why?

Showing it to others is something most writers like to do. Virginia Woolf, for example, read her autobiographical writing to the Memoirs Club. There is no Memoirs Club today, to my knowledge, but you can usefully invent your own informal one. The prefaces to many lifestories show how much writers have relied on others to comment on their work. Reasons for you to show your work include:

- other people may point out what you've missed
- they can help you to be realistic about its worth
- they can assess the likely responses of others – not least of family members
- for encouragement
- they may be able to offer practical suggestions about publication

You almost certainly wrote your lifestory for other people to read, so it's time to start.

When?

Choose your timing well. This has been such a big effort, it would be a shame either to rush the last stages or to hold back for too long. Show it once you are satisfied you've got down most of what you need to say. By then you are less likely to be swayed by anyone else's idea of what should be included. Read it at least three times right through and wait until you've had a chance to digest it. Don't wait until you feel nothing can be changed as this will encourage you to reject any feedback, however useful, because it's too much trouble to rewrite (this is when it really pays to have a word processor).

If you leave it too long (say, over a year), you're no longer the same you who wrote it.

To whom?

It may be that you choose to show it to individuals you know, or teachers, or that you read bits out in a group. Taking it to a group has the great advantage that you'll get many opinions, not one (though you should be aware that group members always strongly influence each other's responses and time is limited). You may also find some generous people who will read work outside the class.

Here are some points to bear in mind when you are considering the best person to read it right through:

- Identify the kind of knowledge you need them to have. Someone who knows about writing lifestory? Someone who knows about you? Someone who's never met you? Someone hot on grammar?
- Decide whether you want frank critical feedback or praise and appreciation. Don't be falsely brave. Getting the wrong kind of feedback at this stage can be disabling, so look after yourself by choosing someone who can give what you need.
- Don't show it first to the person who matters most to you. He or she may have a separate agenda that could get in the way of giving you what you need. Choose someone whose response won't affect you so deeply.
- When you're feeling brave, ask someone whose opinion you most value. Even if they're famous, ask them. People's responses are often surprisingly kind.
- Don't ask someone who's currently too tired or going through a difficult time. Be fair on them.
- Be aware of the potential for rivalry and resentment.
- Be aware also that a friend may not want to offend you. Flattery is all very well at first, but then ask for feedback from people who will look you in the eye and criticise frankly.

How?

It's your decision whether to show it to people chapter by chapter as you go along or as a whole.

Bear your reader in mind. Can s/he cope with a messy, even a handwritten draft or should you type it up first? S/he may respond better if it's bound (say in a ring-binder), especially if s/he has trouble keeping things in order or can't hold heavy weights. Do you want to make it look like a book already – with photos, title and covers – so that it can be appraised as a whole object rather than a clump of papers?

You may like to give your reader a list of questions to consider. I'd recommend no more than ten, and try to frame them so that you get full and unmanipulated answers rather than yes/no. They might include:

- What do you think of the tone?
- Are there areas you'd have liked to know more about?

- If you saw this in a bookshop, what would you say were its strengths?
- Which bits did you like best and where – if anywhere – would you like to see more of those inserted?

Be clear about what you want to get out of this process and not only ask for it but set up ways of getting it. For example, if you need a fast, positive response within a week, and then a detailed and more critical one in three months, then ask for it, in writing, with dates underlined. Enclose a stamped addressed envelope. Always ask first – don't send the manuscript out of the blue.

BENEFITING FROM OTHERS INDIRECTLY

Other people can help not only by giving direct feedback, but also by example. There comes a stage in most people's autobiographical process when they want to read or re-read others' books as models. Such reading can provide help with content, structure and style. Appendix 2 lists some of the best published lifestories I know. They taught me because they use exciting approaches to thinking and writing autobiographically and they talk about their lives in ways I want to hear. Don't rely just on published lifestories but also try the mini-autobiographies that women wrote for the Mass-Observation Archive[1] or your favourite letter writers.

It may help to read about people very unlike you. Read some of the earliest self-analytical autobiographies, such as that by St Theresa of Avila. Choose ones that inspire you. Change genres and look at self-portraits in paintings and photographs. The National Portrait Gallery has many traditional ones but contemporary artists are also creating stimulating installations and photomontages to show their view of themselves and their lives.

Living observantly

People can help you more obliquely; the stories they tell (and the way they tell them), and the fragments they let slip, can indirectly influence you. When I'm in lifestory mode I hear all sorts of things that help me make unexpected connections.

Chris has found that everyday life works:

Writing my lifestory is an organic process, I'm doing it as it comes. Sometimes many poems, sometimes long periods of narrative writing – often stimulated by some key occurrence in my everyday life. For me it is good to be in touch with other people, hearing their news, working, riding on the bus: this triggers memories of my own.

Again, go out with a notebook when you are at this stage.

Classes

You could attend adult education classes on autobiography and work alongside others for a year or even a term. If you prefer not to attend regularly, some institutions run weekend workshops, or Saturday schools. The point is to share with others your dilemma about how to express particular things. You receive support and helpful criticism and, above all, you have the pleasure of the company of people engaged in a similar process. One of the best courses is at the City Literary Institute in London.[2] If your local adult education centre or Workers' Education Association does not run courses on lifestory, then you can request such a course. Most centres are responsive, provided that they know enough people (usually twelve) are interested to make it cost-effective to run a class.

Gatherings

If you can't get to a regular class, try going to where writers congregate. There are organisations for writers such as the Writers' Guild, the Society of Authors and the Women Writers' Network, which sometimes hold workshops or lectures, occasionally by autobiographers.[3] This enables you not only to question the speaker but to identify other people in the audience who are also writing their lifestories. They may well become useful colleagues. Similarly, conferences of writers or literary festivals offer workshops with opportunities to hear speakers and make contacts. Southampton hosts a jam-packed writers' conference annually, and the Federation of Worker Writers and Community Publishers holds an annual conference which includes help on publishing.[4] Your local arts organisations will give you details of literary festivals in your area, and the public library should have information about these and similar events.

Reading theory

If you want to learn more of what women, academics and writers, have said about the process of creating autobiography, then consult some of the book on autobiographical theory listed in Appendix 2. Join the Auto/Biography study group of the British Sociological Association which publishes a journal and runs conferences. (See page 285 for the address.)

Women's History

The Women's History Network is a friendly organisation that puts on conferences several times a year in different parts of the country, has a newsletter and publishes occasional notebooks, usually of work in progress.[5] You can join very cheaply and become part of a gang who share information and support each other in their research. The conferences have lively sessions and provide opportunities for making new contacts. There are always stalls full of relevant books and you might like to consider giving a paper or a poster presentation talking informally about your findings (which you have illustrated by sticking key images on to a large piece of card).

Lifehistory theories and techniques

There are several relevant courses if you want to continue thinking about the nature of lifehistory. The University of Sussex in Brighton runs a one-year Certificate in Life History Work one evening a week; it includes documents, oral history and reminiscence. Birkbeck College at the University of London organises a two-year part-time Masters Degree in Life Course Development – understanding why certain things happen at certain times in our lives.[6] The University of Manchester Sociology/Women's Studies Department can supervise higher research degrees (masters and doctorates) if you want to approach your lifestory in a more theoretical way. Several universities, such as Lancaster and York, have women's studies departments where autobiography plays a big part in the courses.

Use other people to help you improve the telling of your lifestory. They can give you fresh insights, support and technical information. On the other hand, they can destabilise your confidence and divert you on to a course that isn't right for you. Use other people sparingly and judiciously – and be grateful to them. Remember them and the writers who have influenced you in your section of acknowledgements. Not only is this fair, but it gives your readers new leads too.

Relationships can be changed by this sharing process. I hope they change well for you.

Saying goodbye

Ending your lifestory can be deeply enjoyable. At last this big task is done and can be put aside so that you can move on to something new. There's relief at getting it all down and into shape. Some people, though, experience it as an amputation or like the ending of a relationship. If it helps, try seeing the end as *au revoir* not 'goodbye'. This lifestory will continue to be your lifetime companion. Going out into the wider world and hearing what other people make of your lifestory is an illuminating process. There are mixed feelings, there are revelations, there is the complex joy of being published. You can develop useful strategies to handle the public stages, thriving on the responses you receive.

WHAT IS AN ENDING?

The ending is the point at which you decide to stop the story. It may not be the end of your long writing process. You may write the final chapter quite early on, or you may polish each chapter in order, completing the last one only when all the others are finished.

A good point at which to finish

The ending does not necessarily bring you up to the present day, but only to the point where you feel you need to go no further. There will be odd ends to tie in, but you have said the bulk of what you wanted to say.

You may end with a watershed – say, your fiftieth birthday or a major realisation that puts your history in perspective. It can be the point where you survey the territory of your life in one last sweep of your eye. It's a truism that you can never write the very end of your actual lived life, because you won't be around to do it.

Sometimes people finish their autobiographies for practical reasons. Harriet Martineau completed her autobiography in just three months in 1855 because she was told by doctors she would die of heart disease very soon (she lived another 20 years). If you're having trouble finishing your final chapters you could try asking yourself what you would do if you were up against a deadline.

Some people want to finish because they've worked on it so long that that they're sick of it. Again you could try giving yourself a fixed period in which to finish. Name a precise date and write it down, leaving it prominently displayed. Bear in mind that you can finish it quickly, certainly after a particular stage when most of the internal thinking, growing and evaluating has been done.

Not necessarily the end

The final chapter may be a tying up of loose ends, or it may make it clear to you that you still have a lot more to do, perhaps another volume, or a fictionalised account of your life. Also, if your book is to be published then your editors will probably want changes. So the ending you write is often a provisional one. For now. Lifestories in particular have a habit of resurrecting themselves and demanding new endings – if only private ones.

If you really can't end it, don't worry. There must be a good reason. Find out what's obstructing you. Talk about it and to it. Make friends with the blockage. And if you still can't end it, then OK. Some things refuse to be ended before their time so you'll just have to leave it unfinished for as long as it takes. However, if you are being held back by a fear, I recommend being aware of it.

WAYS TO WRITE ENDINGS

Before writing the final chapter, I suggest you read all the preceding ones at a sitting. Do this several times, and make notes on what occurs to you each time. Check:

- Have I said all I needed to say (given the limitations of space)?
- Is there anything else I need to make clear to readers?
- What are the key things I want to make sure they have understood?
- What might I regret having omitted/included and shall I put that in the conclusion?

You may decide to write the final chapter, or even a piece of paper simply saying 'the end', long before you have finished the rest. If you are scared about finishing, this is one way to deal with that fear.

It might just be that during the writing you come across a sentence or a story that you think sounds like the final word. Store it. This neatness is gratifying. It can be very enjoyable to have the end sitting there waiting like a car parked outside ready to take you home when you leave the party.

If you're really stuck ...

I hesitate to offer any formula for endings. You must find your own and I believe that it will come to you when you are ready. If you are really stuck, try any of the following as topics for your final chapter:

- The ten key things about my life have been ...
- My epitaph should read ...
- I think/feel now, after writing all this, that what I was actually doing all the time/what I really thought was/is ...
- Here I am, then. Here you see a ...
- I hope you'll go away from this book remembering ...
- Looking back at all the wise/under-informed/generous/ enterprising, etc. things I've done, I think ...
- The pluses were ... the minuses were ... mixed blessings were ...
- This was my life and now ...
- The most unexpected lessons I have learned, in living and writing about living, are ...
- The best, worst and most telling things were ...
- What emerges of my deepest self here is ...
- This writing process has, for me, been about ...
- What I have not managed to say in this book includes ...
- I hope what shows through in these pages is ...
- On balance, what the life of someone like me shows is ...

- The underlying themes of this book have been ...
- Now you have read this book, I'd like you to feel ...

Reflect on any or all of these questions, including the ones you flinch from. There is a kind of triteness about some of them that makes me unhappy. That's because attempting to sum up can be a rather cliché-ridden process. Do something better. Or consult Frank Kermode's *The Sense of an Ending: Studies in the Theory of Fiction.*[1]

TYPES OF ENDING

There are many different ways to end a lifestory. Look at your favourite, or least favourite, endings and see what will work for you.

The no-end ending

You may not want to construct a 'The End'-type end. You may prefer no conclusion, no rounding-up statement. This approach works fine if you have written a collection of essays, but as the whole lifestory process has been about reflecting and appraising it may be important to sum up what you have discovered.

Epiphanies and triumphs

Some endings are like epiphanies: visions of the progress you have made and what the future might be. Elly Danica wrote very movingly in the epilogue of her book about surviving years of silent suffering over abuse by her father: 'Beginning. Always. From the secret place. Soul dwelling: found. Self: found. Heart: found. Life: found. Wisdom: found. Hope, once lost: found. Process: never lost.'[2]

Sometimes autobiographies, particularly ones written long ago when all stories were supposed to have a 'proper' ending, finish triumphantly. Mrs Pankhurst's last page and a half express her belief in a positive future: 'Our battles are practically over, we confidently believe ... No future government ... will be willing to undertake the impossible task of crushing or even delaying the march of women towards their rightful heritage of political liberty and social and industrial freedom.'[3] While we may find it ironic that the early feminists did not realise how prolonged the struggle would be, any grand pronouncements like this can leave the writer looking naive. Give some thought to how much you want to proclaim and predict as you bow your way off stage.

Summing up

For many people, writing the ending to their lifestory is a summing up. I think this is hard to do without being reductive. But if you want to do it, consider: What precisely are you totting up? Make a list. Identify the key element in each chapter or in the major episodes in your life, noting them on what you could call the 'summing-up' list.

You might want to say what you have learned. Or perhaps write what you think 'on balance' – even though that is only today's balance. You may want to summarise the one or two things that have mattered most of all in your life. For some people, this may be the point where they consider if they would do it all the same way again if they had the chance to relive their lives.

Echoing the start

Some endings echo the start of the lifestory. In Mercy's chronological autobiography she decided:

I have always loved stories that refer to something that happened on the very first page and so I decided to do that in my book. I'd begun by referring to the swim down to the birth canal into life and the world. So I finished it by writing about the waters of life, and learning to swim in them – every possible stroke I've had to pick up. And my anger at having to be so ingenious – and wondering if I could have floated through life, if I'd had a less combative vision of what I'd had to do.

Pleasing endings

Theorists of women's autobiography have found that women sometimes try to deny life's difficulties in the closure of a story, especially if they have complained, exposed injustices and been frank about pain. Canadian critic Janice Williamson looked at a number of lifestories of father–daughter incest. She found that Charlotte Vane Allen in *Daddy's Girl* 'constructs a counter-narrative to deflect the pain of her own history, a story of compensation with "tributes to her saviours" and the promise of a happy ending'. Similarly, Sylvia Fraser in *My Father's House* 'enacts her own splitting into a multiple personality "the girl who knows" and the "girl who doesn't know". This split female subject is reconciled finally in a version of the "happy ending", an epiphanic sense of forgiveness in which the child imagines the father as victim also.'[4]

You may well find that you have reached a good resolution by the end of your story but if not, there's no need to feel obliged to make light of tragedy. Try to find a way of ending that accepts the pain in what you have written. It doesn't have to be melancholy or humourless; it can be proud, funny or wry, but still real. I don't think that ending with an acknowledgement of how hard it has been will result in readers flinching or appreciating the story less. My reaction is always: 'Thank heaven for her courage!' Your lifestory will be the more accepted and trusted by others if it ends true to the spirit of the whole rather than splitting away, denying pain with the falsely cheery shrug of a woman taught not to complain. What kind of lifestory endings do you prefer reading?

Departing

Finishing telling the story of your life is a kind of departure. Hilda Bernstein ends her book, *The World That Was Ours*, with her physical departure from the South Africa that was so dangerous for anti-apartheid activists like herself:

We thank them all for all they have done, we say goodbye and climb into the plane. As we bump across the field, they raise their fists and cry '*Amandla! Amandla!*' And we too raise arms and shout '*Ngawethu! Afrika – Mayibuye!*' Our voices are subjugated by the noise of the plane. We see them standing there with upraised arms, diminishing in size as we rise higher and higher, as our plane trembles against wind and space; until they are scarcely marks on that boundless land and we are alone with the never ceasing wind and the white-hot blaze of the African sky.[5]

Returning to the title

You might want to end with some reference to the title, if you have
found your title yet. Try making a list of what the titles implies. Then
think how you could counter or confirm that in your ending.
Alternatively, your ending may upset the beautiful title you have
fondly relished throughout all these months or years.

Ending with a question

Artist Stella Bowen's autobiography, *Drawn from Life*, ends with a
question. It's July 1940, wartime, and her country cottage might be
commandeered as a first-aid post. 'Do we go or stay?' she writes.
'Tomorrow when I have finished this book, I must decide these things.'[6]
Her daughter Julia Loewe answers the question in the introduction
to a much later edition of the book, explaining that Stella Bowen
returned to London, lived another seven years, painting but in
deteriorating health. So the last lines do not necessarily have to be your
final statement. You can end on a note of uncertainty and even with
a question.

Alternative endings

Some fiction writers give their novels an alternative ending; you read
whichever one you choose. This isn't a real option in autobiography
but you might like to try playing with the idea that there are different
versions of your ending, depending on your mood. For example, what
about those fairy-tales that influenced our early thinking? They ended
with everything resolved: everyone lived happily ever after. Theorist
Vladimir Propp argues that such stories always end in the restitution
of the status quo; the thing that had been lost was found. The princess
marries the prince who can restore to her father all the lands he once
possessed. Red Riding Hood and her grandmother return to their
tranquil lives. As your lifestory is far more complicated and real than
any fairy-tale, you have no easy way of ending it. You might like to
end by contrasting what you thought you'd get out of life with what
you actually got. Or you could write yourself a fairy-tale ending to make
further contrasts and comparisons with your real life.

FEELINGS ABOUT THE FINISHED BOOK

Releasing your book into the open can also be a hard stage. You have lost a certain sort of privacy by publicly revealing your whole life. Some women never want to finish, because they don't want to be judged. Jean Rhys, who wrote autobiographical fiction, found such difficulty at this stage that her husband physically took the manuscript from her, told her it was truly finished and sent it off to the publisher so that she couldn't tinker with it any longer. This fear can be realistic, especially for women and marginalised people. It can also be phobic. Either way, it needs to be tenderly respected, challenged and overcome. Some older people may feel depressed that they have no time to remedy a life. Others feel proud and impressed, but unsure as to whether that's OK.

Your completed autobiography is now an object that has a separate identity and a life of its own, as it were. That's hard enough to cope with if you have written a novel or non-fiction book, but with an autobiography people can feel split apart for a while. Julia wrote:

> The immediate impact on my subsequent life was to feel totally bereft, to the extent of grief at the loss of this embellishment in my life. I did feel a sense of catharsis that I had revisited a very significant phase in my past life and put it into the context of current experience. Despite the jarring effects of the disintegration of the former Yugoslavia on my inner sense of stability, the fact that my feelings about it have been shared openly with those of other women at least provides a record and a documented testimony.

Disclosure

When you show your lifestory to other people – be they friends or likely publishers – you may feel that it is not just your writing that is being judged, but that *you* and your life are being evaluated. Here are some ideas that can help:

- Write a list of what you want to happen to the book, for example mass publication or private contemplation. Know what you want. Then go for it.

- Take as much time as you need between finishing it and showing it to anyone else.
- If it is accepted for publication, stay as involved in the publication process as you can so that the book does not become alien to you.
- Protect yourself from hostile feedback if you think it is likely. For example, Elly Danica avoided discouragement and lawsuits by calling *Don't: A Woman's Word* 'autofiction' rather than autobiography.[7] Another technique is to list where you think your critic is coming from. Get clear what are their values and what are yours.
- Accept that this could be an anxious time, a kind of trial, and treat yourself extra nicely.
- Divert yourself by starting a new hobby or another book so that you are not focusing too heavily on what will happen next to your lifestory.
- List your concerns about letting your lifestory go public and then deal with them.

For example, Cathy's list went:

1. Fear of exposure as the scared and uneasy person I am. Solution: maybe accept that I can't hide it for ever and it's not so exceptional anyway?
2. Recognition – even fame. Solution: stay as private as possible, restrict use of photos of me now. Arrange that agent accepts any prizes on my behalf!
3. Blame by people named in it. Solution: accept that some will be cross. Ditch those paragraphs that aren't important. Face out the row over the bits I believe should be in there.
4. Accusations of pomposity and arrogance, for writing a whole book about me. Solution: disregard. It's their agenda.
5. Terror that the publisher will edit it to pieces. Solution: refuse when reasonable, through agent.

- Get informal legal advice if you are worried about being sued for libel. You can get advice for free if you are a member of the Writers' Guild. A large publisher will have its own libel lawyers to check any passages you are worried about. If your life has involved famous and litigious people, you may (as Miss Whiplash

claimed at the start of her autobiography)[8] find there's hardly any of your book left after the lawyers have made prudent cuts.
- If you are worried about offending your family you must work this out for yourself. Talk to friends who can give you an informed opinion.
- Learn to accept that readers will make of you what they will anyway. Their criticism will be at least as much about them as it is about you.

After publication

Your work has become a piece of evidence, an artefact, one among the thousands of manuscripts and books in the publishing world, on bookshelves, in bestseller lists. You might feel proud, elated, fearful, confused, shocked, released or a mixture of all these and many more.

Betty, on publishing her first book, said:

> The stages I found challenging were: going for the first meeting with the publisher and not really liking her, not wanting to trust my baby to someone who seemed to have a very limited understanding; signing the contract – because it was yet another official document; breaching it could end me up in court again; publicity that seemed to make a bit of a fetish about my 'foreign upbringing'. I didn't want my book marketed as the product of someone remarkable or exotic. I changed bits of the book jacket blurb and the press release to stop them doing this.
>
> I felt good about: working with the copy-editor – who had some very wise ideas about what I was saying and put it better than I had, sometimes; being recognised by some people in the bookshop who were encouraging to me; having 'my life' in Foyle's famous bookshop, in the capital. I felt that I had been allocated a more central place in the world at last.

If you feel hesitant about the publishing stage, the following things may help:

- Reading about other women's experiences of being published.
- Reading therapy books about being successful. (See *A Life in the Arts*, especially the chapter 'Obscurity and Stardom'.)[9]

- Talking to a counsellor or trusted business adviser.
- Talking to other women writers in networks.
- Identifying your abilities and desires. Could you appear on TV? Can you give public talks? Write a strengths and needs list, maybe several times, so you can be very sure of your ground.
- Attending an assertiveness class or re-reading an assertiveness book.[10]
- Looking after yourself well enough to keep stress levels down (good food, exercise, aromatherapy oils, relaxation, diversity, company).
- Making sure you're confident and prepared before interviews. Write down the questions you feel you'd have most trouble with and then practise responding to them. Rehearse with a friend.

Women have very different responses, and different experiences of publishing their autobiographies. A useful thing you can do for others is to write about your experience and share it. Writers' magazines (which usually don't pay) love stories like this. It encourages others and gives them guidance. It might even educate the editors of future autobiographies and keep lifestory publishers on their toes in dealing with writers. Even if you don't publish anything, at least keep a diary of this stage of your autobiography's life. It's a very important time. Reflection and records are useful to you now and in the future.

Section IV

Reaching a wider audience

Getting published

For many people, the most important reason for creating an autobiography is to have it published, because it seems like a validation of the life lived. Many of us write lifestories because we need others to see and understand precisely what we've been through. We long for acknowledgement and witnesses to acclaim the lifestory – and, implicitly, the life – that we have created. Being published can appear to offer the validation and esteem we should have received long ago. Having a life turned into a proper book can seem like the obvious, indeed the only, way to get such necessary recognition.

Some people love the idea of media interviews, of signing copies in bookshops, of study groups painstakingly discussing the meanings of what they have written. Others shrink from publicity and stay out of the limelight, feeling that a lifestory is a private outing, not a public one. Others hover between the two positions. In this chapter I look at the options available to you.

COMMERCIAL PUBLISHING

Mainstream publishers

How do you find possible commercial publishers? Step one is to browse in good bookshops (not libraries; you need up-to-the-minute news), looking at who publishes autobiographies of people like you. Jot down names and look up the addresses later in the *Writers' & Artists' Yearbook.* This is the main source for information on publishing and is available at all libraries or costs around £12 to buy. Read the current edition, then phone likely publishers to find out their policy on submissions and the name of the commissioning editor to whom you should send your work. Publishers change rapidly, staff turnover is high and you need the most up-to-date information you can get.

I'm stressing the word 'commercial' to indicate that publishing is just another business, so economic success is the goal. Publishers may be gate-keepers who have the power to let us in or out but they are not arbiters of our value. They are business people trying to create products to sell.

This is not a good time to get published. The world price of paper has gone up so much in the last few years that books cost far more to produce. The ending of the net book agreement is enabling booksellers to sell books at whatever price they choose, so publishers' and booksellers' profits are even smaller. Book-buying in shops is declining; the trend of the future is direct mail, approaching potential customers with news of books they might like. When publishers see your lifestory they will ask themselves 'Will it sell? Will 10,00 people buy it at £15 a copy?'

No statistics are kept on how many autobiographies are published each year, let alone on how many are by women and how many are rejected. I telephoned some commercial publishers to ask what they were really looking for and how they handled proposed autobiographies. I discovered that around two-thirds of the autobiographies published were by men and that women's published autobiographies fell into the following categories (approximately this order of popularity):

- actresses and movie stars (such as Katharine Hepburn, Joyce Grenfell, Sarah Miles)
- arts people and writers (such as Penelope Mortimer)
- adventurous, daring women in exotic places (such as 'castaway' Lucy Irvine – Warner are far and away the leading publisher here)
- women who'd experienced tragedy, often a near-death illness, especially if they had been famous beforehand
- women whose lives were dished up tabloid-style – usually by a ghost writer
- people conjuring past rural idylls (such as Dacia Maraini, Alice Taylor)
- politicians (such as Margaret Thatcher, Helen Suzman)

- non-famous working-class women, especially those who presented their lives as remarkably impoverished, or in evocative or comic ways
- famous feminist figures (such as Kim Chernin, Erica Jong)

Feminist publishers

The main feminist publishers, who publish a little autobiography, are the Women's Press and Virago. The former is willing to look at synopses and sample chapters. So do send them in. Virago has impressively led the field in publishing the testimonies of working-class women. These include Kathleen Dayus, Hilda Hillinsworth, Joyce Storey (some of whose three-volume autobiography was initially brought out by a community publisher) and Frances Clarke. Telephone before sending your autobiography as policy changes.

Academic publishers

Academic publishers seldom publish whole lifestories but they often publish anthologies that include theorised autobiographical chapters. You will need to find out what is in preparation and contact the editor, who will not be a company employee but an academic with her/his own career.

Find out what academic conferences are scheduled that include topics ('strands') relating to your interest. Good ones are the Women's Studies Network and the Women's History Network.[1] You can find out about their next conferences by looking in academic journals or by being a member of the network. Arrange to give a paper on your subject at the conference. Make sure the organisers know you would like it go in a book as most conference organisers now try to get the papers published. Some of these publishers include Polity Press, Taylor and Francis, Macmillan, Sage, Routledge and the various university presses.

If the organisers are not putting together a conference book then try getting your essay/paper published in a related journal. There will usually be no fee for this, or perhaps £50. The pay-off is that people in academic jobs can get promotion and security of tenure by being well published. You will have the pleasure of being thoroughly challenged and critiqued, and you will be assisted with honing and refining your work, something that may teach you a lot. And you may be invited to write something else.

How to go for publication

The kind of advice about seeking publication given in any handbook on creative writing also applies to autobiography.

Prepare a proposal and several sample chapters. A proposal should include the following:

- title
- author (at this point you may want to decide on a pseudonym)
- length (number of words)
- illustrations (type and number, if any)
- estimated date of completion
- brief summary of contents (you could write a line or two about each chapter)
- distinctive qualities/selling points
- similarity to other books on the market
- types of readers likely to buy it
- information about the author

Include an SAE for return of your work (if publishers receive unsolicited material with no SAE they may not reply at all).

Make this proposal succinct. Type it out beautifully and lay it out well. You might want to send a laser photocopy (not an original) of one arresting photograph. A brief covering letter should tell them about any previous publications (including magazine articles). You should aim to convince them that they really want to know more.

Study your potential publishers well before you send them anything. Choose those who have published similar autobiographies, but nothing too close to yours (unless it's a bestseller and you think the publisher will want to continue the trend). Consider whether you should send it to a big hardback publisher, a feminist publisher, a small (maybe regional) publisher or an academic publisher.

Acceptance

Publishers pay authors a royalty on each copy sold, usually between 7 and 10 per cent of the published price for paperbacks. Most trade (general) publishers will agree to pay an advance against future royalty earnings. Smaller publishers and academic publishers may not. This means you would have to wait until copies of your book have sold before you receive any royalty payment. Well-known authors can demand large (some say too large) advances, but for new and unknown writers the sums are usually quite modest and in the region of £1,000 to £3,000, depending on how many books the publishers are intending to print.

In the process of being published, several editors will work with you. Probably one will assist on your overall ideas, one on the fine-tuning (copy-editing) and one on the pictures, cover, etc. This process can be very satisfying – you can feel you have finally arrived. However, it can also be frustrating and alienating as you see your book being shaped into something different from the one you have written. Negotiating with your publisher can be a tricky business and some flexibility is usually required on both sides to achieve an outcome that satisfies all parties.

Rejection

A business adviser recently told me that most businesses offering their services find that they have to make around 100 proposals in order to get four or five responses. Out of those four or five responses might come one or two people who will actually buy their services. The same applies to writers seeking publishers. It takes many attempts and many dead ends. Most of us just have to keep sending out proposals routinely, week after week. If you make it into an automatic task it can hurt less. Indeed, you might like to ask a reliable friend to be the person who sends the proposal to a list of publishers that you've supplied. You don't need to be involved in this process. You could try doing it for each other if she is writing too.

If your proposal is returned, read the letter very carefully. It's easy to imagine that faint praise is no praise and that a guarded 'Yes, but ...' is a rejection when actually it's a green light. Don't be discouraged by rejections. Keep trying. Pat Barker won the 1995 Booker Prize at 52. She had 13 years of rejections until Virago published her first book, *Union Street*, in 1982. The publishing world is full of stories like this.

Conversely, be realistic about rejections. Talk each one through with a friend. Consider suggestions that seem valid, and act on them. Discard those that your intuition tells you are not helpful.

If you are rejected by commercial publishers try remembering:

- You did this process primarily for you – so you got a lot out of the process and you can present the book for others to read in other ways, e.g. self-publishing.
- Rejection is about commercial bets in a world that does not care much about the struggles of women it deems unexceptional. It is not about your intrinsic value.
- It's their loss. They could have had the honour of publishing you.
- There's always the next one. Keep sending out the proposals. Thirty times is not too many.

COMMUNITY PUBLISHING

One solution to the problem of commercial publishing is to eschew it. Try looking instead at the less glitzy, more human-sized side of the market.

Join a community writing group that publishes books regularly. There are many of these in the Federation of Worker Writers and Community Publishers.[2] You can find out about them either through the Federation or by asking at your local library. Local bookshops usually stock recent community-published books. In Brighton, for example, Queenspark Books publish about ten or twelve autobiographies a year which sell well at an affordable price (£1.50).

Inadequate funding for the voluntary sector means that not all community groups can afford regular publication, but one may well publish your story. It is advisable to become an active group member working on other people's books too, rather than someone who's there only to be published. The point is collectivity and skills shared among people who work together, learning.

Benefits and drawbacks

Community publishers can't afford to pay you. Their raison d'être is to ensure 'ordinary' people's lives are given a public forum. The gain is usually in the attention you get from local newspapers – and even on the street. Working on your publication with others, especially co-editing it with peers and friendly professionals, means that the publishing process is far less alienating than is usual in mainstream publishing. You learn so much about the book production process that you see all books differently afterwards; you become an insider. It can be hard work but it's usually fun too. There is nothing precious about this type of publishing.

Also, some books which start off as community publications can be taken up by bigger companies. When Canadian writer Elly Danica wrote *Don't: A Woman's Word*, it was initially published by a small feminist company. It went on to sell over 10,000 copies in Canada alone, was republished as a mass-market paperback in the USA and has now been translated into four languages.[3] Elly Danica had hesitantly taken her writing to a workshop thinking it was just incomplete notes towards a book.

Community publishing may seem like a less glamorous option but in fact it can be a much more satisfying one and it is one that offers a lot of room for women. It can even bring you prizes and acclaim: for example, Caribbean British writer Pauline Wiltshire's lifestory won the Raymond Williams Prize for Community Publishing.[4]

VANITY PUBLISHING

You can get your book published if you are prepared to pay for it. There's no reason to be ashamed of vanity publishing, despite current snobbery about it; if it serves your purpose that's good enough. But some vanity publishers are confidence tricksters and all of them are in it for the profit, so do be very cautious about those that demand huge sums of money or try other ways of ripping you off. Be wary of the small print in the contract and don't be manoeuvred into having more books printed than you can realistically handle. Shop around. Talk to your local legal advice centre about the contract before you make a major commitment.

There are also a number of printers who will print 'short runs' of 100 or so copies. The text for this printing would not necessarily have to be typeset, just reduced from A4 pages to a smaller size. However, it could be designed for you if you produce your typescript on disk and pictures could be scanned and included for an additional fee. You can find such printers either through advertisements in 'quality' newspapers or through the Yellow Pages.

PRODUCING YOUR OWN BOOK

One of the most warming things you can do for yourself and those you love is to publish your own lifestory. You could create a book that is a mixture of artwork and scrap album – a one-off book or just a run of five or 20. People get enormous pleasure from creating these auto-biographical objects, full of photos and drawings, tied with ribbons, necklaces or macramé, with pages of text decorated with fancy headings in different inks on different shades of paper. It may feel like a poor substitute for a 'proper' book, especially if you have a political or educative goal in writing, but in fact it can be far more pleasing.
    Helen took this route:

I'm not very arty but I did have a sense of how I wanted it to be – essentially like a very carefully designed patchwork quilt of me, full of all the metaphorical fabrics of my experience. But I knew it would probably have to be a paper thing that people could easily handle. So I spent a long time dreaming of what I wanted, including night dreams ... In the end I created a book as fat as an old-fashioned photo-album, covered in a kind of mosaic of scraps of my favourite old clothes. I copied it on to the thickest cream paper I could hand-feed into the photocopier (120 gsm). Each chapter was interleaved with laser-copied colour photos sandwiched between tissue paper – as I'd seen in the antique art books of my childhood. I wanted it to look and handle like a precious volume. It was. Luckily I found a binder – through the local art college – who could cope with binding weird objects and I ended up with something quite sturdy to handle, for all that it was stuffed so full. I love it.

Other people create something quite simple and make just enough copies for friends and family.

The writing

It doesn't have to be typewritten or typeset. If you are going to do it on a computer then do explore all the different typestyles that it can offer you. You could learn a desktop publishing program such as Quark XPress, or pay someone to type and design the book for you on a computer.

You may decide to photocopy the whole thing yourself. A community print shop or a copy shop may have several colours of toner that it can offer you, so that your black text can come out green, red, blue or brown. This looks particularly effective on coloured paper: I love scarlet on sunshine yellow.

You may like to letter it by hand in italic script using Indian ink, or write with different coloured inks in different chapters. You could illustrate the first letter of paragraphs or decorate the margins. Look at illuminated medieval manuscripts and books of typefaces for ideas.

Paper

First think of what you'd ideally like, then consider what you can afford, what will last and how you want it bound. Thick paper will mean you can have fewer pages in each volume. Ordinary typing paper is 80 gsm (grams per square metre) in weight. Heavier paper, such as 100 gsm and above, will stand more handling. Coated paper, with a glossy feel, will last longer because it will resist sticky finger-marks but it costs more. Look round specialist paper shops, such as Paperchase, and art shops. Printers and artists' materials shops have catalogues of papers. Shop around: the paper of your dreams may be just round the corner. Even a new roll of good quality brown wrapping paper might work well if you use heavy black Indian ink on it. It's a good idea to see your paper as an investment: think as a conservator here.

Alternatively, as a lifestory is such a product of you, you may want to make your own paper. Local authorities often run paper-making courses – it's a rejuvenated craft. You could make the sheets of your book from remnants of your old clothes, pressed with flowers and grasses between them.

Some people like writing over pictures, including ones that they have bleached out slightly. You can easily bleach out a picture by photocopying it at the lightest setting the machine will allow.

Illustrations

Photographs, drawings, small decorations and cuttings can all make your book rich. This is when colour (laser) photocopiers are really useful – and cheap. One A4 sheet costs 75p to £1.25. If you're hard up you can, with care, fit four small images on to one sheet, then later cut them up and re-mount them on a sheet of your choice.

The cover

Like a movie poster, covers tempt you to sample the contents. Or if you want to be more focused on expressing yourself – to hell with the viewers – then you might want to consider a cover that sums up how you think you are: be it black rubber with a nail-varnished title and a graffiti-covered xerox of you, or a mirror-tiled collage, or silk rosebuds on an old sampler.

Covers can be made of exotic fabrics – velvet, fake leopardskin, beloved old patchwork stuck on to stiff card. They can be painted and varnished. Covering pictures with a self-adhesive transparent sheet such as Fablon or Libraseal (available from art shops, about £1.50 for a roll that might do four or five books) will last for a decade. If your book is a standard shape, use plastic slide-on book covers from big bookshops (my local Dillons has them for about 75p).

Binding

The way you bind your book is primarily affected by what you can afford and do for yourself.

At the lower end of the scale, the edges of the pages can be glued together with a very fine layer of carpet glue from a DIY shop. Use a clamp to ensure it's even. Or you can collect your pages together with a plastic slide-binder (10p, but it won't take more than 20 pages without springing off). Stapling works well on thinner books. If you get long enough staples they might go through 30 to 40 thin pages. You can borrow long-arm staplers which enable you to turn sheets of A4 into an A5 booklet by stapling them in the middle. Staple guns can be hired from DIY shops and these shoot staples into very thick wads of papers and covers. Or you can sew the sheets down the centrefold. Look at books on bookbinding for information on the kind of thread to use and how to attach each section together.

For 50p you can buy a comb-binder which can cope with up to 400 pages; you need to have access to a machine that can punch the right-sized holes for the comb (universities and colleges often do, or a print shop will do it for you for about £3). This is a permanent job, so it pays to spend a long time getting the pages thoroughly aligned and the right way up. I speak from experience of too many mistakes made in haste that ended with me having to photocopy the pages all over again and repeat the process.

You can even just keep the lifestory in a decorated ring-binder. Or develop your own version of this, threading ribbon or a plait of favourite fabrics – or even hair – through punched holes in paper and card covers.

You may want to do a really attractive permanent job and have it bound by a bookbinder. Some people do this as a family present for a birthday or fête day. Or several people club together to fund the price of one copy that they share. It needn't be a cost borne solely by you.

Bookbinders are quite a rare breed now. You can find them in the Yellow Pages. The kind of bookbinders who bind theses for universities will make a fine job of sewing up 500 pages (2.5 inches thick) together in a 'case book' and sticking hard covers on with gold lettering from £25. Some places use lightweight card for only £5.

If you wanted as many as 20 copies of a hard-cover case book, the price would go down to about £18 each. Try R.G. Scales in central London.[5] For £200 they offer leather binding, with gold frames on the covers. The sky is the limit. They are used to dealing with customers who have little technical knowledge but loads of ambitious ideas. Quotes are free.

In the medium price range, other alternatives are less permanent and less costly. Perfect binding – meaning a booklet with a stiff spine – can be done at print shops such as some branches of Prontoprint. Your book should not be more than 1.5 inches thick if you want to use this method. If you were to fold 70 double-sided sheets of A4 in half, the cost of binding them into an A5 booklet would be about £8. The price goes down substantially with every additional copy, because the main cost to the company is in setting up the machine to do the job. For example, you might be able to negotiate 20 such A5 booklets for £6 a copy. Shop around for quotes. All the companies who do this kind of work expect customers to request quotes first.

Prontoprint also offers channel binding as glue can crack. Channel binding means sliding a metal channel over the left-hand side of the pages. It costs slightly more than perfect binding (about £10) but lasts longer. If you have your heart set on a particular but awkward cover, you may need to either shop around or compromise. I do recommend that if you are making your own book you take your time at this stage, especially over something so final as the binding. It's easy to be rushed into wrong choices by people concerned with the techniques with which they can best complete the job and not with the spirit of what you passionately desire. If your goal is to create the most beautiful, appropriate and enduring book you can, then this stage merits careful research and reflection.

Bear in mind other ways of connecting the pages. Try concertina folds or a book in a box (reader selects the order) or a giant paper jigsaw.

Turn your private process of lifewriting into something other people can share and enjoy. It can be a great delight and the pinnacle of your process. While the most personally satisfying outcome might be a self-published book, community publishing or commercial publishing might be the final product that you prefer. There will be many challenges and pleasures at this stage. The next chapter talks about how your book can reach all the people you want it to reach.

Sharing and selling

Whether or not you are commercially published you will probably want others to see your written lifestory. If you are commercially published, the publishers will look after distribution. Make friends with the publicity department staff and offer suggestions to them as well as accepting their ideas for promoting the book. These include readings to interested groups, signing sessions in local bookstores, radio and TV appearances, even international lecture tours. If you are one of the many who doesn't get published but who wants multiple copies of her lifestory to be seen, the following ideas could be tried.

IF IT'S NOT REALLY A BOOK

Have you written many autobiographical pieces which do not constitute a complete book, yet still want your work to be read? This desire is quite a difficult one to meet as autobiographical fragments don't fit easily into any category. Below are some suggestions about dealing with this situation but first, a word of warning. Whatever use you decide to make of your writing, always keep one copy intact. You may be so unhappy with what you've written that you feel it's OK to chop bits off and put them to another use. But you may change your mind later. If you want to work on a particular section, then either save it separately in a fresh document if you are using a computer or photocopy the original and store it somewhere safe.

Magazine articles

Look carefully at what you've written in relation to what magazines are publishing. Who would take what? Women's magazines sometimes carry autobiographical pieces, as do specialist magazines. For example, the Step-families' Association Newsletter sometimes has pieces about step-mothering. They also – like many such newsletters – carry appeals from researchers who want to hear from people with a particular experience. So even if you don't get to show your whole work, you may get the chance to talk about what you have found out during the exploring process. Read any likely magazines and write a brief letter of enquiry to the features editor, listing clearly what you've done and asking what they are interested in. The bigger the magazine, the more likely it is to pay.

Don't overlook the letters page. Write about your lifehistory in response to something that is mentioned there or is happening in the news. For example, Pat wrote about what she did in the war, and got widely published in VE Day anniversary specials. If your letter is under 200 words it is less likely to be cut. Pictures (black and white) can help. Only send a (good) copy. Publishers notoriously lose precious original photos.

Local newspapers

Local newspapers sometimes welcome nostalgia pieces, usually no more than 300 words long. If you want to work a bit of your lifestory up into something suitable for this market then look at what previous writers have done. Make sure you write something with lots of references to the locality, evoking as much of the period feel that you can: modes of transport, clothes, shops long gone, the old watermill where Safeway now stands, for example. Or sort out decent quality photographs you think the paper might like to use – then write extended captions (say 150 words) to back up each picture. They needn't necessarily be your pictures, they could come from a public archive, but do check the copyright position or you may end up having to pay a reproduction fee. Only go to the trouble of acquiring pictures once you have established that the newspaper is interested. Such speculative endeavour can be fun but it can cost time and money.

Radio and TV

The more you become known locally, say as a contributor of autobiographical pieces to the town's newspaper, the more you will be invited to speak about your life on radio and TV programmes. For example, BBC national radio programmes such as *Woman's Hour* have people on for three to ten minutes. All local stations have a list of rent-a-quote people who they use regularly. One way to become established on such a list is to become known as someone who can speak authoritatively and interestingly, is expert at delivering 30-word soundbites and is a journalist's dream: friendly, available (an answering machine or reliable message-taker helps enormously), patient, flexible and reliable.

One of the main ways people's lifestories get broadcast, for minutes rather than in brief soundbites, is through programmes such as *Video Diaries*. Write to Video Diaries, BBC TV, Wood Lane, London W12 7RJ for an application form. A programme like Carlton's *Your Shout* (tel: 0121 643 4000) offers people the chance to speak, from personal life experience, about a social change they want to see. If you have done something extraordinary recently – for example, having been held prisoner abroad (and written a diary/autobiography in captivity or shortly afterwards) – then a production company might be interested in basing a programme on your experiences. One way to make an approach is to note, from TV programmes you like, the name of the production companies making this sort of programme. Then phone or write to them with a one-page typed outline of your experiences, giving information about sounds and images that could illustrate your story.

The community team at the BBC (0181 743 8000) or at your commercial TV channel are useful people to contact. Use the *Writers' & Artists' Yearbook*, the *Radio Times* and the local Yellow Pages for addresses and telephone numbers. Most TV stations have an extension for general enquiries, so you can ask about any opportunities coming up. Be ready to do a hard sell on this. Companies are interested in obvious winners so make yourself sound exciting. Work on your line in advance with a dynamic friend.

Alternatively, you could make your own video. Either rent a video camera and talk your friends into filming you in various locations, or contact the head of the film and television studies department at your local further education college to see if any students would like to video your life. Quite often students are casting round for ideas for programmes as part of their training. Why shouldn't they focus on you?

Archives

The local history libraries in every borough have a collection of manuscript autobiographies which they especially value for detailed descriptions of the locality. If you don't finish your lifestory for some reason but want it to have a public use, then deposit it with this library. It doesn't matter how short it is. There are other archives too, specific to particular interests, for example the Lesbian Archive, the Black Cultural Archive and those of professional bodies such as film-makers at the British Film Institute.[1]

Make an appointment with the archivist and discuss in what form they'd like to receive the material, how it will be stored, and if you want to restrict access to it. For example, some people stipulate it's only to be made available to serious students, or not until after they're dead. Present the material neatly – there may be no staff member available to sort it out into reader-friendly shape.

Tapes

You may have audio-taped some bits of your lifestory. Where to put it? Local history libraries often don't have the right conditions to store tapes, but if you want to leave the tapes there, you can. Include a summary of each tape's contents. The main place to deposit lifestory tapes for posterity is at the National Sound Archive's Lifestory Collection.[2] This department of the British Library will copy your tapes and return a set to you – free – if you like. Its purpose is to guard such audio evidence of personal history for the nation.

IF IT'S A ONE-OFF BOOK OR ALBUM

If you have put together your lifestory so that it is simply one book or album of which there are no copies, then how are you going to share and take care of this precious artefact? Try the following:

1. Make sure everyone involved knows where the copy of the book is being deposited so that they can have access to it. You might want to photograph it or write a short leaflet about it to show farther-flung friends and relatives. You may like to personalise it by adding 'and the bits about you, Aunty Willa, are on pages 24, 47 and 189'.

2. Hold a party to celebrate the book being finished and to thank everyone involved for their help. Have the book on display there; away from the booze. Make sure your guests know they can look at it and photocopy anything they like. Decide in advance who is to do the photocopying and when. You could even hire a desktop photocopier for a couple of days, so that all the photocopying can be done safely at home.

IF IT'S A SELF-PUBLISHED BOOKLET OR SMALL BOOK

Are you having your lifestory made into a booklet or small book and will you have a number of copies to distribute? If you're having them printed, gauge the quantity carefully: 70 to 100 is actually quite a lot to sell and give away. Make a list rather than an estimate. While it's tempting to take advantage of a printer's offered economies of scale, it may be wiser to just ask the printer to keep the plates and give you a quote for running off more copies at a later date if needed.

Launch it with a splash

Organise a launch party at a local arts venue and/or a signing session at a local bookshop. Invite the press, councillors, regional arts board officers, other writers and, above all, people who'll share in your pleasure. However small and badly attended you fear it might be, set it up. Ask a friend with promotional skills to hype the book on your behalf if you find doing this embarrassing. Expect to give away at least 20 free copies; some will be an investment because the recipients will recommend them, others will create goodwill.

Local newspapers

Send an advance copy of the book to the local paper (the arts editor, the women's editor or the features editor – or all three) with a press release. Ideally do this at least a month before it is due to come out. A press release should include no more than a side and a half of A4 paper, double-spaced, with two sentences to a paragraph, and no paragraph longer than 35 words:

- first paragraph: announces a new autobiography entitled xx
- second paragraph: says something about the author
- third paragraph: gives a summary of the book
- fourth paragraph: gives a relevant quote from the book
- fifth paragraph: suggests why people would like to buy it
- final paragraph: gives information about where it can be bought, price and cost of postage and packing (don't forget to include the cost of padded envelopes as well as the stamps) and who the cheque should be made payable to
- the bottom: states 'Press contact' in bold, followed by your name and telephone numbers, especially a daytime number if possible

Offer a photo (black and white, 8in x 10in, ideally professionally done). Local papers are always short of pictures, especially as few now have their own photographers. List some suggestions for exciting photo-opportunities. For example, if your story is about becoming the first woman butcher in the area, then suggest pictures of yourself at your counter or you with a local meat supplier.

Follow up the press release with a phone call three or four days later. Get the journalist's name if you can. It's usual to say something like, 'I sent you a press release, Jackie, about my new autobiography. I wondered if you had received it ... Have you got queries I can help you with? When do you think you might run it?'

Personal contact is a good way of increasing your chances of getting coverage. If they say they've lost it send or fax another one with a friendly note attached, on first-name terms. Ring again within three days. Judicious persistence pays.

The library

Take or send a copy of your autobiography to your public library and ask if you can donate it. Usually they'll be happy to agree. If your book is just stapled and small, they may make it a reference-only book as it could be damaged by going out on loan.

If you want, and can afford, to make multiple copies, you could do enough for every library in your borough (not forgetting the mobile library). The central library will usually arrange for your books to be sent out on their regular van round to the branches, so you won't have to pay postage to each branch. Get your friends to go in and ask for it. Put the book face out if it's not visibly on display. The point of giving free copies to libraries and making sure that they are seen and mentioned is that word of mouth is the best publicity. You may get quite a few sales as a result.

Take it with you

If it's light and small enough, carry two or three copies of your book/let wherever you go. Mention you've written a lifestory, then get it out, offer to sign it and sell it. Some writers make a resolution before going to any event: 'I'm going to take ten copies and sell every one of them. I won't bring a single one home.' Try it. I've seen it work.

Local organisations

Brainstorm with a friend on what local organisations might be interested in knowing about your book, even reviewing it in a newsletter or asking you to speak about it at a meeting. Try, for example, the council's Women's Unit, the local history society, organisations in which you're an active member, from the Women's Institute to a lesbian network, from a hospice fund-raising team to a political group.

Alternative book distributors

Some cities have an alternative, rather than a commercial, book distribution network, which handles radical books, community-published books, books on homoeopathy, local walks and other things of local interest. Find the one in your area by asking your local bookshop or by looking inside likely books to see if there is a notice saying 'Distributed by ...' Phone and ask if they will handle your book. They will expect to take a small commission.

Set up a stall

Take a stall, or part of a stall, at a local market, car boot sale, village fête. Such stalls can cost between £3 and £10 for the day. Lay your books out well and make a clear and large placard with your photo, book title and offer of signed copies. Be there to chat and sign. Suggest people might like to buy multiple copies as Christmas presents for relatives or neighbours who have now moved away. Offer a small cumulative discount for this, 5 per cent off two copies, 10 per cent for five and so on.

Find out all you can about how to handle self-published and community-published books. There's no technique specifically for distributing autobiography. Getting your work seen is an interesting process that is most successful when you can give it energy, enterprise and commitment. You'll learn from it as well.

What next?

There is no real end to writing a lifestory because usually we keep on doing it in our heads (and sometimes on paper) all through life. Having completed this version you may now feel the need to do something else that is in some way related to it. Sometimes writing a lifestory can free you up to write a novel or a very different kind of non-fiction. Writing and completing your lifestory can both open floodgates and illuminate next steps. Some people want to continue to explore themselves, others may be interested in taking a sociological and historical approach which can lead to studying family history or women's history or local history. Alternatively, you may want to lie fallow, like a field that needs to rest before a new crop grows in its temporarily exhausted soil. Some people like to take a holiday or go into a retreat, as a way to mark the ending of the process.

Whatever you decide to do, your lifestory writing will have expanded and deepened your knowledge about yourself, about your ways of working and about others. The enhanced wisdom will stand you in good stead.

FURTHER EXPLORATIONS OF YOURSELF

If you want to explore your personal depths and currents a bit more, try any of the following:

Art

Go to art workshops, or an art therapy group.[1] This approach explores in images what you may not be able to express in writing. Jung had many ideas about imagery and mythology that you might study and use in painting your lifestory.

Music

Go to music workshops[2] or experiment with the wordless sounds you can utter, the kinds of rhythms you can make, the way you might dance your history. Writing is a largely silent and physically static process; you may now like to explore the deep sounds of you.

Other versions

You may want to write another version of your autobiography. There are various ways you can tackle this:

- write as many additional volumes and versions as you like
- on a smaller scale, write poems or brief essays that contradict or expand the existing material
- add a new introduction every year, or rework the conclusion
- insert new material into an unbound copy of your book
- write autobiography for the Mass Observation Archive[3]

Don't feel hide-bound by conventions. If you want to add to your book, do so. However, don't make changes for the sake of it; this isn't really in the creative spirit. Leave it and start something else.

Fiction

Many people find that they can't say enough in straight autobiography and write stories, novels, poetry or plays to express themselves. See if fiction will work for you. If you're stuck, start off by writing: 'Once upon a time, there was someone nothing like me, and she ...' Or try the basic idea Doris Lessing used in her novel *The Golden Notebook*. Keep four different notebooks/diaries/stories 'by' four different aspects of you (for example, the striving worker, the spiritual you, the wild lover, the campaigning activist). Keep them separate. Then, when you're ready, in a fifth 'golden notebook' write the synthesis; make it by the woman who knows/is all those parts and more. Call her 'she' if that works better.

FURTHER EXPLORATIONS: YOUR CONTEXT

Sometimes after writing a lifestory people can feel tired of focusing so much on themselves and weary of writing subjective accounts. They want to look more broadly and see what life was like for others, or understand what they would have been like if their early experiences had been different.

Family history

If you want to explore your family's history, go back to Chapter 14, on resources, which explains the basic steps which may be appropriate for you now, such as courses on genealogy, drawing genograms and interviewing key family members. If your particular interest is in the effect of the family group on individuals, then many university centres for continuing education and counselling bodies offer courses on social psychology, the sociology of organisations, an introduction to family therapy and group dynamics. Additionally, there are workshops on moving on from your birth family and developing other aspects of yourself.

Helping others

Having learned so much from writing your autobiography, you may want to help others with theirs. Apart from teaching at nightschool as part of the creative writing syllabus, another informal way to do this is as a reminiscence worker. Some old people's homes welcome volunteers. You can get training and information and a range of publications based on others' reminiscences, as well as the journal *Reminiscence* from Britain's main centre for reminiscence work: Age Exchange.[4] If you want to listen to others' lifestories, the National Lifestory Collection at the National Sound Archive has thousands of tapes you can listen to for free.[5]

You may have decided that completing your lifestory is quite enough. Fine. You are free never to write again. Whatever you do next, you will be doing it with more expertise and more self-knowledge, having already undertaken such a major piece of work.

The ideas in this book have been suggestions, not commandments. You will, in the process of working from it, have come up with many ideas of your own. I hope they worked for you, and that you will pass them on to others too. Good luck with your process. I wish you joy in reflecting, writing and sharing your lifestory. You will have done it in good company and I hope it has brought you the satisfaction you deserve. I like the idea that some of the autobiographies I see in the bookshops in the future will have been helped by this book.

Appendix 1

Useful ideas for when you get stuck

Everybody has times when they can't write or can't stand what they have written. These times are temporary. They are normal. They pass all the more quickly, and more fruitfully, if you accept them and turn your attention to something else for a while. It's just a fallow patch before the next fertile season. It will probably help the lifestory process if you keep yourself approximately on course, so try any of the following:

- look at pictures – not of yourself; visit a gallery or look through any art or photography book at random until an image jars you out of your stuck spot
- telephone friends – it's important to remember that other people like you
- use essential oils to lift yourself out of the rut and alleviate the distress you may feel about it; the oils can be burned or used in a massage.[1]
- read poetry – not your own – preferably aloud
- dance, move, exercise
- give yourself treats and comforts[2]
- paint a picture of what you are having trouble writing about

The following are some helpful things to ask yourself:

- What useful things is this problem telling me?
- What is it that I don't want to say?

- What might someone else be feeling if she couldn't write at this point?
- What would the very best friend in the universe advise?
- What is it that I need before I can move on to my next stage (for example, more food, sleep, stimulation, fresh air, music, silence)?
- What can I do to look after this person who can go no further for now?
- What length of break do I need?
- What kind of fierce self-discipline do I need for this next stage?
- What has come up or is coming up that is making it so hard for me to continue?
- Whose permission do I need at this point – and for what?
- Have I reached a natural pause for reasons not yet known to me? If so, how and when do I want to proceed?

Appendix 2

Further reading

INDIVIDUAL AUTOBIOGRAPHIES

Angelou, Maya, *I Know Why the Caged Bird Sings*, Virago, London, 1984.
— *Gather Together in My Name*, Virago, London, 1985.
— *Singin', Swingin' and Getting Merry like Christmas*, Virago, London, 1985.
— *The Heart of a Woman*, Virago, London, 1986.
Barthes, Roland, *ROLAND BARTHES by Roland Barthes*, translated by Richard Howard, Hill and Wang, New York, 1977.
Cardinal, Marie, *In Other Words*, translated by Amy Cooper, Indiana University Press, Bloomington, 1995.
Chernin, Kim, *In My Mother's House: A Daughter's Story*, Virago, London, 1985.
— *Crossing the Border: An Erotic Journey*, Women's Press, London, 1994.
Colette, *Earthly Paradise: An Autobiography*, compiled by Robert Phelps, translated by Herma Briffault, Derek Coleman et al., Farrar, Straus and Giroux, New York, 1966.
Derrida, Jacques, *The Post Card: From Socrates to Freud and Beyond*, translated by Alan Bass, University of Chicago Press, 1987 (first published by Flammarion, Paris, 1980).
Dillard, Annie, *An American Childhood*, Harper Perennial, New York, 1988.
Erdrich, Louise, *The Blue Jay's Dance: A Birth Year*, Flamingo, London, 1996.
Forster, Margaret, *Hidden Lives*, Penguin, Harmondsworth, 1996.
Frame, Janet, *Janet Frame: An Autobiography*, Women's Press, London, 1990.

Fraser, Ronald, *In Search of a Past: The Manor House, Amnersfield, 1933–1945*, Verso, London, 1984.

Gornick, Vivian, *Fierce Attachments: A Memoir*, Virago, London, 1988.

Hellman, Lillian, *An Unfinished Woman: A Memoir*, Bantam, New York, 1970.

— *Pentimento: A Book of Portraits*, New English Library, New York, 1973.

— *Scoundrel Time*, Little, Brown, Boston, 1976.

Hoffman, Eva, *Lost in Translation*, Minerva, London, 1993.

— *Exit into History*, Minerva, London, 1994.

Karpf, Anne, *The War After*, Heinemann, London, 1996.

Kincaid, Jamaica, *The Autobiography of My Mother*, Vintage, London, 1996.

Kuhn, Annette, *Family Secrets: Acts of Memory and Imagination*, Verso, London, 1995.

Lazarre, Jane, *On Loving Men*, Virago, London, 1981.

— *The Mother Knot*, McGraw-Hill, New York, 1986.

Lessing, Doris, *Under My Skin*, Flamingo, London, 1995.

Lorde, Audre, *Zami: Another Spelling of My Name*, Sheba, London, 1984.

— *The Cancer Journals*, Sheba, London, 1985.

McManus, Anne, *They Said I Was Dead*, Scarlet Press, London, 1994.

Meigs, Mary, *Lily Briscoe: A Self-portrait*, Talonbooks, Vancouver, 1981.

Modjeska, Drusilla, *Poppy*, Serpents Tail, London, 1983.

Sarton, May, *I Knew a Phoenix: Sketches for an Autobiography*, W. W. Norton, New York, 1959.

Shapley, Olive, *Broadcasting a Life*, Scarlet Press, London, 1996.

Spence, Jo, *Putting Myself in the Picture*, Camden Press, London, 1986.

Steedman, Carolyn, *Landscape for a Good Woman*, Virago, London, 1986.

Stein, Gertrude, *The Autobiography of Alice B. Toklas*, Bodley Head, London, 1933.

— *Everyone's Autobiography*, Virago, London, 1985.

Walker, Alice, *The Same River Twice: Knowing the Difference*, Women's Press, London, 1996.

Wilson, Elizabeth, *Mirror Writing: An Autobiography*, Virago, London, 1982.

COLLECTIVE AUTOBIOGRAPHIES

Ainley, Rosa (ed.), *The Death of a Mother: Daughters' Stories*, Pandora, London, 1994.

Bennett, Jackie and Forgan, Rosemary (eds), *There's Something about a Convent Girl*, Virago, London, 1991.

Caignon, Denise and Groves, Gail (eds), *Her Wits about Her: Self-Defence Success Stories by Women*, Women's Press, London, 1989.

Ford, Janet and Sinclair, Ruth (eds), *Sixty Years On: Women Talk about Old Age*, Women's Press, London, 1987.

Goodare, Heather (ed.), *Fighting Spirit: The Stories of Women in the Bristol Breast Cancer Survey*, Scarlet Press, London, 1996.

Heron, Liz (ed.), *Truth, Dare or Promise: Girls Growing up in the Fifties*, Virago, London, 1985.

McCrindle, Jean and Rowbottom, Sheila (eds), *Dutiful Daughters: Women Talk about Their Lives*, Penguin, Harmondsworth, 1979.

McNaron, Toni A. H. and Morgan, Yarrow (eds), *Voices in the Night: Women Speaking about Incest*, Cleis, San Francisco, 1982.

McNeill, Pearlie et al. (eds), *Women Talk Sex*, Scarlet Press, London, 1992.

Malone, Caroline et al. (eds), *The Memory Bird: Survivors of Sexual Abuse*, Virago, London, 1996.

Morris, Jenny (ed.), *Able Lives: Women's Experience of Paralysis*, Women's Press, London, 1989.

— *Alone Together: Voices of Single Mothers*, Women's Press, London, 1992.

Oguntoye, K. et al. (eds), *Showing Our True Color: Afro-German Women Speak Out*, Open Letters, London, 1992.

Rakesh Ratti (ed.), *A Lotus of Another Colour*, Alyson, Boston, 1994.

Rooney, Frances (ed.), *Our Lives: Lesbian Personal Writing*, Second Story, Toronto, 1991.

Sistren Theatre Collective and H. Ford Smith, *Lionheart Gal: Life Stories of Jamaican Women*, Women's Press, London, 1986.

Stanley, Jo (ed.), *To Make Ends Meet: Women over 60 Write about Their Working Lives*, Older Women's Project, London, 1989.

Wandor, Michelene (interviewer), *Once a Feminist: Stories of a Generation*, Virago, London, 1990.

Washington, M. H., *Invented Lives: Narratives of Black Women, 1860–1960*, Virago, London, 1989.

BOOKS ABOUT AUTOBIOGRAPHY, ESPECIALLY ABOUT WOMEN AND THE AUTOBIOGRAPHICAL PROCESS

Bell, Susan Groag and Yalom, Marilyn, *Revealing Lives: Autobiography, Biography and Gender*, State University of New York Press, 1990.

Benstock, Shari (ed.), *The Private Self: Theory and Practice of Women's Writings*, Routledge, London, 1988.

Brodzki, Bella and Schenck Celeste, *Life/Lines: Theorising Women's Autobiography*, Cornell University Press, Ithaca, NY and London, 1988.

Buss, Helen, *Mapping Ourselves: Canadian Women's Autobiography*, McGill-Queens University Press, Montreal and Kingston, 1993.

Gilmore, Leigh, *Autobiographics: A Feminist Theory of Women's Self-Representation*, Cornell University Press, Ithaca, NY and London, 1994.

Gusdorf, George, 'Conditions and Limits of Autobiography', in Olney (ed.), *Autobiography*.

Heilbrun, Carolyn G., *Writing a Woman's Life*, Women's Press, London, 1989.

Holmes, Katie, *Spaces in Her Day: Australian Women's Diaries 1920s–1930s*, Allen and Unwin, London, 1995.

Jelinek, Estelle C., *The Tradition of Women's Autobiography: From Antiquity to the Present*, Twayne, Boston, 1986.

— (ed.), *Women's Autobiography: Essays in Criticism*, Indiana University Press, Bloomington, 1980.

Kadar, Marlene, *Essays in Life Writing: From Genre to Critical Practice*, University of Toronto Press, 1992.

Milner, Marion, *A Life of One's Own*, Virago, London, 1986.

— *Eternity's Sunrise: A Way of Keeping a Diary*, Virago, London, 1987.

Neuman, Shirley (ed.), *Autobiography and Question of Gender*, Frank Carr, New York, 1991.

Olney, James (ed.), *Autobiography: Essays Theoretical and Critical*, Princeton University Press, NJ, 1980.

Personal Narratives Group (eds), *Interpreting Women's Lives*, Indiana University Press, Bloomington, 1989.

Plummer, Ken, *Documents of Life: An Introduction to the Problems and Literature of a Humanistic Method*, Allen and Unwin, London, 1983.

Rainer, Tristine, *The New Journal*, Angus and Robertson, London and North Ryde, NSW, Australia, 1978.

Selling, Bernard, *Writing from Within: A Unique Guide to Writing Your Life's Stories*, Hunter House, Alameda, California, 1994.

Smith, Sidonie, *A Poetics of Women's Autobiography: Marginality and the Fictions of Self-Representation*, Indiana University Press, Bloomington, 1987.

Spacks, Patricia Meyer, *Imagining a Self: Autobiography and the Novel in Eighteenth-Century England*, Harvard University Press, Cambridge, Massachusetts, 1976.

Stanley, Liz, *The Auto/biographical I*, Manchester University Press, 1991.

Stanton, Domna (ed.), *The Female Autograph: Theory and Practice of Autobiography from the Tenth to the Twentieth Century*, University of Chicago Press, 1987.

Steedman, Carolyn, *Past Tenses: Essays on Writing, Autobiography, and History*, Rivers Oram Press, London, 1992.

Swindells, Julia, *The Uses of Autobiography*, Taylor and Francis, London, 1995.

PERIODICALS

Auto/Biography, journal of the British Sociological Association Auto/Biography study group. Any issue of this is fascinating. Subscribe by becoming a member through Michael Erben, Dept of Education, The University, Southampton SO9 5NH.

Gender and History, vol. 2, no. 1, spring 1990, Blackwell, Oxford, on autobiography and biography.

Literature and History, vol. 14, no. 1, spring 1988, Manchester University Press (first published by Thames Polytechnic, London), on autobiography and working-class writing, including a useful critique of Carolyn Steedman by Stephen Yeo and a summary of overlooked working-class women's autobiography by Rebecca O'Rourke.

Narrative Study of Lives, Sage, Thousand Oaks, California. Any edition is fascinating. They began in 1993.

Oral History, journal of the Oral History Society, often contains news and articles about oral, collective and individual autobiographies. Subscriptions c/o Department of Sociology, University of Essex, Wivenhoe Park, Colchester, Essex CO4 3SP.

Sociology, vol. 27, no. 1, 1993, Oxford University Press, on autobiography.

Notes

PREFACE

1. I edited the collected writings of Jo Spence, my friend, who had just died (*Cultural Sniping: The Art of Transgression*, Routledge, London, 1995) and I contributed a chapter on what a woman can, autobiographically, do with a pen: 'Accounting for Our Days' in Jo Spence and Joan Solomon (eds), *What Can a Woman Do with a Camera?*, Scarlet Press, London, 1995.
2. An element of this, 'Where Troubles Melt like Lemon Drops', was published in Pearlie McNeill, Marie McShea and Pratibha Parmar (eds), *Through the Break: Women in Personal Crisis*, Sheba, London, 1986, pp. 233–4.
3. The Wandsworth Women's Working Lives project is written up in Jo Stanley and Bronwen Griffiths (eds), *For Love and Shillings*, London History Workshop Centre, 1991. Aspects of the process are described in 'Just an Old Picture of Me at Work', in Jo Spence and Pat Holland (eds), *Family Snaps: The Meaning of Domestic Photography*, Virago, London, 1991. The video, exhibition and archives of the project are at Wandsworth Museum. Also see Jo Stanley (ed.), *To Make Ends Meet*, Older Women's Project, London, 1989.
4. See, for example, Peter G. Coleman, *Ageing and Reminiscence Processes: Social and Clinical Implications*, Wiley, Chichester, 1986. Joanna Bornat edited *Reminiscence Reviewed*, Oxford University Press, 1993.

INTRODUCTION

1. For further discussion of this notion of simple seeing and complex seeing, see Simon Denith and Philip Dodd, 'The Uses of Autobiography', *Literature*

and History, vol. 14, no. 1, spring 1988 – a special issue on autobiography and working-class writing. 'Complex seeing' is a phrase used by playwright Bertolt Brecht; he saw it as a necessary political choice.

2. See Estelle C. Jelinek, *The Tradition of Women's Autobiography: From Antiquity to the Present*, Twayne, Boston, 1986, for a good overview of women's lifestory history using this idea.

CHAPTER 1 WHAT IS IT ANYWAY?

1. Marlene Kadar (ed.), *Essays in Life Writing: From Genre to Critical Practice*, University of Toronto Press, 1992, pp. 17–18.

2. In her introduction to the section on recording a life and the construction of the self, Marlene Kadar discusses what some of the contributors to her book do as critics: 'Here life narratives – sometimes called lifestories – may be defined as alternative (to the canon) texts within the over-determined or canon-reliant contest and disciplines. The self-conscious scholar, historian, anthropologist then uses life writing in order to voice complaints and observations about various theories that have been used in their disciplines and that have predetermined the status and voice of the "subject" who is not viewed as an individual.' Kadar (ed.), *Essays in Life Writing*, p. 81.

3. Christl Verduyn discusses this in 'Between the Lines' in Kadar (ed.), *Essays in Life Writing*. The original source on which she bases her discussion is an earlier work edited by Kadar also called *Essays in Life Writing*, Robarts Centre for Canadian Studies Working Paper no. 89–WO3, York University, North York, Ontario, 1989.

4. Louella O. Parsons, *The Gay Illiterate*, Doublen, Dorian and Co, Garden City, NY, 1944, p. 7.

5. Sidonie Smith, *A Poetics of Women's Autobiography: Marginality and the Fictions of Self-Representation*, Indiana University Press, Bloomington, 1987.

6. Helen M. Buss, 'Anna Jameson's "Winter Studies and Summer Rambles in Canada" as an Epistolary Dijournal' in Kadar (ed.), *Essays in Life Writing*, p. 43. Buss's quote comes from Smith, *A Poetics of Women's Autobiography*, pp. 45–6.

7. The ideal of the autobiographical pact, which has been crucial in academic thinking about autobiography, comes from Georges Gusdorf, 'Conditions and Limits of Autobiography', in James Olney (ed.), *Autobiography: Essays Theoretical and Critical*, Princeton University Press, NJ, 1980.

CHAPTER 2 WHAT IS IT FOR? WHO IS IT FOR?

1. Elizabeth Cady Stanton's (1815–1902) autobiography, published in 1898, is *Eighty Years or More: Reminiscences 1815–1897* (p. xiv). It is discussed at length in Estelle C. Jelinek's *The Tradition of Women's Autobiography: From Antiquity to the Present*, Twayne, Boston, 1986.
2. For example, see Valentine Ackland's autobiography *For Sylvia, An Honest Account*, Chatto and Windus, London, 1985. Her prologue says: 'My love ... it is strange to think that this is probably all I have to give you, this record of blundering from shame to shame', referring to her infidelities and drink problems.
3. Alexandra Kollontai, *The Autobiography of a Sexually Emancipated Woman*, Orbach and Chambers, London, 1972, translated by Salbator Attanasio.
4. The last three beneficial side-effects of lifestorying are listed by writers Lieberman and Tobin as being true of aging but I think they are actually true of us at any time. M. A. Lieberman and S. S. Tobin, *The Experience of Old Age: Stress, Coping and Survival*, Basic Books, New York, 1983, p. 348.
5. Shirley Dex (ed.), *Life and Work History Analyses: Qualitative and Quantitative Developments*, Routledge, London, 1991, p. 125.

CHAPTER 3 SPEAKING OUT

1. Estelle C. Jelinek, *The Tradition of Women's Autobiography: From Antiquity to the Present*, Twayne, Boston, 1986, p. 99.
2. Sidonie Smith, *A Poetics of Women's Autobiography: Marginality and the Fictions of Self-Representation*, Indiana University Press, Bloomington, 1987. See also Domna Stanton (ed.), *The Female Autograph: Theory and Practice of Autobiography from the Tenth to the Twentieth Century*, University of Chicago Press, 1987.
3. Mary Wollstonecraft, *Letters Written during a Short Residence in Sweden, Norway and Denmark*, Carol H. Poston (ed.), University of Nebraska Press, Lincoln, 1976.
4. I am grateful to Marlene Kadar for this idea, in 'Whose Life Is It Anyway', in Kadar (ed.), *Essays in Life Writing: From Genre to Critical Practice*, University of Toronto Press, 1992, pp. 154–5.
5. Discussed in Jelinek, *The Traditions of Women's Autobiography*, p. 74.
6. Stephanie Dowrick, *The Intimacy and Solitude Self-Therapy Book*, Women's Press, London, 1995.
7. Deena Metzger, *Writing for Your Life: A Guide and Companion to Your Inner Worlds*, Harper, San Francisco, 1992.
8. Kate Millet, *Flying*, Paladin, London, 1978, p. 444.

CHAPTER 4 INGREDIENTS

1. Mike Parkinson (ed.), *Mike Parkinson's Confession Album*, Sidgwick and Jackson, London, 1973.
2. To see these entries contact the NSA at the British Library, National Lifestory Collection, 96 Euston Road, London NW1 2DB (tel: 0171 412 7440).
3. Emmeline Pankhurst, *My Own Story: The Autobiography of Emmeline Pankhurst*, Eveleigh Nash (ed.), Virago, London, 1979, p. 108 (first published 1914).

CHAPTER 5 HOW DO I START?

1. Viki King, *How to Write a Movie in 21 Days: The Inner Movie Method*, Harper and Row, New York, 1988. The Vancouver three-day novel contest can be contacted (send SAE) via Brian Kaufman/Lisa Sweanor, Anvil Press, 204, 175 East Broadway, Vancouver, BC, V5T 1WZ, Canada.
2. An accessible book on the creativity of your brain's right hemisphere is Sally P. Springer and George Deutch's *Left Brain/Right Brain*, W.W. Norton, New York, 1985. Dillons bookshop in London has three shelves of books on creative thinking. Try J. Geoffrey Rawlinson, *Creative Thinking and the Art of Brainstorming*, Gower, Aldershot, 1994.

CHAPTER 6 WRITING ABOUT YOUR BODY

1. Dinora Pines, *A Woman's Unconscious Use of Her Body*, Virago, London, 1995, and Joyce McDougall, *Theatres of the Body, a Psychoanalytic Approach to Psychosomatic Illness*, Free Association, London, 1989.
2. See, for example, Jo Spence, *Putting Myself in the Picture*, Camden Press, London, 1986, and *Cultural Sniping: The Art of Transgression*, Routledge, London, 1995.
3. Mary M. Gergen and Kenneth J. Gergen, 'Narratives of the Gendered Body in Popular Autobiography', *Narrative Study of Lives*, vol. 1, Sage, 1993.
4. Peter Redgrove and Penelope Shuttleworth, *The Wise Wound: The Myths, Realities and Meanings of Menstruation*, Grafton, London, 1986.
5. Gergen and Gergen, 'Narratives of the Gendered Body in Popular Autobiography', p. 201.
6. Joan Baez, *And a Voice to Sing With: A Memoir*, New American Library, New York, 1987, p. 43.

7. Laura Davis, *The Courage to Heal Workbook*, Harper Perennial, New York, 1990.

8. Lifestories about sexual abuse include:

Charlotte Vale Allen, *Daddy's Girl: A Very Personal Memoir*, McLelland and Stewart, Toronto, 1980; Louise Armstrong, *Kiss Daddy Goodnight: Ten Years Later*, Penguin, New York, 1987; Elly Danica, *Don't: A Woman's Word*, Gynergy, Charlottetown, Prince Edwaed Island, Canada, 1988 and the Women's Press, London, 1989; Sylvia Fraser, *My Father's House: A Memoir of Incest and Healing*, Collins, Toronto, 1988; and Jacqueline Spring, *Cry Hard and Swim: The Story of an Incest Survivor*, Virago, London, 1987. For a discussion on these see Janice Williamson, 'I Peel Myself out of My Own Skin', in Marlene Kadar (ed.), *Essays in Life Writing: From Genre to Critical Practice*, University of Toronto Press, 1992.

CHAPTER 7 THE WORLD OUTSIDE

1. Storm Jameson, *Journey from the North: The Autobiography of Storm Jameson*, vols 1 and 2, Virago, London, 1984 (first published in 1969 and 1970).

2. Carol Dix, *Say I'm Sorry to Mother: The True Story of Four Women Growing up in the Sixties*, Pan, London, 1978.

3. Michelene Wandor (interviewer), *Once a Feminist: Stories of a Generation*, Virago, London, 1990.

4. Carolyn Steedman, *Past Tenses: Essays on Writing, Autobiography and History*, Rivers Oram Press, London, 1992, p. 44.

CHAPTER 8 TIMES IN YOUR LIFE

1. A recent anthology is devoted to this theme: Gloria Norns (ed.), *The Seasons of Women: Stories, Memoirs and Essays from Girlhood to Maturity*, Viking Penguin, London, 1996.

2. Bernard Selling with Jim Strohecker, *In Your Own Voice*, Hunter House, Alameda, California, 1994.

3. Shakespeare's 'seven ages of man' speech appears in *As You Like It*, Act 2, scene vii.

4. Gail Sheehy, *Passages: Predictable Crises of Adult Life*, Bantam, New York, 1977. Pioneering midlife work was done by Bernice Neugarten, *Middle Age and Aging*, University of Chicago Press, 1968. For a survey of the

controversies surrounding adult development, see Anne Rossenfeld and Elizabeth Stark, 'The Prime of Our Lives', in *Psychology Today*, May 1987, pp. 62–72.

5. Gail Sheehy, *New Passages*, Random House, New York, 1996.

6. Erik Erikson, *Identity and the Life Cycle*, W. W. Norton, New York, 1980; *Childhood and Society*, W.W. Norton, New York, 1963. Daniel Levinson et al., *Seasons of a Man's Life*, Knopf, New York, 1978. 'Man' really does mean man, not people, in lots of cases. Beware of the studies based on men's stages – unless of course you are using the gender differences in an exploration of your gendered behaviour or looking at men you'll be including in your autobiography.

7. Iris Sanguiliano, *In Her Time*, Knopf, New York, 1978.

8. Carol Gilligan, *In a Different Voice: Psychological Theory and Women's Development*, Harvard University Press, Cambridge, Massachusetts and London, 1993.

9. For example, the two Karnac psychology bookshops in London at 56 Gloucester Road, SW7 (tel: 0171 584 3303) and at 118 Finchley Road, NW3 (tel: 0171 431 1075). Also Silver Moon at 68 Charing Cross Road, WC2 (tel: 0171 836 7906) and Dillons at 82 Gower Street, WC1 (tel: 0171 636 1577) have good psychology sections: the latter very large, and the former specifically related to women.

10. Emmeline Pankhurst, *My Own Story: The Autobiography of Emmeline Pankhurst*, (ed.) Eveleigh Nash (ed.), Virago, London, 1979, pp. 2–3, first published 1914.

11. Emily Hancock, *The Girl Within*, Pandora, London, 1990.

12. Annie G. Rogers, Lyn Mikel Brown and Mark B. Tappan, 'Interpreting Loss in Ego Development in Girls', in *Narrative Study of Lives*, vol. 2 *(Exploring Gender and Identity)*, Sage, 1994.

13. For a full discussion of this and useful references to psychologists' studies of such ideas, see ibid. and Carol Gilligan, *In a Different Voice*.

14. Jane Loevinger, *Ego Development*, Jossey-Bass, San Francisco, 1977.

15. Don S. Browning sums it up in *Generative Man: Psychoanalytic Perspectives*, Westminster, Philadelphia, 1973, pp. 145–228, and Erik Erikson in *Identity, Youth and Crisis*, W.W. Norton, New York, 1986, p. 130.

16. Lillian Rubin, *Women of a Certain Age: The Midlife Search for Self*, Harper and Row, New York, 1979.

17. The Growing Old Disgracefully network can be contacted via Piatkus Books, 5 Windmill Street, London W1P 1HF. The Older Feminist Network can be contacted via Astra Gordon, 54 Gordon Road, London N3 1EP (tel: 0181 346 1900). Please include an SAE. The OFN meets on the second Saturday of every month in central London.

18. Simone de Beauvoir, *All Said and Done*, Penguin, Harmondsworth, 1974.

19. Some of the myths in Allan B. Chinen's *In the Ever After: Fairy Tales and the Second Half of Life*, Chiron, Wilmette, Illinois, 1989, offer some interesting ways to re-vision old age.
20. Janet Ford and Ruth Sinclair (eds), *Sixty Years On: Women Talk about Old Age*, Women's Press, London, 1987.
21. See, for example, Peter Coleman, 'Aging and lifestory: the meaning of reminescence in later life', in Shirley Dex (eds), *Life and Work History Analyses: Qualitative and Quantitive Developments*, Routledge, London, 1991, pp. 120–141.
22. May Sarton, *Journal of a Solitude*, Women's Press, London, 1983 (first published 1973).

CHAPTER 9 IT HAPPENED TO ME THEN

1. Abigail Stewart, 'The Women's Movement and Women's Lives: Linking Individual Development and Social Events', *Narrative Study of Lives*, vol. 1, 1993, p. 248.
2. Ibid., p. 239.
3. Ibid., p. 233.
4. Sarah Schulman, *Lesbian and Gay Life during the Reagan/Bush Years*, Cassell, London, 1994, p. 3.
5. Stewart, 'The Women's Movement and Women's Lives', p. 234.
6. Ibid., p. 234, referring to a study by W. Chafe.
7. Ibid., p. 235.

CHAPTER 10 WHO SHALL I INCLUDE?

1. Margaret Mead, *Blackberry Winter: My Earlier Years*, Angus and Robertson, London, 1973.
2. Sally Cole, 'Autobiographical Lives', in Marlene Kadar (ed.), *Essays in Life Writing: From Genre to Critical Practice*, University of Toronto Press, 1992, p. 114.
3. Mary Meigs, *Lily Briscoe: A Self-Portrait*, Talonbooks, Vancouver, 1981.
4. Gertrude Stein, *The Autobiography of Alice B. Toklas*, Bodley Head, London, 1933.
5. Lilian Faderman, *Scotch Verdict: Miss Price and Miss Woods v. Dame Cummings Gordon*, Quill, New York, 1983.
6. The journal *Gender and History* devoted a whole issue to autobiography and biography, spring 1990.

7. Hilda Doolittle, *Tribute to Freud*, Pantheon, New York, 1956.

8. Jane Lazarre, *On Loving Men*, Virago, London, 1981.

9. Margaret Cavendish, *A True Relation of the Birth, Breeding and Life of Margaret Cavendish, Duchess of Newcastle, Written by Herself*, privately printed, Lee Priory, Kent, 1814; and *Observations upon Experimental Philosophy*, to which is added *The Description of The New Blazing World*, A. Maxwell, London, 1666. *The Life of the Thrice Noble Prince William Cavendishe, Duke, Marquess and Earl of Newcastle* (some few notes of the authoresse), A. Maxwell, London, 1675.

10. Drusilla Modjeska, *Poppy*, Serpents Tail, London, 1983.

11. Polly Young-Eisendrath, *Hags and Heroes*, Inner City Books, Toronto, 1984, is fascinating for its Jungian approach to ways we relate.

12. Rebecca West, *Family Memories*, Lime Tree, London, 1992. The book was published posthumously, edited by Faith Evans.

13. Victoria Hughes, *The Ladies Mile*, Absom Books, Bristol, 1977.

CHAPTER 11 WRITING ABOUT SPECIFIC PEOPLE

1. Colette, *Break of Day*, Women's Press, London, 1979; first published as *La Naissance du Jour*, Paris, 1928.

2. Vivian Gornick, *Fierce Attachments: A Memoir*, Virago, London, 1988 (try also Louise M. Wildchild, *The Mother I Carry: A Memoir of Healing from Emotional Abuse*, Seal Press, Washington, 1993); Carolyn Steedman, *Landscape for a Good Woman*, Virago, London, 1986; Kim Chernin, *In My Mother's House: A Daughter's Story*, Virago, London, 1985; Nancy Friday, *My Mother, My Self*, Fontana, London, 1979.

3. The phrase comes from Janice Williamson, in 'I Peel Myself out of My Own Skin', in Marlene Kadar (ed.), *Essays on Life Writing: From Genre to Critical Practice*, University of Toronto Press, 1992, p. 143. She is referring to some Canadian women writers' autobiographies, for example Gail Scott's *Spaces like Stairs*, Women's Press, Toronto, 1989.

4. Judith Arcana, *Our Mothers' Daughters*, Women's Press, London, 1981.

5. Karen Payne (ed.), *Between Ourselves: Letters between Mothers and Daughters*, Picador, London, 1984.

6. *Mother to Daughter, Daughter to Mother: A Reader and Diary*, 'shaped and selected' by Tillie Olsen, Virago, London, 1985.

7. Maxine Hong Kingston, *The Woman Warrior: Memoirs of a Girlhood among Ghosts*, Random House, New York, 1975; see also Jamaica Kincaid, *The Autobiography of My Mother*, Vintage, London, 1996.

8. Penelope Mortimer, *About Time: An Aspect of Autobiography*, Penguin, Harmondsworth, 1979, p. 147.

9. Germaine Greer, *Daddy, We Hardly Knew You*, Hamish Hamilton, London, 1989. You may also like to read Victoria Secunda, *Women and Their Fathers*, Cedar, London, 1996.

10. Steedman, *Landscape for a Good Woman*, p. 72.

11. Ibid., p. 71.

12. Judy Hill Nelson, *Choices: My Journey after Leaving My Husband for Martina and a Lesbian Life*, Birch Lane Press, New York, 1995.

13. Gornick, *Fierce Attachments*, p. 176.

14. Jane Lazarre, *The Mother Knot*, McGraw-Hill, New York, 1986; Adrienne Rich, *Of Woman Born*, Virago, London, 1977.

15. Steedman, *Landscape for a Good Woman*, p. 91.

16. Gornick, *Fierce Attachments*, pp. 180–1.

17. Sarah Schulman, *Lesbian and Gay Life during the Reagan/Bush Years*, Cassell, London, 1994, p. xvii.

CHAPTER 12 WRITING ABOUT PLACE AND SPACE

1. As your starting point, try Gillian Rose, *Feminism and Geography: The Limits of Geographical Knowledge*, Polity Press, Cambridge, 1993. Doreen Massey, an Open University lecturer, has written many articles and books about geography and gender. Her *Space, Place and Gender*, Polity Press, Cambridge 1994, is a difficult but important work.

2. Virginia Woolf, *Three Guineas*, Penguin, Harmondsworth, 1977, p. 125.

3. She spoke of this with me in an interview in 1983. I have not seen it written up elsewhere.

4. Yvonne Mitchell, *Colette: A Taste for Life*, Weidenfeld and Nicholson, London, 1975, p. 35 and Colette's *My Apprenticeships and Music Hall Sidelights*, Secker and Warburg, London, 1957, p. 21.

5. Elizabeth Wilson, *The Sphinx in the City*, Virago, London, 1991.

CHAPTER 13 INCLUDING DEEPER THOUGHTS

1. Sigmund Freud, *The Interpretation of Dreams*, George Allen and Co., London, 1913, translated by A. A. Brill, 1913, and Carl Jung, *The Structure and Dynamics of the Psyche*, in his Collected Works, vol. 8, Routledge and Kegan Paul, London, 1960.

2. Lucy Goodison, *Dreams of Women: Exploring and Interpreting Women's Dreams*, Women's Press, London, 1995. See also Tony Crisp, *The Instant Dream Book*, Neville Spearman, Suffolk, 1984; and the 'Dreams' issue of *Self and Society*, vol. IX, no. 3, May–June 1981, available from 39 Blenkarne Road, London SW11 6HZ.

3. If you feel stuck on this then try glancing at one of the most famous anthologies on women's (sexual) desires: Nancy Friday, *My Secret Garden*, Quartet, London, 1976; and its successor, *Forbidden Flowers: More Women's Sexual Fantasies*, Arrow, London, 1996.

4. Morwenna Griffiths, *Feminisms and the Self: The Web of Identity*, Routledge, London, 1995; or Morwenna Griffiths and Margaret Whitford (eds), *Feminist Perspectives in Philosophy*, Macmillan, London, 1985; Carol Gilligan, *In a Different Voice: Psychological Theory and Women's Development*, Harvard University Press, Cambridge, Massachusetts and London, 1993; Dorothy Dinnerstein, *The Rocking of the Cradle and the Ruling of the World*, Souvenir Press, London, 1978; Nancy Chodorow, *The Reproduction of Mothering*, University of California Press, Berkeley, 1978.

5. Marlene Kadar (ed.), *Essays in Life Writing: From Genre to Critical Practice*, University of Toronto Press, 1992.

6. Tereska Torres, *The Converts*, Rupert Hart-Davis, London, 1970.

7. An invaluable guide to a whole other way of seeing mythologies is Barbara G. Walker, *The Women's Encyclopedia of Myths and Secrets*, Harper, San Francisco, 1983. A feminist introduction to spirituality is Ursula King's *Women and Spirituality: Voices of Protest and Promise*, Macmillan, London, 1989.

8. Alison Halford, in Jackie Bennett and Rosemary Forgan (eds), *There's Something about a Convent Girl*, Virago, London, 1991, p. 101.

9. Katie Boyle in Bennett and Forgan (eds), *There's Something about a Convent Girl*.

10. Gail Scott, *Spaces like Stairs*, Women's Press, Toronto, 1989.

11. If you want to know about scripts, try reading some basic books on transactional analysis, the therapy developed initially by Eric Berne. Ian Stewart and Vann Jones, *TA Today*, Lifespace Publishing, Nottingham and Chapel Hill, North Carolina, 1987. Some personal development counsellors also use the inventions of new scripts as a way to progress beyond pain and old self-destructive habits: see, for example, Ursula Markham, *Life Scripts*, Element Books, Longmead, Dorset, 1995.

12. Catherine E. Warren, *Vignettes of Life: Experiences and Self-Perceptions of New Canadian Women*, Detselig Enterprises, Calgary, 1986, p. 50.

CHAPTER 14 GETTING BACKGROUND INFORMATION

1. Sarah Gristwood, *Recording Angels: The Secret World of Women's Diaries*, Harrap, London, 1988 (extracts from women's diaries over several centuries); Lyn Lifshin (ed.), *Ariadne's Thread: A Collection of Contemporary Women's Journals*, Harper and Row, New York, 1982, is much more biting.

2. Alessandro Portelli, *The Death of Luigi Trastulli and Other Stories: Form and Meaning in Oral History*, Suny Press, Albany, NY, 1991.

3. Virginia Woolf, *A Writer's Diary*, Leonard Woolf (ed.), Triad/Grafton, London, 1978. (First published by Hogarth Press, 1953.)

4. Marion Milner, *A Life of One's Own*, Virago, London, 1986; and *Eternity's Sunrise: A Way of Keeping a Diary*, Virago, London, 1987.

5. Tristine Rainer, *The New Journal*, Angus and Robertson, London and North Ryde, NSW, Australia, 1978.

6. Kim Chernin, *Differential Levels of Listening*, Harper and Row, London, 1996. The book she is most famous for, in which she discusses the extent to which women's troubling relationship with food can be about fear of surpassing the mother, is *The Hungry Self: Women, Eating and Identity*, Virago, London, 1986.

7. Janet Frame, *An Angel at My Table*, Women's Press, London, 1984; Kate Millet, *The Loony Bin Trip*, Virago, London, 1993.

8. Ronald Fraser, *In Search of a Past: The Manor House, Amnersfield 1933–1945*, Verso, London, 1984.

9. Annette Kuhn, *Family Secrets: Acts of Memory and Imagination*, Verso, London, 1995; Jo Spence, *Putting Myself in the Picture*, Camden Press, London, 1986.

10. See also Jo Spence's *Cultural Sniping: The Art of Transgression*, Routledge, London, 1995.

11. Cynthia and Arthur Koestler, *Strangers on the Square*, Hutchinson, London, 1984; Barbara Pym, *A Very Private Eye: An Autobiography in Letters and Diaries*, Macmillan, London, 1984. Her editors were colleague Hazel Holt and her sister, Hilary Pym.

12. Useful books on oral history include S. B. Gluck and D. Patai (eds), *Women's Words*, Routledge, London, 1991; Paul Thompson, *Voice of the Past*, Oxford University Press, 1988; and V. R. Yow, *Recording Oral History*, Sage, London, 1994. See also H. Roberts, *Doing Feminist Research*, Routledge and Kegan Paul, London, 1981. Back issues of the journal *Oral History* will show you how illuminating oral history can be and some of the challenges and delights of the process.

13. Michael Gandy, *Short Cuts in Family History*, 1994; George Pelling, *Beginning Your Family History*, 1995; John Titford, *Writing and Publishing*

Your Family History, 1995; Pauline Saul, *Tracing Your Ancestors: The A–Z Guide*, 1995 – all published by the Federation of Family History Societies, Birmingham, in conjunction with Countryside Books, Newbury, Berks; Ruth Finnegan and Michael Drake (eds), *From Family Tree to Family History*, Cambridge University Press/Open University, 1996; Kirk Polking, *Writing Family History and Memoirs*, Better Way Books, Cincinnati, 1995.

14. Deirdre Beddoe, *Discovering Women's History: A Practical Guide to the Sources of Women's History 1880–1945*, Pandora, London, 1993.

CHAPTER 15 PULLING IT INTO SHAPE

1. If you would like to read more about this, see Carolyn Steedman's *Past Tenses: Essays on Writing, Autobiography and History*, Rivers Oram Press, London, 1992, pp. 41–50.
2. Margaret Powell, *Climbing the Stairs*, Peter Davis, London, 1970, p. ii.
3. Jane Lazarre, *The Mother Knot*, McGraw-Hill, New York, 1986. Louise Erdrich, *The Blue Jay's Dance: A Birth Year*, Flamingo, London, 1996.
4. Lucy Irvine, Castaway, Gollancz, London, 1993. Linda Lovelace and Mike McGrady, *Ordeal*, Star, London, 1982.
5. Morales and Morales, *Getting Home Alive*, Firebrand, New York, 1986; S. Greval et al. (eds), *Charting the Journey*, Sheba, London, 1988.

CHAPTER 16 WAYS TO ARRANGE THE ORDER

1. Mary McCarthy, *How I Grew*, Penguin, Harmondsworth, 1987.
2. Hilda Bernstein, *The World That Was Ours*, Heinemann, London, 1967.
3. Harriet Martineau, *Autobiography*, 2 vols, Virago, London, 1983 (first published by Smith, Elder and Co, 1877).
4. Joyce Johnson, *Minor Characters*, Picador, London, 1983.
5. Amryl Johnson, *Sequins on a Ragged Hem*, Virago, London, 1988; Audre Lorde, *The Cancer Journals*, Sheba, London, 1985.
6. Huda Shaarawi, *Harem Years: Memoirs of an Egyptian Feminist*, translated by Margot Badan, Virago, London, 1986, pp. 165–6.
7. Michèle Roberts, *During Mother's Absence*, Virago, London, 1993, p. 158.
8. Annette Kuhn, *Family Secrets: Acts of Memory and Imagination*, Verso, London, 1995.
9. Annie Besant, *Annie Besant, An Autobiography*, T. Fisher Unwin, London, 1893.

CHAPTER 17 POLISHING AND FINE-TUNING

1. Gloria Anzaldúa, *Borderlands/La Frontera: The New Mestiza*, Spinsters Inc/Aunt Lute, San Francisco, 1987.

2. The main male theoretical writers on autobiography, such as James Olney and George Gusdorf, made this point, as do feminist writers today, such as Marlene Kadar and Sidonie Smith. For titles, see Appendix 2.

3. Sue Limb, *Love Forty: How I Turned over a New Life*, Transworld, London, 1987.

4. Hilda Bernstein, *The World That Was Ours*, Heinemann, London, 1967, p. 89.

CHAPTER 18 GETTING FEEDBACK

1. Mass-Observation Archive, The Library, University of Sussex, Falmer, Brighton BN1 9QL (tel: 01273 678157).

2. City Literary Institute, 16 Stukely Street, London WC2B 5LJ (tel: 0171 242 9872). The excellent current (1997) tutor there is Carol Burns.

3. Writers' Guild of Great Britain, 430 Edgware Road, London W2 1EH (tel: 0171 723 8074). Society of Authors, 84 Drayton Gardens, London SW10 9SB (tel: 0171 378 6642). The Women Writers' Network meets every month at Conway Hall, Red Lion Square, London WC2. Membership secretary is Cathy Smith, 23 Prospect Road, London NW2 2JU. They should be able to tell you about similar groups outside London.

4. Federation of Worker Writers and Community Publishers, PO Box 540, Burslem, Stoke on Trent ST6 6DR (fax: 01782 822327).

5. The Women's History Network can be reached through Gerry Holloway, Centre for Continuing Education, Education Building, University of Sussex, Brighton, Sussex, BN1 9QT.

6. Anne Jamieson, Course Director, CFMS, Birkbeck College, 26 Russell Square, London WC1B 5DQ (tel: 0171 631 6649; e-mail: a.jamieson@cems.bbk.ac.uk).

CHAPTER 19 SAYING GOODBYE

1. Frank Kermode, *The Sense of an Ending: Studies in the Theory of Fiction*, Oxford University Press, 1967.

2. Elly Danica, *Don't: A Woman's Word*, Gynergy, Charlottetown, Prince Edward Island, Canada, 1988 and the Women's Press, London, 1989, p. 93.

3. Emmeline Pankhurst, *My Own Story: The Autobiography of Emmeline Pankhurst*, Eveleigh Nash (ed.), Virago, London, 1979 (first published 1914), pp. 363–4.

4. Janice Williamson, 'I Peel Myself out of My Own Skin', in Marlene Kadar (ed.), *Essays on Life Writing: From Genre to Critical Practice*, University of Toronto Press, 1992, p. 188, referring to Charlotte Vale Allen, *Daddy's Girl: A Very Personal Memoir*, McClelland and Stewart, Toronto, 1980, and Sylvia Fraser, *My Father's House: A Memoir of Incest and Healing*, Collins, Toronto, 1988.

5. Hilda Bernstein, *The World That Was Ours*, Heinemann, London, 1967, p. 247.

6. Stella Bowen, *Drawn from Life*, Virago, London, 1984, p. 253. (First published by Collins, London, 1941).

7. Williamson, 'I Peel Myself out of My Own Skin', p. 137.

8. Lindy St Claire, *It's Only a Game: The Autobiography of Miss Whiplash*, Piatkus, London, 1995.

9. Eric Maisel, *A Life in the Arts: Practical Guidance and Inspiration for Creative and Performing Artists*, Putnam, New York, 1994. Also Susan Schenkel, *Giving away Success: Why Women Get Stuck and What to Do about It*, Harper Perennial, New York, 1991.

10. See Anne Dickson, *A Woman in Your Own Right*, Quartet, London, 1996.

CHAPTER 20 GETTING PUBLISHED

1. Women's Studies Network, Jill Webster, School of Social and Policy Sciences, University of Westminster, 309 Regent Street, London WIR 8AL. Women's History Network, Gerry Holloway, Centre for Continuing Education, Education Building, University of Sussex, Brighton, Sussex BNI 9QT.

2. Federation of Worker Writers and Community Publishers, PO Box 540, Burslem, Stoke on Trent ST6 6DR (fax: 01782 822327).

3. Janice Williamson comments on this process in 'I Peel Myself out of My Own Skin', in Marlene Kadar (ed.), *Essays on Life Writing: From Genre to Critical Practice*, University of Toronto Press, 1992, p. 137. Elly Danica's book, *Don't: A Woman's Word*, was published by Gynergy, Charlottetown, Prince Edward Island, Canada, 1988.

4. Pauline Wiltshire, *Living and Winning*, Centerprise, London, 1985.

5. R.G. Scales, 5 Kings Bench Walk, Inner Temple, London EC4Y 7DN (tel: 0171 853 7770). If you have trouble finding bookbinders, contact their professional association: BATMAR, 12 Roy Road, Northwood, Middlesex HA6 1EH.

CHAPTER 21 SHARING AND SELLING

1. The Lesbian Archive is at Glasgow Women's Library, 109 Trongate, Glasgow, G1 5HD (tel: 0141 552 8345). The Black Cultural Archive is at 378 Coldharbour Lane, London SW9 8LF (tel: 0171 738 4591). The British Film Institute is at 21 Stephen Street, London W1P 2LN (tel: 0171 255 1444).
2. National Lifestory Collection, British Library National Sound Archive, 96 Euston Road, London NW1 2DB (tel: 0171 412 7440).

CHAPTER 22 WHAT NEXT?

1. The British Association of Art Therapists can be reached at 11a Richmond Road, Brighton BN2 3RL. Try reading Tessa Dalley (ed.), *Art as Therapy*, Routledge, London, 1994; or Liesl Silverstone, *Art Therapy, the Person Centred Way*, Autonomy Books, London, 1995.
2. You can find out about them through the Association of Music Therapists of Great Britain, 48 Lancaster Road, London N6 4TA. A good book to start with is Olivia Dewhurst-Maddock, *The Book of Sound Therapy*, Gaia Books, London, 1993.
3. The Mass-Observation Archive has an introductory booklet, *Mass Observation in the 1990s: How to Take Part*, which includes a useful bibliography. The Mass-Observation Archive, The Library, University of Sussex, Falmer, Brighton BN1 9QL (tel: 01273 678157); or see Dorothy Sheridan, 'Writing to the Archive: Mass Observation as Autobiographic', *Sociology*, vol. 27, no. 1, February 1993.
4. Age Exchange, 11 Blackheath Village, London SE3 9LA (tel: 0181 318 9105/3504).
5. National Lifestory Collection, British Library National Sound Archive, 96 Euston Rd, London NW1 2DB (tel: 0171 412 7440).

APPENDIX 1 USEFUL IDEAS FOR WHEN YOU GET STUCK

1. Christine Westwood, *Aromatherapy: A Guide for Home Use*, Amberwood Publishing, Christchurch, Dorset, 1991.
2. Jennifer Louden, *The Woman's Comfort Book: The Self-Nurturing Guide for Restoring Balance in Your Life*, Harper, San Francisco, 1992.

Index